CÉAC
BIO

D1539871

CHICKENS IN THE ROAD

CHICKENS
IN THE
ROAD

An Adventure in
Ordinary Splendor

. . . .

SUZANNE MCMINN

HarperOne
An Imprint of HarperCollins*Publishers*

HarperOne

CHICKENS IN THE ROAD: *An Adventure in Ordinary Splendor.* Copyright © 2013 by Suzanne McMinn. All rights reserved. Printed in the United States of America. No part of this book may be used or reproduced in any manner whatsoever without written permission except in the case of brief quotations embodied in critical articles and reviews. For information address HarperCollins Publishers, 10 East 53rd Street, New York, NY 10022.

HarperCollins books may be purchased for educational, business, or sales promotional use. For information, please e-mail the Special Markets Department at SPsales@harpercollins.com.

HarperCollins website: http://www.harpercollins.com

HarperCollins®, 📖®, and HarperOne™ are trademarks of HarperCollins Publishers

FIRST EDITION

Designed by Greta Sibley

Library of Congress Cataloging-in-Publication Data
    McMinn, Suzanne.
        Chickens in the road : an adventure in ordinary splendor / Suzanne McMinn.
    — First edition.
            pages cm
        Includes index.
        ISBN 978-0-06-222370-8
        1. McMinn, Suzanne. 2. Walton (W. Va.)—Biography. 3. Walton (W. Va.)—Social life and customs. 4. Farm life—West Virginia—Walton. 5. Country life—West Virginia—Walton. I. Title.
    F294.W25M35   2013
    975.4'36—dc23   2013007366

13 14 15 16 17 RRD(H) 10 9 8 7 6 5 4 3 2

In Memory of Clover
May 29, 2007—September 10, 2012

This book is dedicated with love and gratitude to each and every one of my readers at Chickens in the Road. You carried me through this journey on your wings of unflagging support and encouragement. Thank you always.

CONTENTS

· · · · · · · · · · ·

FOREWORD

It was a cold late autumn day when I brought my children to live in rural Walton, West Virginia. The farmhouse was one hundred years old, there was already snow on the ground, and the heat was sparse—as was the insulation. The floors weren't even either. My then-twelve-year-old son walked in the door and said, "You've brought us to this slanted little house to die."

Products of suburbia, my three children wondered why there was no cable TV or Target, not to mention central heat. My daughter, hungry from the trip, tried to call Domino's. My cousin Mark explained gently and without laughing that "they don't deliver pizza out here." I think it took her a good thirty minutes to believe he wasn't making that up.

I was at a turning point in my life, a crossroads where for the first time I could choose where I would live, not simply be carried along by circumstance. I was born in Texas, grew up in Maryland, Alabama, and California, and had since lived everywhere from Idaho to the Carolinas. When people used to ask me where I was from, I would go blank, like a foster child passed around to too many families to know which one was home. Where did I come from? I longed, deeply, to find a place to call mine. And as a writer, my office was my laptop. I could choose anywhere.

So why did I choose West Virginia, a state that has notoriously *lost* population in the past century?

When I was a little girl and we lived in a suburb of D.C., my father took us every summer to an old cabin in West Virginia. It stood on the last family-owned piece of a farm that had belonged to my great-grandfather, a farm once spanning hundreds of acres on the banks of the Pocatalico River. My father was born and raised on that farm in Stringtown, an early twentieth-century gas and oil boomtown in rural Roane County, rising up out of the backwoods between Walton and the county seat of Spencer. Back in his day, what are now wild woods were cleared farm fields. There was a church, a school, a store, and even a hotel. The gasoline plant employed fifty men. There were wooden sidewalks down the dirt road and a public walking bridge across the river. The one-room schoolhouse where my grandmother taught still stands, but the Stringtown where I played during those long-ago summers was much different otherwise. It was like some kind of lushly forested alternate universe filled with the ghosts and tales of my ancestors—the now-overgrown hills and meadows they once farmed, the caves where they hid their horses from Confederate soldiers, the graves in hidden cemeteries where they were buried.

I loved those summers in West Virginia. I loved the trees and the quiet. I loved swinging on grapevines over the river and learning to skip rocks. And most of all, I loved that sense of history and place. My father clearly felt enough sentiment for the land to share it with me by bringing me to visit. Yet despite its charms he—like so many of his generation, drawn like moths to the flame of cosmopolitan life beyond those simple hills—grew up and moved away, never to return but for those brief times. He used to say about West Virginia, "I got out of there as soon as I could."

But when I stood at that crossroads in my life and decided to move to the boonies of West Virginia, to the countryside outside the tiny town of Walton just over the hill from my great-grandfather's old farm, I took a deep breath of the clean air, looked up at the sky littered with stars you could actually see, felt the far-reaching pull of my family's roots, and said, "I *got* here as soon as I could."

The tiny town of Walton takes, oh, a minute and a half to drive through. Most people might think there's not much there, but there's all we need. If we actually want something from the city, we can drive the winding road to the interstate and get it, but that doesn't happen too often. There is a cute little one-room library, a cute little grocery store with half a dozen aisles, a couple of small churches, and a bank, all flanked by country roads so narrow you have to pull off to pass. The school is so small, when my younger son graduated from eighth grade and I asked him who his friends were, he looked at me as if that was a stupid question and said, "There are only thirty-six students in the whole grade. I have to be friends with everyone."

And he was right—everyone is friends with everyone. Walton was like one big *Cheers* bar. Everybody knows your name. At first, I found this disconcerting. Why were these strangers at the Thriftway, Walton's one little store, talking to me as if they knew me? And how did they know my name? When my oldest son totaled my car two days after he got his driver's license, all the kids at school knew about it by the time he got there the next morning. When I arrived at the accident scene, a paramedic I'd never laid eyes on before was calling me by my first name. Mark, my cousin, heard about it at his office and drove down to check on the scene. Mark's wife, Sheryl, a nurse at the nearby hospital, ran down to the emergency room in case we needed to come in. It's like everyone knows everything by some kind of osmosis. Everywhere I went for the next month, people asked me about the accident. I was a world away from the anonymous suburbs. Here, people were connected—to the land, to the history, to one another.

My kids ate sandwiches sitting in apple trees. They jumped fully clothed into the river. They skated on frozen creeks and learned how to pick a hoe out of the shed. They knew what a low-water bridge was and how to set a turtle trap. They piled corn on the cob on their plates and remembered planting the seeds. We didn't worry about burglars at night—just raccoons.

People around here don't have much if you compare them to suburbanites. Even if they can afford it, they don't buy granite countertops or designer clothes, and there's not much competition at the high school for the swankest car. As my older son liked to say (in his exaggerated teenage way), "They're all driving cars their grandfathers bought in 1950." But for all they don't have, what they do have is one another, along with that deeply held pride in community and family and plain living that has been largely lost in the contemporary world.

And that's exactly why I wanted to bring my once-pampered suburban children here, to grow up knowing what matters, what is real. The rural landscape of Appalachia is still an alternate universe from the rest of the country. Here, you don't call for pizza. You call your neighbor.

Other people may have chosen to leave, but I chose to come, and I choose to stay. When people ask me where I'm from now, I have an answer. I'm from West Virginia. And my children, who once wondered if I brought them to this Slanted Little House to die, bloomed like flowers taken from a sterile hothouse and put out in the natural sun.

We didn't come to this Slanted Little House to die. We came here to live.

CHICKENS IN THE ROAD

CHAPTER 1

I want to live where I can have chickens in the road." I made this pronouncement one day while driving down a dusty back road bordered by weedy woods and intermittent dilapidated farms. A big red rooster led a line of hens across the lane, lending a charming, storybookish air to the run-down scenery.

I was so smitten.

52, by my side, said, "You can have all the chickens you want."

Maybe I loved him. Maybe I just wanted the chickens. I thought I wanted both, but it was hard to tell. They were deeply intertwined.

He and I were cousins six or seven times removed, which isn't unusual in West Virginia. Unless you are talking to someone fresh from Alaska, you are probably related. He'd grown up in Roane County and his family roots went back as far as mine, though he was living in Charleston then. At the time we met, he was 52, which became my endearment for him. He was more than a decade older than me, with an air of calm wisdom. He was bespectacled, gray haired, and he smoked cherry tobacco in an old pipe. Tall, neatly dressed on workdays in an ever-present button-down white shirt and the day's choice of navy blue or khaki slacks or his weekend uniform of worn jeans and a plain T-shirt, he was my soft place to land.

He liked the nickname I'd given him. "I'm 52 forever," he liked to say.

We'd started out as friends, but our relationship gradually deepened. He told me a story one day about a feral cat that had shown up outside his door in Charleston. The cat wouldn't let him come near her, but one day he left his back door open. The cat came inside. For three weeks, he didn't even try to touch her.

He was, just simply, kind to her. "And eventually," he said, "she was mine."

It was how he got me, too.

I'd had a couple of hard years. I'd left my marriage and my life behind to move "home" to West Virginia, a place I'd visited often during childhood but had never lived. I could already point to a jury of family and friends who would say I'd lost my mind. Now I was going to buy a farm.

With 52.

Who was so kind.

I couldn't think of anyone with whom I'd rather start a flock of chickens.

He got me. He completely understood my crazy desire for a farm. He wanted one, too. We were, most of all, mutual enablers, ready to pull each other by the hand as we leaped into the mist.

I could never remember later who first said, "Let's buy a farm together," but we were both on board. I'd dreamed of a farm all my life, though my motivation wasn't that simple. I was lost and trying to find myself in my childhood memories of West Virginia. I'd come to test myself, to discover the real me. He'd actually owned a farm in the past, which had ended badly in a broken marriage, and he was ready to go back to a farm again and do it right.

I was the one who found the real estate listing online. Forty acres, free gas, green meadows, blue skies, a dirt-rock road. In my imagination, I added butterflies on the breeze, chickens in the road, and bluebirds on the windowsill. I was instantly transported to fantasyland. I was going to be a pioneer! All I needed was an apron and a bonnet!

The free gas turned out to be a lie, and the best house site was halfway up a hill with a steep, terrifying access. But the property was in my family's long-ago stomping grounds of Stringtown.

Even the real estate agent got lost trying to find it. The fact that the sign had been knocked down didn't help. The farm was on a two-and-a-half-mile stretch of dirt-rock road that ran between two paved roads. To reach the hard (paved) road on one end, you had to ford a river.

To reach the hard road on the other end, you had to cross three creeks.

There were no bridges.

Bridges were for sissies.

This was rural Roane County, West Virginia. It was only about thirty miles outside the capital city of Charleston, but there was a world of twisty, curvy roads and wild terrain between them. In the hills of West Virginia, barriers don't take up much mileage. Once you hit the back roads, go country or go home. I had only recently figured out the difference between hay and straw, but I was going country all the way.

From a population perspective, West Virginia is a small state. The total population is slightly under two million, which is roughly the same number it held a century before—and that is after some slight recent growth. The largest city in the state, the capital of Charleston, boasts just over fifty thousand residents—which is but a medium-size town in many places. Roane County is a typical county within the state, its heyday in the gas and oil age of the late nineteenth and early twentieth centuries long gone, leaving a population of only around fifteen thousand. Most of that population is centered in and around the county seat of Spencer, with a few small towns in the outlying areas, including the tiny town of Walton, outside of which my cousin's farm is located. It is a very rural county with many small communities that long ago disappeared, such as Stringtown.

Walton has its little store, an elementary/middle school, a post office, and a couple of tiny churches. In Spencer, one can find the courthouse, the one high school in the county, a Walmart, a few fast-food restaurants and mom-and-pop diners, and the

Robey Theatre, which holds the distinction of being the longest continuously operating movie theater in the United States. (In 1941, when my dad was sixteen, he could take a date to the Robey with twenty-five cents—tickets, popcorn, and Cokes included.) If you need more, Charleston is less than an hour away, but from those lost communities like Stringtown, tucked away on near-impassable rock roads in the depths of the hills and hollers, you might as well be on the moon. I was attracted to the isolation, the challenge, and the charm of the unspoiled land.

I went home to the Slanted Little House and told Georgia I was buying a farm in Stringtown. She was Mark's mother, and my stand-in mother, adoptive grandmother, constant friend, and waking nightmare. Georgia had grown up in West Virginia, and she was smarter than me.

Georgia said, "How will you get out in the winter?"

"Other people live out there! They must be able to get out! If I can't get out sometimes, I'll stock up!"

Georgia said, "Well."

In Georgia-speak, "well" could mean many things. That day, it meant, "You don't know what you're doing, girl."

Georgia was a woman of few words and she said a lot of them with her eyeballs.

Not that I was listening. I was about to buy the most magical farm in all the land! Or, in fact, I was about to embark on an intense experience of hardship, deprivation, passion, danger, and romance gone awry.

But it was a good thing I didn't know any of that right then.

I'd been living in the Slanted Little House for well over a year by that time. The Slanted Little House was—and still is—a one-hundred-year-old farmhouse that stands on a farm in Walton, West Virginia. The current owner is Georgia's son, my cousin Mark, who built his own home next door. He's actually my second cousin, but in West Virginia, almost everyone is your cousin to one degree or another, so we don't usually get that detailed.

Back in the day, Mark's grandparents, my great-aunt Ruby and great-uncle Carl, lived in the Slanted Little House. Carl Sergent was a farmer and an oil field worker, and he was also active in local politics, which meant he got his road paved. When the road crew arrived, they told Carl to cut a nine-foot rod for them to use to make the width of the road as they paved. Carl didn't want a nine-foot road so he cut a twelve-foot rod. Nobody double-checked him, so he got a twelve-foot road. Carl knew how to get things done.

The original farmhouse (dubbed the Slanted Little House by my younger son because of its uneven floors) was built sometime around the turn of the twentieth century and consisted of what are now the front rooms. The construction was typical of its era—a simple white clapboard home with a small front porch that was later expanded to become quite large, stretching across the entire front. Porch swings hung on each end, and large rocking chairs with peeling green paint lined up in front of the wide banisters. It was the kind of porch that begged you to sit a spell in its shaded cocoon.

An old-fashioned well, the kind with a pail on a chain enclosed in a quaint well house, still stands to one side. On the other side, there is a stone cellar, which was later attached to the house through the cellar porch and the addition of back rooms. No hallways exist—all the rooms open onto each other, one doorway leading to the next. (Where there are doors, that is. Ruby didn't like doors.) A small bathroom was added at some point. The kitchen was remodeled sometime in the 1950s or 1960s and remains a testament to Formica and linoleum.

During my childhood, family trips to Stringtown, where we camped out in an old cabin, were always bookended with visits to the Slanted Little House, which was only a few miles away and over the hill. Ruby would be outside doing strange things, like taking corn off an actual cornstalk. Who knew you could grow your own corn? And truly, I didn't think anyone did, except for my great-aunt Ruby. She grew all kinds of things I didn't know people could grow, plus some other things I'd never heard of and didn't want to eat, like beets and rhubarb. Then she'd do some trick where she'd get the stuff into jars and keep it in the cellar. The old stone cellar had a short medieval-style door that latched with a chain. The ceiling was low and inside it was dark. Cobwebs lurked in the corners. The sagging shelves were always lined with jars filled with Great-Aunt Ruby's garden witchery. As a child, I found it both creepy and mysteriously alluring.

At home, we had a bright, clean pantry full of food with labels from Green Giant and Kellogg.

In earlier days, Carl and Ruby raised chickens, cows, sheep, and pigs, but by the time I was a child, they'd retired from farming and just kept a pony around for the grandkids and other visiting children. For some reason I can't imagine, I was allowed to take off down the road with the pony one day. The road just past their farm was dirt, because of course Carl only had the county pave the road to his farm and no farther. The pony got away from me. It had been raining, and I can still see the puddles in the dirt road as I ran screaming and crying after it. The pony kept running, and I went sobbing around the back of the house to find Ruby in the garden. She said, "It knows where it belongs. It'll come home." And it did.

I never saw Ruby get excited or upset about anything. She was an ocean of calm on her farm of wonder. She wore an apron all day every day, and her table groaned with bowls and platters of food at every meal. She was comfort personified, and her house was a beacon of everything I thought home was supposed to be, from the huge, shady front porch with rocking chairs to the ticktock of the grandfather clock in the slightly shabby sitting room, from the sheets hanging on the line in the sunlit breeze to the fat, juicy tomatoes in the biggest garden I'd ever seen.

By the time I came to live in the Slanted Little House, it stood empty but for its crowded collection of antique furnishings. Ruby had been dead for over ten years, and Carl more years than that, but the Sergent farm, like so many family farms in West Virginia, was well populated. Rural Appalachian farms commonly have two, three, even four homes. Grandma and Grandpa in one, their child or two in others, then their child or two in yet others. West Virginia is often said to have higher home ownership than any other state because so many families have generations-old family farms—and everybody lives there. By the time Ruby died, her son Bob and his wife, Georgia, had built a house on the farm, as did their son Mark after that. Bob had passed away, and Mark was married with a son around the age of my sons. I was never alone. The kids went to school. Mark went to work at the courthouse. His wife, Sheryl, went to her job as a nurse at the local hospital. But Georgia, in her late seventies by then, was always there.

She was the lady of the manor, a workhorse, a slave driver, Miss Marple, and Martha Stewart rolled into one. Her hair was short and white, and she had it styled like clockwork every Tuesday at the old folks' home. She wore a sweater unless it was the hottest of days, and she was always, constantly, doing something. She came over to the Slanted Little House ten times a day, and if I was in the bathroom, she waited outside the door. With my mail. Or a plate of sandwiches. Or orders to come help her hoe.

She suffered from macular degeneration, and she liked me to drive her places.

She'd come over and say, "What time did you say you were going to town?"

Because I'm slow, I'd always say, "I wasn't planning to go to town."

She'd say, "Yes, you were. I need to go, too. Let's go at ten."

There were only a couple hundred people in town and she knew them all. Usually, she was taking some kind of food basket to somebody, so we'd have to make deliveries. I'd play her Secret Service detail, chauffeuring then hanging around outside, wait-ing. I'd take her to the bank and the post office and the little store,

then we'd run out of places to go on parade because the town is
that small. Sometimes, just to exasperate her, I'd ask if she wanted
to joyride and find a bar.

She thought I was funny. Or crazy. In any case, I was entertaining.

Back home, she'd turn into the chore Nazi. Time to hoe. Time
to can. Time to climb on ladders and clean out the gutters. Time
to rake, time to drag branches to the brush pile, time to sweep
something. If she couldn't think of a good chore, then she'd come
into the house, walk into my bedroom where I'd be sitting at my
laptop trying to write, and just stand there.

ME: What are you up to?
GEORGIA: Nothing.

Then I knew she just wanted to talk, and I learned to listen.

Anytime I went anywhere, when I came home, she was right
there, like she'd transported herself to the porch from the *Star-
ship Enterprise*. She'd bring my mail to me whether I wanted her to
or not, and she'd donate all her leftovers to me, whether I needed
them or not. She checked up on my kids, whether they liked it or
not, and none of them could get away with anything because she
was half blind with laser vision.

When I came back to West Virginia as an adult, leaving a broken
marriage behind me, whether it was instinct, fantasy, or pure in-
sanity, the first thing I did was go "home" to the Slanted Little
House, like a pony finding my way back to the barn. I'd never lived
in West Virginia, but it was home to me all the same. My childhood summers there had filled me with the intoxicating fantasy
of its hills and woods and gurgling streams, and something about
it felt just right. I was supposed to be there. I didn't need a rhyme
or reason, and I didn't really have one. I was following my heart,
pure and simple, and at that most difficult point in my personal
life, my heart led me like a heat-seeking missile to my roots in
West Virginia. Here, I was certain, I could find the real me.

I barely knew Georgia when I asked her if I could live in the Slanted Little House. She and Bob had lived in various parts of West Virginia during Bob's career before retiring back to the farm, so I had spent little time around them during my childhood visits, but she didn't blink. She said, "Of course, you're family."

I had always loved that old house, though I found it wasn't easy to live there. There are a number of things nobody tells you about living in a hundred-year-old farmhouse before you move in.

· ·

TEN THINGS NOBODY TELLS YOU

1. Somebody probably died there. Maybe a couple people. Maybe they're still there. Maybe in that ammo box on top of the pie safe. People are practical in the country. Why buy a fancy urn when there is a perfectly good empty ammo box available?

2. It's cold. And it's going to get colder. And the house is not going to get warm. Remember when you were five and you thought living in an igloo would be so neat? Try to be cheerful. Buy an electric blanket and a space heater no later than November. You can forget about finding any in the store after that.

3. You're going to be cold anyway.

4. Those noises in the wall? That's mice. Huge, giant, evil mice with flaming red eyes and poisonous fangs. Your cats aren't going to get them out of the wall for you so just forget about that, but you can stock up on scented candles because when they die there? You'll be the first to know.

5. Buy really, really long wooden matches. You'll be less scared that you're going to blow yourself up if you have long matches when it's freezing and you're lighting the gas stove in the cellar porch every night in the winter to keep the pipes from freezing.

6. The pipes are going to freeze anyway.

7. Don't get excited about buying ten extension cords with multiple plugs to make up for the lack of existing outlets in the house. You're just going to go home and blow all the circuits.

8. Those slanted floors that were the first thing you noticed when you moved in? You'll totally forget about them after a few years. So be careful when you're drinking.

9. No matter the inconveniences, no matter the hardships, living in a slanted little house is a privilege. It might change your life. It will certainly change your perspective.

10. If you can move out before anyone puts you in an ammo box, it's all good.

By the time I met 52, I was longing for a home of my own (with insulation and outlets), a fresh start, a new life . . . a farm. A real working farm, like Carl and Ruby's used to be.

We met at the farmers' market in Charleston, or one day when he pulled over at the Slanted Little House to ask directions—depending on which story we were telling that day. In fact, we met online at a dating site. Neither of us liked that story, so we had a few alternate versions.

I had regretted signing up for the site nearly as soon as I'd done it and quickly removed my profile, but not before receiving a message from 52. We began to correspond. I thought he was funny.

"Funny ha-ha or funny strange?" he wanted to know.

Maybe a little of both.

We did, indeed, meet in person for the first time at the farmers' market in Charleston. We had lunch at Soho's, a trendy Italian restaurant located inside the Capital Market. He had the minestrone, which I later found he always ordered there, and I had a sandwich. He was supposed to go back to work, but we talked for three hours. He spent much of that time describing his failed marriage. He had three grown children. His relationship with them had been strained in the past but had since grown closer. It was the continuing bitterness with which he spoke of his ex-wife that was off-putting.

On the drive home, I decided not to see him again, but no sooner had I gotten back to the Slanted Little House than he'd e-mailed me.

He'd been satisfied alone, he said, but he wouldn't be as happy that way as he could be.

He told me I was cute and thanked me for giving him a chance.

I didn't have time to respond. Georgia was waiting for me out-side the farmhouse when I got home, nearly in a fit because she was worried about where I had been all that time. The kids had just gotten off the bus, and I had to figure out what in the world I was doing with 52 and why I still wanted to talk to him. I'd promised myself I wouldn't, but later that day I e-mailed him back.

We met for the second time when he did, indeed, pull over in front of the Slanted Little House. And maybe he was looking for directions, in a sense. I had admitted my conflicted feelings about a relationship that was anything more than friendship with him.

"You're not finished with your experience with me yet," he said. "Once you're sure you're done with that, you can move on."

"If you're nice," I said, "I'll never move on."

Aside from my doubts about him, my kids were ten, thirteen, and fifteen. My daughter, Morgan, was my youngest, and I had two boys, Weston and Ross. I didn't think they were ready to see me involved with a man, but at the same time, I wanted to go on with my life. I wasn't sure if 52 was the one with whom I wanted to go on, but we had enough in common to make me curious. We had discovered our distant family relationship along with our shared interest in simple living. We took long drives to nowhere on back-country roads, picking blackberries and looking for old barns. We took walks, holding hands, while he told me all the names of the wildflowers and trees. We went to the New River Bridge, Dolly Sods, Blackwater Falls, the Canaan Valley, Spruce Knob, Seneca Forest. He was my West Virginia tour guide.

I had come empty, looking for West Virginia to fill me up, and he became the epitome of my West Virginia.

We were friends, and eventually lovers, though I kept my relationship with him mostly to myself, seeing him on weekends and summertimes when the kids were visiting their dad.

By the time I'd become enamored of chickens in the road, we were looking for a farm of our own.

He wrote down a beautiful dream and gave it to me. The cats would sleep in the road. We'd leave our doors unlocked and feel safe. We'd have a smokehouse and a woodstove. We'd be so warm we'd open our windows in the winter. There would be cows and horses, and kids playing ball in the meadow bottom. If we needed help, we'd call the neighbors and they'd come 'round the hill in the middle of the night or a Sunday afternoon.

We'd rock grand-babies on the porch swing, can from the garden, and have a giant corn patch, and flowers—so many flowers. There'd be sled riding and Christmas lights, a tire swing and a big rooster.

"And we'll just sit on the porch and get old together—and we won't care if we're fat and old and worn out because we'll love each other too much to care."

The sum of it all, he told me, was that I was his dream.

I wanted it all—the sweetness of him, the corn patch, the Christmas lights, the big rooster, and the love. I was a romance writer, and I was ready for my own storybook. He was my hero.

We signed the papers at the bank and we had a farm . . . without so much as a tumbled-down fence post with which to begin.

CHAPTER 2

Soon after we'd bought the farm, my father called and said, "Whatever you do, don't buy a farm in the country. Buy a house in Charleston."

It took me a few months to get up the courage to tell him that not only had I bought a farm in the country, I'd bought a farm in Stringtown.

And really, it was his fault.

I didn't grow up there, but I was indoctrinated in the West Virginian's reverence for roots by my father, who not only took me "back home" every summer of my childhood to the old cabin and Ruby's Slanted Little House, but told me the stories as he did it. Here is where your great-great-grandfather hid his horses from the Confederate soldiers, here is where he built a log cabin, here is where he is buried.

When I was growing up, I can recall the occasional resentment of my mother for the emphasis my father placed on his family's roots as opposed to her own.

She would sometimes stamp her foot and say, "I have a family history, too."

But she was from Oklahoma, and the same way a Texan swaggers into a room with the confidence that everything is bigger in Texas, a West Virginian quietly and yet emphatically lets you know there are no roots like West Virginia roots. My father, who frequently repeated, "I got out of there as soon as I could," was a West

Virginian to the bone nonetheless. I'd grown up on the tales of Stringtown, and now I was moving there.

52 came up with the farm's new name, Stringtown Rising Farm. Stringtown would rise again! I felt an immediate, intense sentimental attachment for the property, located as it was in the midst of my family history and childhood memories.

There was a two-and-a-half-mile unpaved road between the Slanted Little House and Stringtown Rising. The road was icy and barely passable in the winter (and certainly not without a four-wheel-drive). There was no U.S. mail, UPS, or FedEx delivery. No cell phone, cable, or DSL service. No school bus. No trash pickup. And, as I later learned, no local television satellite service. Stringtown Rising was hemmed in by three creek crossings in one direction and a river ford in the other, but it was directly across the river from my great-grandfather's old farm, across the road from our old family cemetery with its beaten-down tombstones, and within a mile of the house where my father grew up and the old cabin where I had spent so many of my childhood summers.

Not only that, but my grandmother had lived on this farm in one of the oil company worker houses that once lined the road, and she had later taught in the little white church that doubled as a one-room schoolhouse that had once stood on the farm. My father attended that little community church throughout his childhood and went to school there to first grade, after which a new school was built across the river.

I wrote sentimentally about the road to our new farm on my website, not yet smart enough to fear it.

"There are no guardrails, no pavement beneath your wheels. It's a hard road to travel. You can't speed down it even if you want to, but there are things to discover along the way, and something beautiful at the end.

"Many of the people on this road are passers-through. The road is scattered with weekend cabins. They come in the fall with their orange coats and their deer rifles. They come in the summer with their ATVs and their beer. If you wait long enough, they'll go away.

"The handful of people who stick around for the isolating snows of winter and the pounding rains of spring are an optimistic bunch. They put out mailboxes at the ends of their driveways as an affirmation to the universe that someday the post office will deliver mail down this road. They know anything is possible if you believe. Even mail.

"Don't be scared by the first creek. The creeks get bigger. Keep going. You're not going to drown. Don't forget to look around. You might see a black bear or a wild turkey. Or maybe the first sweet pea leaning its pretty bloom over a fence post.

"Some people want to stop at the second creek. But you can't turn around. There's no place to go but forward. Do you see a bunch of abandoned vehicles? People have gone down this road before you and they made it.

"Look around and see the foundation stones of the old gasoline plant that employed fifty men a century ago in the gas and oil heyday of this now-deserted area. They didn't have cars. They had to walk this road every day.

"The last creek is the biggest. Flash floods can make it temporarily impassable, but if you just wait a little while, the water will go down. If you can get past this final obstacle, there are better things ahead. Maybe even a brand-new farmhouse."

52 and I had decided not to marry, having both experienced divorce, but we had few qualms about going into a property purchase together—or at least few that we discussed. I was, in truth, afraid of tackling a farm on my own. I knew nothing about farming, and I'd spent most of my life being taken care of by other people—first by my parents, then by my husband, then, in a sense, by my cousin Mark. I was having a hard time breaking that habit and was only

even vaguely aware that I was, again, counting on a man to take care of me. Defying a marriage certificate was a false independence to which I clung.

We hired a builder and began construction. The property boasted no remaining structures, but it did have a nice meadow bottom large enough for a pasture and a barn (in my imagination), with a creek winding along the foot of the hillside. The new house was built on a plateau halfway up the hill, accessed by a driveway carved into the hill by loggers a few years earlier when the property had been selectively timbered. The loggers had also created the plateau where the house was built, which provided enough semiflat space around the house for a vegetable garden, chicken house, duck pond, and a few small fields to keep animals, but building a house in such a remote and inaccessible location created one obstacle after another.

One day, an 18-wheeler from Ohio arrived at the Slanted Little House, where the kids and I continued to live during the construction, with the kitchen cabinet delivery for the new farmhouse. Two big men got out of the truck and one of them said, "I stopped at the little store in town and they told me we'd have to drive through three creeks to get to your farm."

I said, "Oh. Yeah." Well, he wasn't so sure about that and decided he'd better hop in my SUV and let me take him out there for a look-see.

We didn't get a quarter of a mile down the road before he said, "I'm not taking my truck down this road."

I said, "That's okay. You can just go around the other way. That way, you only have to drive through a river." That last sentence seemed to disturb him.

I tried to convince him it was only a small river, but by the time we got to the Pocatalico for a look-see there, he was shaking his head, no, no, no, he was not crossing the river. I said, "It's only like a foot deep. It's got a rock bottom. I've driven through it lots of times. It's hard road all the way if you go this way except for when you cross the river."

The farm borders the river, so from that direction, all you had to do was drive through the river—and you were there. There was no convincing him.

In the end, the two men and their truck drove around to the ford, and our builder, Steve, made repeat trips across the river in his pickup to off-load the cabinets one truckload at a time and take them back across to the house. Meanwhile, the two men in the 18-wheeler stayed on the hard road across the river. One of them got out a video camera and took footage of the ford to take back home to Cleveland.

I went home to the Slanted Little House and told my cousin the story of the two big men in their big truck who wouldn't cross the river. I said, "Well, you know, they were from the city."

Mark said, "You really are a country girl now."

This wasn't entirely true, of course. In fact, while the house was under construction, I'd totaled my previous SUV by driving across when the water was too high. I learned to respect the river and not take crossing the ford for granted. The Pocatalico River, which finds its source in Roane County not far from the ford, is a long, narrow river that flows eventually into the Kanawha River. The old-timers called it the Poky, and a lot of the new-timers call it a creek. It's a river by length, not width, and in many spots really doesn't look like much more than a big creek. The ford, in common use for horse and vehicle traffic for at least a hundred years, was usually no more than six inches deep and safe about 99.9 percent of the time. But right after a heavy rain, it could kill your car and possibly you if you didn't pay attention, and, as I learned after living at the farm, once or twice a year the Pocatalico floods, transforming it into a truly terrifying force of nature. I was really glad to have a house halfway up a hill the first time I saw that happen.

The ford was, and is, the beating heart of old Stringtown. In the old days, when my father was growing up, there was a swinging bridge across the river near the ford for foot traffic. Not far down the river from the ford is a deep spot that has served as a swimming hole from before my father's day to today. The one-room schoolhouse was across the river, the little church on this side of the river. There were stores and a hotel and a gasoline plant not far down the road. Men congregated at the river to shoot marbles in the evenings. Women gathered to talk.

In what remains of Stringtown today, neighbors still gather at the banks of the ford. There was a lot of talk when the new farmhouse was built.

"Who knew there was that much room to put a house up on that hill."

"They should have made that roof red."

And my favorite one: "It's that romance writer, you know."

A few years earlier, when I was still a summertime visitor to the Slanted Little House, Georgia had engineered an article in the county paper about me. I'd written a novel set in West Virginia, so she used that as a springboard to talk the editor into doing a piece. She'd set up a book signing at the one-room library in town and got the high school principal to bring me in to talk to a few classes about writing. Georgia was a one-woman promotional machine, and people still remembered that I was "that romance writer." If that wasn't enough, now I was building a house in Stringtown, and everybody knew it.

I was at a school function with Morgan one evening when a massive man wearing a flannel shirt with sleeves torn off at the shoulders and tattoos on his bulging biceps approached me. He didn't look like a West Virginia mountain man. He looked like a West Virginia *mountain*.

"Are you Suzanne?"

A number of possible responses ran through my mind, including, "No, I'm her twin sister," and, "I think she moved away."

Morgan said, "That's her name!" I gave her the evil eye.

The man said he was a friend of my cousin's, which might have made me feel better except my cousin was an attorney, so he knew a lot of criminals. Then he asked me if he could have my derrick.

Oil and gas exploration in the 1890s in this area of West Virginia made Beverly Hillbillies out of countless families—including my own, who were so overcome by their surprising wealth-from-nowhere that they threw their clothes away after wearing them to buy new rather than trouble themselves with laundry. One would think they could have set aside some of their loot for their descendants. My great-grandfather, at least, spent a good portion of his oil dollars buying up land. It wasn't his fault that his descendants sold out, leaving nothing for my generation. All that remains today of Stringtown's gas and oil heyday is its historic junk, covered in grapevines and multiflora rose. My favorite pile of junk was the old oil derrick on our new farm. It was situated up on the hill, not far from where we were building the house. It soared through the trees, a testament to a different time in that old place.

Flannel-and-Tattoos said the former owners of our farm had promised the derrick to him.

"I'm going to tear it down and sell it for scrap metal," he explained. "They said I could have it."

The derrick came complete with a flywheel and a gearbox that would have transmitted power to the walking wheel. The gearbox is inscribed with the forging date of July 18, 1898. The walking wheel ran the beam and rods that pulled the oil up out of the ground. A wire line wheel held cable that drew various tools in and out of the well.

The well was lined with wood and was open when we found it. We'd covered it with a board and a heavy rock for safety.

All this huge, heavy equipment had been hauled to Stringtown down narrow, rocky back roads and over countless hills by teams of horses and oxen. I could hardly imagine the event it must have been to construct that derrick on our hill.

To me, it wasn't scrap to be sold for dollars. It was history.

"It's not their derrick anymore," I said firmly. "It's ours, and I like it right where it is."

He looked disappointed, and I worried about whether he might sneak out to the farm and take it anyway. I mentioned him to my cousin.

"He won't take it if you told him no," Mark told me. "Everybody knows it's your farm now."

So many people knew about our new farm, in fact, that they became a nuisance. The builder put up a gate on the driveway to protect the materials and tools at night, but sometimes he had to lock it during the day to keep people from driving up, taking his work time to gawk and gossip. Then they'd drive real slow up and down the road in front of the farm and look up through the trees. They even sat on the hill across from the farm with binoculars.

Then there were the people who couldn't even find the farm.

The electrical inspector called me at the Slanted Little House, lost on his way to inspect the electric at the new farm.

I said, "Where are you?"

He told me he'd gone past where the hard road stopped and then it had turned to hard road again. After a few more questions, I figured out where he was, which was about three miles past the river ford. He'd found a bar of cell service there.

He said, "How do I get to your house from here?"

I'd already learned that people didn't react well to being told to drive across the river, so I said, "I'll be right there."

When I found him, I rolled down my window, and he said, "The map doesn't show this road even going to your farm."

I said, "Yes, it does. It's just kind of like an adventure."

He said, "What do you mean?"

"Don't worry about it. Just follow me."

Sometimes it worked better to lead people across the river and let them see me bring my car out on the other side. Then they knew they would survive.

The road in the other direction was no easier, stretching for two and a half miles of unpaved, steep, rocky terrain. There were a handful of residents on the first half mile, close to the hard road. Once you got past that, heading out toward the ford and our farm, there were just a few scattered hunting cabins until you reached a small trailer and then Stringtown Rising Farm and the ford. I came from the rocky road direction most of the time since the Slanted Little House was just around a few bends once you hit the hard road. Between that first half mile and cluster of homes and the ford, there was little regular traffic.

Since the woman who lived in the trailer near our farm drove her kids to the bus stop at the hard road every morning and went out again in the afternoon to pick them up, she was one of the first Stringtown neighbors with whom I interacted. She was a plain but attractive woman with three young children. She looked to be in her early thirties, her brown shoulder-length hair often pulled back, her body sturdy—neither thin nor fat—and an air of stubborn self-reliance that permeated her every expression.

The first time I met her, her car had broken down after she'd picked up her kids from the bus. I was on my way out to check on our under-construction house and I took her and her children home in my SUV. My second interaction with her, months later, was when we met on the road, going in opposite directions. We met at a wide spot where I was able to pass. I happened to have my window down and she rolled her window down to tell me that I drove too fast on this road and she didn't like it. I thanked her for letting me know and went on. Having been stuck behind her on the road a few times already, I knew that her idea of fast was anything swifter than five miles an hour.

Sometimes three.

There were no posted speed limits on the road, though I'd been told it was commonly considered a twenty-five-mile-an-hour limit on unpaved roads in the area. It would be difficult to go any faster than that without careening over a cliff, and I supposed no sign was posted because the rough, winding road formed its own limit and for much of it, even twenty-five was too high, but creeping along at five miles an hour or below wasn't necessary unless it was winter. Two and a half miles is a long way to go at creeping speed. There were various points along the road where I could go around her if she stopped or even pulled over just a little, but she refused, leaving me to creep along behind her.

If I had to pass her on the road coming from the other direction, it was always me who had to move over, not her, even if it was harder for me and sometimes required backing up to find a place wide enough. One time I came across her and she stopped her car in the middle of the road when she saw me. I waited for her to move over at least a little to help me pass her. She didn't move. Eventually, she got out of her car, marched up to my window, told me I had four-wheel drive and she didn't, so she wasn't going to move over and I'd better just figure out how to get around her. I asked her if she could move over just a bit since there was a cliff there and she was in the middle of the road. She refused to budge.

I sensed her resentment. I was an outlander, "that writer" who was building that house on the hill to pretend to be a farmer. I was an oncoming blight upon the community, and she let me know, in her way, that I wasn't welcome.

In the house where this woman lived with her husband and young children, they had electricity, but little else. At the time, they had no phone service and no satellite TV. Their house was made up of two old single-wide trailers put together, and there was mildew almost completely covering the outside of the trailers. Their living situation was the classic image of stark Appalachian poverty.

I was appalled, fascinated, and a little bit scared of her, but I soon discovered she was the least of my worries.

CHAPTER 3

I was terrified of driving on the road to our new farm once the snows started. 52 still lived in the city, and it was up to me to keep tabs on the construction progress and to meet with the builder when he needed a quick consultation on-site about one detail or another. I was often so scared and exhausted after the three-mile trip from the Slanted Little House to our farm on its icy, unpaved road that I would get to the bottom of the driveway to the new house, blow my horn, and wait for the builder to drive down and take me up.

My cousin Mark took me for a winter driving lesson.

"What if we roll over the hill?" I asked.

Mark sat in the passenger seat beside me in my SUV, his deadpan gaze suggesting he wasn't getting paid enough for this expedition. I had the key in the ignition, my hands on the wheel. The steep, twisting, narrow rural roads of West Virginia- so bucolic in spring, summer, and fall- looked like nightmare sheets of ice.

One-lane back roads were cut into hillsides, bordered by sharp drop-offs—and there weren't any guardrails. The mountainous landscape was breathtaking and scary.

"If you start sliding, stay off the brake so you can steer," Mark said.

"What if we careen off a cliff?"

"Just take it easy. And step on the gas."

"But what if we go over the cliff?"

"We'll call Peewee to come get your car." Peewee was my cousin's mechanic buddy, and I knew the answer was meant to reassure me. I didn't want to be reassured.

"What if we die?" I countered. Some drop-offs were fifty or more feet down.

"What if a meteor hits us? What if a spaceship lands on our heads?"

"Now you understand!"

Lost in the foreign land of rural Appalachia, sometimes I just needed someone to validate my hysteria.

I'd never lived where it snowed much, and the true four seasons of West Virginia had been a big attraction to me. The reality was a big challenge, not just on the road but in the Slanted Little House as we waited for the new house to be finished. Outside the Slanted Little House, it was a gorgeous winter wonderland, crisp and cold. Inside . . . it was crisp and cold. On snow days home from school, the kids would sleep in front of the gas fire in the sitting room. It was the only warm place in the house. Windows were covered in plastic, rugs were shoved along the bottoms of the doors, all to no avail. It was freezing cold, inside and out. There was no such thing as insulation or double-paned glass back in the day that house was built. Pipes, added later when running water didn't mean running out to the well, passed through the cellar porch on their way to the house, and they froze regularly. (The "cellar porch" was not much more than an enclosed porch that connected the old cellar to the rest of the house.) I used an old gas range in the cellar porch to try to keep the pipes warm. The ignition didn't work quite right, so I'd have to turn on the burners, then light them with a match. Most nights, I'd just light one burner.

If it got down into the teens or below, it was a two-burner night.

Usually if it was that cold, the pipes froze anyway.

I'd had a three-thousand-square-foot modern colonial back in the suburbs of Raleigh, North Carolina. I married when I was eighteen years old. I met my husband when I was fifteen. I still loved him like family, but our relationship had spiraled into a disaster. I wrote romance novels for a living—a dream concocted during my teen years reading Harlequins—and I had begun to feel trapped in a happily ever after that wasn't happy or even my own.

My childhood environment had been sheltered and traditional. My father was a Church of Christ preacher, which was a strict denomination. Men were looked upon as the head of the household and the family's religious leader. Marriage was a woman's true calling, and divorce was severely discouraged—for almost any reason. I was a good girl, and I couldn't get married soon enough. My husband was in the navy at the time, and we both finished college after his enlistment ended. Children were next on the to-do list. Three, just how I'd always planned. I had two boys, then the last one was a girl. Perfect.

It was a bad time to realize that I didn't like my husband very much and that marriage might not be my true calling. I worked hard turning out books left and right. The rest of my attention was focused on the kids. My husband felt neglected and became increasingly angry. I buried myself in my shell, pouring all my passion into my writing while my marriage disintegrated around me. He would explode in outbursts of temper that, while never physical, still scared me and scared the kids, too. The night my youngest, Morgan, ran downstairs crying, demanding to know if we were getting a divorce, stopped me in my tracks.

It wasn't the kind of environment in which I wanted to raise my children, and the moment catapulted me into facing the truth I'd been carrying for too long. I was unhappy. At the same time, I knew that a divorce would not be acceptable. I had been the good girl all my life, the one who never caused my parents trouble, the one who always did what was expected, the one who could be counted on to go along to get along.

I was the youngest child. My sister was two years older than me and liked to lock me in the pantry when we were little. My brother was thirteen years older than me and used to hold me upside down by my ankles over dog poop piles when he got home from school. No matter what they did, I never told my mother because then my brother and sister would have been mad at me. I knew how to tolerate trouble and keep it a secret.

While my brother and sister rebelled against our strict upbringing and had been in frequent conflict with my parents during childhood, I behaved like the ideal child, the one who ate her peas, made perfect grades, and kept her mouth shut. And by the time I was thinking about moving to West Virginia, I'd realized that I could either keep behaving like the ideal child for the rest of my life or I could find out who I was if I stopped doing what everyone expected me to do just because they expected me to do it.

The decision to divorce was selfish or courageous, depending on whom you asked.

I lived in the Slanted Little House for two and a half years after leaving my husband. During my early days there, sometimes when the kids went to school I just stretched out on the tattered couch and stared at the ceiling. For hours. Crying. I'd made a sudden, radical change in the course of my life—and I had no idea how to live outside the perfect good girl box I'd spent my entire life building. I blamed myself for the pain the divorce caused—hurting my husband, hurting my kids, hurting my parents. I couldn't do what was expected of me anymore, but I couldn't accept my decision to do differently. I was in desperate need of inner peace, which I sought in various avenues of simplicity in my new country life. I started baking, which I hadn't done much in years, and learned to make West Virginia staples like corn bread in an iron skillet and big pots of beans.

I started walking. I walked two miles from the Slanted Little House to the main road, then back, every day. I walked when it was hot. I walked in the rain. I walked in blowing snow.

I loved to walk past the neighbors who had cows.

Moo.

The cows did not judge me, and the fresh air and exercise helped vanquish my deep feelings of guilt, at least for a little while each day. Old childhood longings, based on storybooks, for a farm and a cow and chickens awakened and stretched within me as

I walked and walked and walked past the farms. A farm was just a dream, not something I had ever seen as a reality. Realistic plans were things like going to college, getting married, having kids, even getting books published. I grew up in the outlying suburbs of major metropolitan areas. I'd never known anyone who had moved to a farm. It seemed completely unrealistic. But if I had the courage to leave my marriage, what else could I do?

After I moved into the Slanted Little House, anything I could imagine suddenly seemed within reach. Coming back to the world of my childhood, I was like a child again, with my life open before me, the future a story I could write fresh.

Neighbors stopped by often, especially when I first moved in. I was the new local attraction. My favorite was a woman named Faye who lived several miles up the road. She wore lumberjack shirts and jeans, kept her hair tied back, and applied no makeup; she worked at the hardware store. She was good to "Georgie" as she called Georgia, and she stopped by often to visit her. Afterward, she'd come by the porch of the old farmhouse and tell me stories, spitting hulls off sunflower seeds all the while. Her husband had become disabled. She told me that he used to be mean.

She got sick of his behavior and thought about leaving him.

"I told him he needed to call his mother and see when she could come," she said.

"Why?" I asked.

"He asked that question, too," she said. "I told him he'd need somebody to take care of him when I was gone." She told him that he wasn't a very nice person.

She was doing his laundry one day not long afterward and, as always, she checked his pockets before putting his jeans in the wash.

"He had a little folded-up paper in there," she said. "I opened it up and it was a to-do list. Get gas, stop at the store, things like that—except for one. The last thing on the list was 'Be a nicer person.' That day, I decided to stay, and he did become a nicer person."

I was impressed. Faye was an independent woman, and she'd insisted on how she expected to be treated. She was kind, plain-spoken, and tough all at once. She was like a foreigner to me, and I was fascinated.

One day she told me that they didn't have an indoor bathroom. They had an outhouse. It was time to move it and she was digging a new hole.

When she left, I went straight to my cousin Mark. He was the county prosecutor by day. The rest of the time, he liked to work on old cars, drive his tractor around mowing the grass, and cook. He was six foot four, and a giant of a man. He was only a few years older than me, but his hair was salt and pepper. We hadn't known each other well before I'd moved to the Slanted Little House, but he'd taken me in like his little sister. He did a lot of charity work, both through his church and through the courthouse. He'd help people he'd put in jail after they got out. I was his new long-term project. He'd go shopping and buy milk and other groceries, then come to the door at the Slanted Little House with his arms full and tell me they were having a sale or that the items had accidentally fallen into his cart. He knew I had three kids to feed and some-times not enough money.

"Yes, they use an outhouse," Mark said in response to my flab-bergasted demand. He possessed an eternally calm demeanor.

"That's not possible."

"Of course it's possible."

The tectonic plates of my perception of actual hardship had taken a leery shift then, and they took another every time I drove past the mildewed, dilapidated home of my new abrasive neighbor.

Sure, I wasn't moving into an old trailer. I would be, in fact, moving into a nice, modern home with all the heat and insula-tion of which I dreamed during the cold winters at the Slanted Little House. But these two women, both living on rough, remote roads, were tough, and they represented pieces of who I wanted to become.

And yet I was no tough mountain woman—even as I was heading for those same hills, "moving up a holler with my cousin," as I liked to tell people.

I had 52 to take care of me, which was a substantial comfort, and as spring came around and the house neared completion, I was excited and eager to get started on a farm. The kids were excited, too—at least about moving into a new, modern home. I'd introduced 52 into their lives gradually. They accepted him well enough. He took an interest in them, but he didn't push himself on them. They were as ready as me to move out of the Slanted Little House and have more space. My oldest, Ross, even worked on the house with the builder. He was interested in construction. I was just hoping the house might ever be finished.

Of all the challenges in building a house halfway up a hill on that remote road, water was the last great obstacle. Usually, water is one of the first things you determine you have in hand before you build a house, but the previous owners had had a trailer in the meadow bottom at one time, with a sixty-five-foot well. We depended on the notion that it was what we would use too. The new farmhouse was almost completed before the discovery was made that the well was nearly dry. Possibly the casing had caved somewhere inside. Nobody knew, and it didn't really matter. A new well would have to be drilled.

In rural areas, where no public water lines are available, a private well on your own property is your source of running water. An electric well pump pushes water from the well through buried lines to the house, where it runs through the plumbing and comes out the faucets, just as if you were hooked up to a public water source. Except that with a well, all this infrastructure is the property owner's responsibility.

Steve-the-Builder made the arrangements.

"They're going to witch a well," he said.

I was excited. "I want to see that!"

He said, "I figured you'd seen that before."

Maybe in a movie.

The driller arrived with his witcher. I wanted to try, so I asked him to show me how to hold the two wires, which looked like straightened coat hangers to me. (I think they *were* straightened coat hangers.)

I held the wires out in front of me the way he demonstrated. They didn't move.

I said, "This doesn't work. You're making this up."

The witcher said, "You have to believe."

He walked around with the wires for a few minutes, then said, "There's water right here." He pointed to a spot on the ground.

The driller pulled the rig over and started drilling. The messy innards of the earth churned forth from a pipe set across the creek. I'd parked my SUV near there, with the window down, and watched volcanic-like ash spew into my vehicle, helpless to do anything about it unless I wanted to be covered in volcanic ash, too.

The dust filling the air made our farm look like the set of a rock concert.

Two hundred and forty dry feet later, the driller gave up and capped it off.

There had been water at one time at the site of the old sixty-five-foot well. One possibility was to go back to that site and drill a new well nearby.

Or if the driller could get the rig up the hill, which would put the well closer to the house, he could drill near the natural spring in the hillside. During the weeks of the well saga, every old-timer around here told me, "Drill by the spring."

"Drill by the spring."

"Drill by the spring."

I asked my father for his advice since he'd grown up in this very community. He said, "Drill by the spring."

To get the huge drilling rig up the hill, a bulldozer would have to pull it, which was a scary proposition with added expense. Steve-the-Builder arranged for a dozer.

The driller arrived with his rig. 52 and I told him that we wanted to drill by the spring. He pointed to his witcher, who stood halfway up the meadow between the new dry hole and the old well site, pointing at the ground.

He said, "I want to drill there."

I said, "I'm not poking holes all over this meadow. We've already got one dry hole down here."

The driller crossed his arms and gave us an even stare. "Double or nothing. I drill where I want to drill to a hundred feet. If it's a good well, you pay double. If it's dry, it's free, and I go up the hill this afternoon and drill where you want to drill. If we go up the hill now, you pay for that hole and if it's dry, then I come down here and you pay for this hole, too."

He hit water in the meadow at eighteen feet, but he went down to a hundred because he'd promised a hundred feet. The water was gushing all the way. We'd taken the bet that we might get a free dry hole, but it was a well and a half and we were happy enough at that.

The witcher scooped up a handful of the water spewing from the hole and drank it from his hands. "Tastes good," he said. "Except for the mud."

With the water problem solved, we'd be moved into our new house in no time.

52 said, "I'll come home to you every day and we'll sit on the porch and hold hands." That sounded good to me.

It had taken nearly six months to build the house. I had chicken eggs in an incubator and a pile of homesteading how-to books. I could hardly wait to be a farmer.

CHAPTER 4

Up the road from the Slanted Little House was a farm with chickens. Even as our new farmhouse was still being finished, I called to ask if we could come out to see the chickens and collect some eggs. I couldn't wait to get started on my new self-sufficient farm life. By the time we were getting ready to move in, my sons, Ross and Weston, were nearly seventeen and fifteen, respectively, and, like most teenagers, more interested in their friends and things to do in town than chickens and a farm (or their mother). My daughter, Morgan, had just turned twelve and she was the most engaged by the farm, so I took her with me. Georgia came, too. She always enjoyed an outing.

The "chicken lady" had all sorts of chickens, some obtained by ordering mixed batches from catalogs and others by hatchings on the farm. Her eggs came in all colors—shades of brown from pink to deep umber, as well as white, blue, and green. I'd never seen blue and green eggs before in my life. (Blue and green eggs come from Ameraucana or Araucana chickens, or as they're also known, Easter Eggers.) She had golden chickens, black chickens, red chickens, and even a naked-neck chicken, along with guineas, geese, and ducks.

They all came running when her daughter headed to the feed shed to throw out some corn. I wanted a barnyard full of chickens of my own. I'd always loved animals but had never had a chance to have very many of them. I'd had a dog growing up, but that was it. I'd started keeping cats after I married, and during one point when we lived on a lake in Texas, I raised ducks, so I'd had a small taste of farm animals before and wanted more. Chickens seemed like the quintessential farm animal and the place to start. What Morgan wanted most of all was a horse, but our new farm wasn't set up for one. I told her, maybe someday, when we build a barn, but I wanted to get her involved with the farm however I could. She was curious enough about the chickens to help me collect the eggs.

We filled up a box with chicken eggs from the nesting boxes inside the henhouse. The chicken lady's birds free-ranged during the day all over the farm and up the hills and into the woods. She had several month-old babies in a shed inside a large metal trough with a light, feeder, and waterer.

I had no shed, no trough, no light, no feeder, no waterer, no chicken house, and barely a farmhouse. I had to get the eggs back to my new farm over the rough road and across three creeks. By the time I arrived, I was afraid I'd jostled them too much and ruined them already. I had an old still-air incubator and worked to stabilize the temperature at 102, added water to the wells under the tray, and gingerly placed the eggs inside. On each egg, I marked an X on one side and an O on the other. They would have to be turned three times a day. If they were fertile, they would hatch in twenty-one days.

I set the incubator in a back room of the new house, thinking they would be undisturbed there. I hadn't come to know the light in the house yet and we'd had a series of cloudy days. The first sunny day, I was distressed to walk in to turn the eggs and find sunlight streaming down on my incubator from the back window. The temperature inside the incubator was 107. Panicked, I taped cardboard over the window and quickly brought down the temperature.

I called the chicken lady. She said, "You might have cooked your eggs."

All I'd tried to farm so far were eggs and I'd killed them. Maybe.

Morgan begged me not to throw the eggs away.

I couldn't bring myself to break her heart and toss out the eggs, but I did go back to the chicken farm to pick up more. I crowded the new eggs into the incubator with the others.

While I waited for chicks to hatch (or explode), I watched the farm around me wake from winter. I sat on my big new wraparound porch in the mornings wearing a sweater as the pink light crept over the hills, drinking in the unfamiliar sounds of my new farm as I drank my coffee. There had to be a thousand birds! I wasn't used to hearing so many birds. Mixed in the chorus of birdsong, I could hear the river below. The sound was loud, rushing.

My first morning on the farm, I said, "How can I be hearing traffic? There is no traffic out here. Where is that noise coming from?" It sounded like the interstate. Then I realized it was the river, full from the spring rains.

Sometimes I heard the steady *pump-pump-pump* of an oil well somewhere beyond our farm. The sound carried for miles. My great-grandfather, on his farm across the river, used to say, "That's the sound of money." Back in the day, when Stringtown was a center of gas and oil drilling, my great-grandfather made good money from that *pump-pump-pump* sound. My family still owned a share of the mineral rights on my great-grandfather's farm. I was running on empty financially. What if my great-grandfather's wells started pumping again? Would I do as my ancestors did, poor mountain folk who'd never seen so much money in their lives, and throw my clothes away to buy new every week because I had so much money I didn't need to do the wash? I sat on my porch and fantasized about my imaginary future riches.

Then I looked down at the loud river rushing between my farm and my great-grandfather's farm, in awe that I was even there, and remembered that I was rich already. I was living on a farm, and soon I would have my first farm animals.

On Day 23, I decided it was time to do the right thing with my first batch of eggs. It was nearly time for the second batch to hatch, and I couldn't have bad eggs exploding in the incubator and creating an infected environment. It was easy to pick them out as I had marked them differently—the first batch was marked for turning with X's and O's, the second batch with A's and B's. I got an empty egg carton, opened the incubator, and started removing the X- and O-marked eggs, placing them one by one in their sad little casket.

As I placed yet another egg in the carton of death, I heard something. I looked back at the incubator.

One of the X- and O-marked eggs from the first batch, an egg I was about to pick up and throw away, had a crack in it.

And it was peeping!

I put all the eggs back.

I asked Morgan what we should name the little chick as, after finally making its way completely out of its shell, we watched it flop around inside the incubator, then rest its weary head against a brother egg.

"Lucky," she said.

The chick would have been even luckier if we'd had a brooder, but I was completely unprepared. We got one of the boxes we'd been using to move things from the Slanted Little House to the new house. I got a light and put newspaper down inside the box. But how to get the light fixed over the box to keep Lucky warm?

"I've got some Scotch tape in my room," Morgan said, trying to help.

I rooted around and finally came up with a candelabra that I could hook onto the side of the box to brace the light. I set an old address book on top of it to keep the light directed the right way. I put the box against the wall but still needed something heavy to keep it there so the address book and the light wouldn't change direction.

"Find a phone book!" I told Morgan.

She came up with the teeny tiny county phone directory.

"No! The big one!"

With the light set, I found small dishes to use for water and chick starter. I called my cousin to ask if I could borrow his brooder. Lucky turned out to be the sole survivor from the ill-fated first incubator batch, but twelve more hatched from the second. Within days, I had proper feeders and waterers, and 52 started building a chicken house using salvaged lumber. It felt official. I had chickens.

We had no money, and I was immediately and necessarily fascinated with living off the land. It was spring, so I took a sack and set off across the farm in search of ramps. Ramps (*Allium tricoccum*), or wild leeks, are the superbly stinky April delight of Appalachia. Ramps have broad, smooth leaves with purple stems and small white bulbs just under the surface of the soil. Both the white roots and the leafy greens are edible. They grow in the dark, rich woodland soil near streams or on hillsides across the Appalachian region, and a common saying is to look for them when the trilliums are blooming. Ramps are most often fried in bacon fat with eggs and/or potatoes and served with pinto beans and corn bread, but they can be used in just about any recipe similar to how you would use onions or garlic.

In recent years, ramps have become a trendy gourmet item and in some places can be quite expensive, but in the country, they are simply tradition. In West Virginia, springtime is the time of community ramp festivals and ramp dinners, roadside ramp stands, and, for the intrepid, ramp hunting in the wild. My cousin didn't have any ramps on his farm, but he always brought me a paper sack filled with ramps from a roadside stand. Now that I had my own farm, I was eager to discover if I had my own ramps.

I found plenty of trilliums in bloom, but no ramps despite hours of combing the farm in likely places. I was walking along the creek in the meadow bottom with my empty sack when a man came by on a four-wheeler.

He stopped to ask what I was doing.

I'd met him a few times before, enough to know his name and know he lived across the river and a few miles away. Not quite a neighbor, but close enough.

"I'm looking for ramps."

Larry said, "I'll show you ramps."

I was excited.

The situation was akin to a serial killer asking a child if she wants to get in the guy's car and come see his puppy. After the child hops in, they end up on the evening news. But this was rural Roane County, West Virginia—and ramps—and my citified fear of strangers was slipping away. I climbed on the back of Larry's four-wheeler and we took off. We splashed through the river and headed out the hard road on the other side, spring green whipping past in the woods. Larry's black dog rode shotgun.

The hillsides of his farm lived up to his promise—they were covered in huge, gorgeous patches of ramps, ready for the harvesting.

Larry told me that there weren't a lot of ramps in Roane County, so he'd started his ramps by planting them. I'd never known anyone who'd planted ramps. I was fascinated. While I sat on the ground digging ramps, Larry explained how he'd done it, and when I got home, I cut off the root end of every ramp in the sack. I chose several shady areas on the farm that looked ramp-friendly. 52 helped dig holes and I planted my bounty.

Meanwhile, Morgan got in the car from the bus one afternoon at my cousin's house with a brown paper sack.

"This is from Mark," she said. "Guess what it is!"

Even if the knockout odor emanating from the bag in her hand hadn't already told me, it was April, what else would it be? "Ramps!"

And in the future, I'd have my own on my farm.

My new homestead was off and running, and I was quickly overwhelmed, knee-deep in a farm and in the middle of a career change. I loved writing and I loved country life. Before we'd even moved to the farm, I'd decided to align my life and passions by writing about country living, so I'd relaunched my old romance writer's website as a blog under the name *Chickens in the Road* even while the house was still under construction. I joined an advertising network that placed ads on my website. It was a "novel" approach for a writer. Give the writing away to readers for free, and make the income from advertising. It was my New Age way to earn a living from a farm.

I posted my writing and photography every day on my blog, without fail, and had already attracted a growing audience and media attention with feature stories in the local county paper and the *Charleston Daily Mail*. I posted my favorite recipes and crafts, with step-by-step directions and photos. I wrote stories about country life, the people, the places, and most often, the farm. I wrote about the chickens and my fantasies about dotting sheep.

Writing about the farm helped me focus on the positives, the pleasure in each new day of more leaves greening the woods around me. Flowers blooming. Calves in the neighbor's meadow. Walking in the creek and clambering up the hillsides. Chicks hatching in my incubator. Bulbs planted to begin a garden that would last the rest of my life. Cats in my bed, dogs on my porch. Living in the most perfect place in the world even though most of the rest of that world wouldn't even venture down our country road.

Bread in my oven and pies on my counter. Children laughing. Candles on my tables, butterflies in my yard. Open windows and the sound of the river far below. Looking forward, never back.

Joy in the present and taking the time to just breathe and know it for what it was, a gift—in spite of the fear and worries that plagued me in that same present.

The house had cost more than we'd anticipated. We were in debt up to our eyeballs, and hard work looked like the solution. 52 was employed by the state government on a set salary. Even if he worked harder, he couldn't make more money. I concluded that it was up to me to improve our financial situation. I was determined to make my website a success.

I was making sausage gravy and biscuits one Saturday morning when 52 walked into the kitchen and said, "You're making too much noise."

I said, "I'm just trying to break up the sausage in the pan." I was slightly baffled.

"You're too loud."

He had been awake already, checking his e-mail on the computer in the back room.

I said, "I'll try to cook more quietly."

By the time breakfast was ready, Morgan was awake, pounding up and down the stairs to her room.

He said, "Morgan's being too loud."

We were sitting on the porch, drinking coffee, by this time. I said, "I'll ask her to be more quiet."

He said, "You say that, but you won't."

"I will, too!" It wasn't the first time since he'd moved in that he'd complained about the kids making too much noise. "I always talk to them if they're doing something that bothers you."

"Always? You don't always talk to them if I tell you something bothers me."

"Well, okay, not every single time, but I do talk to them about each issue that you tell me bothers you." I did, even though sometimes I resented it. He had been divorced before his kids were teens, and he wasn't used to living in a house with three teenagers. Maybe he hadn't really known what to expect. I tried to split the middle between sympathizing with his nerves and letting the kids be kids. I didn't want to ignore his feelings, but I didn't want to smother the kids either. It was a difficult balance.

"Don't make excuses," he said.

"I'm not making excuses. I'm just trying to explain that I really do talk to them about issues that bother you."

"Now you're arguing."

"I don't want to argue with you. I just want you to know that I care. We all have to get used to living together, and we all have to give a little. Maybe you're a little oversensitive to noise. Kids aren't naturally quiet."

"So it's all my fault."

"I'm not saying that! I'm saying that we'll all have to compromise to learn to live together."

"No, you're right, it's all my fault."

"I don't want to be right, and it's nobody's fault."

"You're always right," he said. "You have to always be right. That's just the way you are. You're right and I'm wrong. I know that's what you think."

That one had come out of the blue. I needed a few seconds to even formulate a response, but I didn't have that much time.

"You think I'm stupid," he went on. "I can tell by the look in your eyes."

The look in my eyes? I was pretty sure the look in my eyes was saying, *Who are you?* Because I'd never met this man before.

"I'm going to see if the boys are up and want breakfast." I left him on the porch and went inside.

I called the boys to fix their plates and sat down at my computer. 52 was almost finished with the chicken house, and it was time to move the growing chicks to their new home. I read comments on my blog and answered e-mails, hoping 52 would be in a better mood by the time he got up to put the finishing touches on the chicken house and we were ready to move the chicks.

When I heard hammering, I knew he was at work on the final touches and I hoped that meant, too, that his mood would be back to normal. I wanted to talk to him about what had happened, but I was uncomfortable about bringing it up. Everybody had bad days sometimes. I decided to let it go.

He was having a hard time adjusting to life in a house with three kids. Since I was the one with the kids, I felt as if the least I could do was be patient with him. He came in when the chicken house was done.

"Are you ready to move the chicks?" he asked.

"Yes!" I was excited, and he was smiling. I went outside with him to see the finishing touches on the house.

We held hands as he walked me around the chicken house, showing me how everything worked. There were nesting boxes that opened from the back and a little door between the chicken house and yard that operated on a rope attached to the side of the house. He had a light set up on an automatic timer.

"It's beautiful," I said, giving his hand a light squeeze. "Thank you." He kissed me softly and told me he was glad I was happy.

I held his gaze. "I want us both to be happy."

"I'm happy," he said.

"Good." I smiled, starting to get excited and dancing up on my toes a little bit. I was eager to move the chickens to their new quarters. "Now let's go get the chickens and make them happy, too!"

School was almost out for summer, and that meant the kids would be leaving to spend a couple of months with their dad. The time meant a chance for 52 and me to settle in to the house by ourselves. I thought the break would be good, giving 52, in particular, relief from the kids' active spirits, and an opportunity for us to reconnect as a couple. Summer also meant a chance to get to know "the 'hood" around us, the neighbors in closest proximity. With sunshine and warm weather, everyone was working outside.

Our farm was about a hundred yards from the ford, with our house up on the hill. A small community of a handful of homes circled around it. Frank, a retired, wiry, energetic man, lived directly across the ford. 52 and I jokingly called him the honorary mayor of Stringtown because he always seemed to be everywhere and always seemed to know what was going on—though more than half the town wouldn't speak to him. That changed nothing. He was the mayor. (Politicians are notoriously unpopular.) He was a neatnik who mowed and trimmed constantly as if he was somehow lost from suburbia, except he would never have survived there because someone would have shot him.

Next door to Frank was his son Denny. Denny lived in the old one-room schoolhouse (transitioned to a house) where my grandmother once taught. He had an on-and-off girlfriend who was a real estate agent. Denny mostly didn't talk to Frank, then sometimes he did. We didn't understand these things, but we didn't have to. We tried to get along with everyone.

Then there was Sonny, who lived to the left as we looked out at the ford from our house. We didn't know much about Sonny. He was quiet and kept to himself. Sonny didn't speak to Frank. (Are we seeing a pattern here?) To the right from the ford was Ed, who lived in my great-grandfather's new house. (In other words, Ed built a house on the exact same spot as my great-grandfather's house, which had been torn down.) Ed had a wife, but we'd never met her. Ed didn't speak to Frank. (!) Ed owned several hundred acres of my great-grandfather's old farm.

Down the road a bit, Skip owned most of the rest of my great-grandfather's old farm, and he lived in the house in which my father grew up. Skip didn't have a wife. Or TV. Or Internet, and he was thinking about getting rid of his phone. But he did speak to Frank! Skip had a bunch of cows and was my favorite person, hands down, in Stringtown because he could do everything, knew everything, and was a bundle of amazing energy.

The only other family living on our side of the ford was my abrasive neighbor and her family. She was part of the 'hood. In fact, she was arguably the most interesting member of the 'hood, though I was still a little bit afraid of her. She did, however, speak to Frank, so maybe there was hope.

I came across my new abrasive neighbor on the road, stopped, during the final week of school. The last time I'd come upon her stopped, she'd been picking up a turtle to move it out of the road, which had given me the uncomfortable feeling that she was actually a nice person. I'd also come to the conclusion that she was smart, or at least country-wise, and I'd taken to watching her through the trees from my porch on rainy days to see whether or not she would cross the river. I'd already made one mistake crossing the river, and I trusted her to know whether it was safe or not.

On this occasion, she didn't appear to be picking up a turtle. She was just sitting in her car. She could be strange sometimes, so I went around her, then I thought better of it and stopped, too. I told Morgan to run back there and find out if she was just stopped for no reason (or, you know, actually moving and I couldn't tell because she drove so slow the human eye could not detect the motion) or if she was broken down. Morgan ran down the road to her car and back. The woman's car was, indeed, broken down.

With great reluctance, I got out of my SUV, walked back to her car, and said, "You want a ride back to your house until you can get someone to help you with your car?" On that stretch of the road, far past the handful of houses at the head of the road, she was unlikely to find a ride from anyone else.

I looked her in the eye and could see that I was the last person in the known universe from whom she wanted to accept help. But she took it. And I took her home. We drove a mile down the road (at fifteen miles an hour, about which she made nary a complaint) and chitchatted awkwardly about a wild storm we'd had a few days before. I was never so relieved as when we got to her house.

Our phone was out that day, in the aftermath of the storm, and I said, "I hope your phone is working so you can call someone, because our phone has been out."

She said, "We don't have a phone."

I felt a pang of guilt because I knew that but had temporarily forgotten. One of her daughters had told Morgan one day on the bus that they didn't have a phone. Phone service is such a basic that it had slipped my mind.

She said she would use her other car to go get someone to help her with her broken-down car, letting me off the hook for taking further action. Rid of her at last, I drove away and felt good about helping her in spite of the fact that I didn't want to help her. I felt good about it partly because she didn't want me to help her. I thought it annoyed her that I helped her. (Revenge!) And I knew that someday I might need help and she was one of the few people who lived out here. Now she had to help me whether she wanted to or not because I had helped her twice. (Self-serving!)

What a crappy person I was! Then I couldn't even feel good about helping her.

When I told this whole story to 52 after he got home, he said, "Your trouble is that you are supposed to help her because she needs help and you should expect to gain nothing in return, neither revenge nor some reward in the future."

Sometimes he was really annoying. But then, she always moved over for him, so he didn't understand my problem.

I wondered if this woman would be broken down in the road ten more times and each time I would be tested to see what my motivation was for picking her up, and when I finally picked her up with no motivation other than seeking the goodness of humanity, her country-wise, good-hearted, and abrasive self would evaporate as if she had never existed because she was only put here on Earth as a mere figment, an ornery angel, to turn me into a better person.

Which, apparently, I was yet light-years away from becoming as I imagined her entire existence revolving around the improvement of my character.

CHAPTER 5

It wasn't long before I brought home a Nigerian Dwarf dairy goat named Clover, along with her two babies, a doeling and a buckling. A local reader named Missy had e-mailed me, telling me about their farm nearby and their goat babies. I couldn't resist going to take a look. Their farm was beautiful, set on rolling land with a big red barn—everything our farm wasn't even though the two properties were only about ten miles apart. It still hadn't occurred to me yet that we'd set ourselves a mighty task with the steep terrain of our farm. I was eager for livestock, and small goats seemed like a good follow-up to chickens. The goats were so light I could pick them up if need be, and they weren't at all intimidating. They were as friendly as dogs, and about the same size.

I had the buckling, Honey, wethered (neutered) to be a companion, and Clover and her doeling, Nutmeg, would be the start of my new little herd. Soon, my chickens would be laying. I would have my own eggs, and I wanted my own milk, too.

Cheese, here I come!

I bought a Great Pyrenees puppy to protect the goats. I named her Coco and she grew to be larger than they were. The goats were a delight, smart and full of personality and mischief. 52 fenced a goat yard in front of the house and built a miniature goat-sized milk stand. I had dreams of farmstead chevre dancing in my head. When the babies were old enough to be at least partially weaned, I tried milking Clover.

I was excited.

52 came down to the milk stand with me. I was afraid to milk alone. I'd never milked anything before, neither a cow nor a goat. I'd bought a two-quart stainless steel pail and milk filters. I was ready!

I forgot the milk pail up at the house and had to go back for it.

When I came back, Clover scampered right onto the stand and put her head through the opening of the headlock to eat the food in the tray. I locked her in and reached for the first tiny teat. I'd studied milking photos online. I learned to milk on the Internet.

I reached my other hand for the second teat and started milking two-handed. Then Clover kicked me.

And stomped on my hand.

And sat on the pail.

Then she kicked me some more.

52 held on to both of her back legs and I tried to milk while Clover struggled wildly in his hands.

I came away with a tablespoon of milk. And I was still excited! I took my tablespoon of milk back to the kitchen, filtered it, and put it in the refrigerator. I figured I'd start collecting. In another ten years or so, I'd have enough to make cheese!

Or . . . not.

I learned to hobble one leg, tying it to a post on the stand. Then I learned to hobble two. Then three. Believe it or not, a goat hobbled on three legs can still kick. I used a belly band attached to either side of the milk stand to keep her from sitting down. She chewed off the belly band, kicked off all the hobbles, and kicked me. Meanwhile, however, I was highly successful at getting her to wear hats, jewelry, and other accessories in photos for my website, and she loved to be hand-fed cookies. She quickly became the most popular character on my blog for her ability to constantly one-up me and for her adoration of all things sugar sprinkled.

Stubborn, I continued to make adjustments until I was able to manage alone without 52 coming down to the milk stand with me to help with the hobbles. I would sit down and start to milk, listening to the crow of the roosters and the steady squirts of Clover's sweet, warm milk into the pail. This Disneylike scene would last about thirty seconds, and then she'd start kicking.

I persisted, and I felt like a real farmer the morning I stopped in at the little store in town, after dropping the kids off at the school bus, and said to Faye, "I have to go home and milk my goat."

Goat milk is sweet and rich, perfect for cheese and baking and anything else for which you would use store-bought milk. Handling milk was an all-new experience for me, but I was eager to learn.

I assembled the following supplies, in addition to my stainless steel milk pail and milk filters:

a strainer
bleach
dishwashing liquid
small stainless steel bowl for the udder wash
teat dip cup
a strip cup
paper towels
water
glass containers to hold the filtered milk

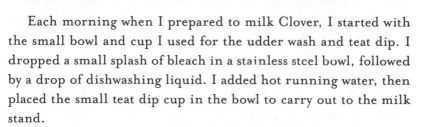

Each morning when I prepared to milk Clover, I started with the small bowl and cup I used for the udder wash and teat dip. I dropped a small splash of bleach in a stainless steel bowl, followed by a drop of dishwashing liquid. I added hot running water, then placed the small teat dip cup in the bowl to carry out to the milk stand.

Next, I would drop a larger splash of bleach into the milking pail in the sink and run hot water into the pail to sanitize. When pouring the water out, I'd pour it over the strainer I would be using later with the filter to sanitize it as well. I dried the pail with a clean paper towel and set the strainer on top of it on the counter.

To the milk stand, I would carry my bowl of udder wash (with the teat dip cup nested inside) and my milking pail (with extra clean paper towels tucked within).

Once in the milking pen, I would remove the teat dip cup from the udder wash bowl, making sure the teat dip cup was filled with some of the solution, and set it aside. I soaked a paper towel with the udder wash and cleaned Clover's entire udder area, drying it with another paper towel. I dipped my own hands in the remaining udder wash solution, drying them on another paper towel. Using the strip cup, I'd draw out the first few squirts.

The first few squirts could contain bacteria that collected in the teat, which should be eliminated. The strip cup also allows you to check the milk for any abnormalities, helping you keep an eye on your goat's health and her milk.

Then I'd set the strip cup aside to milk my lovely Clover, telling her how pretty she looked. In return, she would tell me how many cookies she wanted for this daily violation of her person.

There might or might not (okay, would) be a lot of kicking during the milking, including kicking off the hobbles entirely, which would lead to rehobbling, then resanitizing my hands before continuing. There was often some crying. And some begging. That would be by me, not Clover.

When I finished, I would set the pail aside and pick up the teat dip. I'd dip her teats in the solution, scratch her behind the ears, thank her for not kicking me in the head, and set her free.

When milk leaves the udder, it is at 100 degrees. Ideally, it should be chilled to 38 degrees within one hour.

Before chilling the milk, I'd wash my hands, then take out a fresh milk filter. Milk filters (available at farm supply stores) are somewhat similar to coffee filters, but not exactly. I'd place a milk filter inside the strainer, then slowly pour the milk from the pail into the filter-lined strainer, which was positioned over a glass pint jar. Using a pint jar was an exercise in positive thinking as I rarely got that much milk.

I would then place the pint jar in the freezer to quick-chill for about an hour before moving it to the fridge. After I had stored

my milk properly, the milk pail and the rest of the equipment and
supplies were rinsed in cool water and wiped out, ready to be sani-
tized the next day. And every day, there was Clover, ready with a
fresh supply of her sweet, rich milk. And her kicking.

I wavered between loving it and hating it. I really wanted to be a
farmer, and milking seemed like a farmerish thing to do, though
I was sure in the old days they skipped all the sanitizing and just
filtered through an old shirt, and as much as Clover kicked, she
would have been supper.

Eventually, as I actually started collecting enough milk to make
it possible, I was eager to try my hand at cheese. Missy, who had
sold Clover to me, wanted to learn to make cheese too. She had
a herd of a dozen does, but she hadn't tried her hand at cheese
making yet. We were both nervous, so we decided to do it together.
Like me, Missy hailed from suburbia and had returned to West
Virginia to her family roots.

Missy came over to the farm. I'd ordered supplies—citric acid,
rennet, and cheese salt, which came in a kit from New England
Cheesemaking. I'd already read the directions about twenty times.
Missy and I read them together another twenty times, then we were
ready. We added the citric acid to the milk and began to heat the pot.
Missy's husband, Pete, had come with her, and he and 52 hung out
on the porch, drinking wine while they waited for us to show up with
some bruschetta topped with melted homemade goat mozzarella.

When the milk reached 90 degrees, we added the rennet,
mixing it in with the mysterious instructions for the "up-and-
down" motion with the spoon that we didn't quite understand. We
let the pot sit for five minutes, then returned to see what we'd done.

The milk had turned into this very firm jellylike substance,
pulling away from the sides of the pot where we could see the clear
yellowish whey—the water that releases from milk as it's turned
into cheese.

We were overjoyed! Thrilled! Impressed with ourselves! *The
Little Miss Muffet nursery rhyme finally made sense.* So *that's* what curds and
whey are!

Of course, we weren't actually finished. The mozzarella recipe we were using was a thirty-minute shortcut version of true mozzarella and is the type of mozzarella made by most home cheese makers. After achieving curds, the cheese is scooped with a slotted spoon into a bowl and microwaved three successive times, kneading in between and releasing more whey each time.

Missy and I studied the mozzarella like we were observing a foreign life form. We overheated it and overkneaded it and eventually killed it. It was like a brick by the time I said, "Do you think it's done?"

Missy said, "I don't know. Maybe we should try it."

I cut off a couple tiny pieces and we each took a taste.

We looked at each other.

"This is terrible!" I said.

"Maybe it will be better when it's melted?" Missy suggested.

I had bread for bruschetta prepared for the broiler. We added herbs and our fresh-made awful cheese, then tucked it in the oven and called the men inside.

Luckily, everyone had had a couple of glasses of wine by then or it probably would have tasted worse.

While I tried to conquer goat milking and cheese making, the hot, sweaty summer slipped into fall. I welcomed the cooler weather, but not the endless rounds of sports practices that came with it. Ross had a job and a girlfriend and a car, but Weston and Morgan were avid athletes, keeping me on the run every afternoon and evening.

52 and I had enjoyed a summer, lazy only in the sense that we had been alone together. He'd scratched a garden from a sloped but sunny space near the house, and I had learned to can green beans with a pressure canner. We had very little money, a fact he reminded me about frequently.

I reminded him about something he'd said to me when we first met and I was going through a difficult time. "Things are always harder in the middle," I said. "Remember? I'm going to make my website a success and we'll be all right."

Our bills were paid each month, and I didn't see any reason to wait to be happy until we were out of debt. I wanted to be happy in the here and now, and despite my worries—which were more about his seeming tension with everything and everyone than about our tight finances—I was. I loved living on a farm.

I sat on my front porch and was surrounded by land that belonged to me. I lived on a farm! It was an awesome, and continually surprising, realization. I was raising dairy goats for milk and chickens for eggs. I was, in fact, infatuated with the farm more every day despite the increasing labor involved.

I loved the way its boundaries were defined in the old deed book at the county courthouse.

"Beginning at the road in the Schoolhouse lot, thence with the road of the ford of the run above the mill, thence back in the field about six rods to or near a small black walnut, thence to or just above the white walnut at the spring in the drain, thence just above and with the meanderings of the fence now around the upper side of the lot to a small sugar tree by the old fence going up to the cliff, thence with the creek to the branch below the ford. . . ." And so on and so forth, including references to a pile of rocks, a stump hole, and a dead hickory tree. Need I point out that of course most of these landmarks no longer existed? There was an iron pin referred to in the deed book that remained, as well as some survey flags in a few spots that were placed some years ago. We had relied on the prior owners' directions as to boundaries, and the neighbors had been agreeable to the designations.

Just being in possession of forty acres felt staggering to me. It was far more acreage than we would ever actually utilize, especially since much of it was heavily wooded, but the privacy it afforded was one of its most enjoyable aspects.

I could walk and walk and get tired and still be on my own land. In suburban life, the perspective is more focused on the house and the yard. It's different in the country. There is something so significant about land. Not its value in money, but its sheer substance. There is a weight to it, some kind of primal quality that is ethereal and tangible all at once. It has a life of its own, the land does.

My farm teemed with trees and springs, a creek and a river, wildflowers and vines, birds and chipmunks, raccoons and deer. It held secrets I didn't know yet, and many I would never know. It welcomed me and protected me, and it often exhausted me and sometimes scared me. Mostly, it was patient with me. Land is long-suffering. It knows it isn't going anywhere. It was there before I arrived, and it would be there when I was gone.

No matter how stressed I was some days, writing constantly for my website between spending hours running for the kids' sports, not to mention taking care of the animals, I could sit down on the porch for even a minute, look out at my land, and feel happiness flow over me.

I wanted 52 to feel it, too.

I waited for him on the porch when I expected him home from work.

"Tell me about your day," I invited when he sat down in his rocking chair. Whether I had cut small branches for fall decorations, had come up with a new bread recipe twist, or had managed to keep the hobble on Clover, I was eager to tell him about it.

He often said he had nothing to tell about his day, so I went on with telling him about mine. One day, I'd bought some new rubber boots for the coming winter (for myself), and I had managed to actually get the boots on Clover while she was in the milk stand and take her picture wearing them for a post on my blog. The boots went all the way up her legs, of course, and she looked really cute. I barely got started when he interrupted me.

"I don't want to hear a long story," he said.

I was taken aback. "I wasn't going to tell you a long story. It was kinda like a short one."

"You're not interested in me, are you?"

I was taken aback again. "Of course I'm interested in you. I asked you about your day. You said you had nothing to tell, so I thought I'd tell you about my day."

"You don't care about my day."

"Of course I care about your day. I asked about it, didn't I?"

"You didn't really want to hear about it."

He looked quite angry, and I wasn't sure why.

"The goats need water," he said.

I looked over the porch rail. The main floor of the house was actually on the second floor, with what had originally been intended as a basement on the first floor. During construction, the builder had discovered too much rock to make digging a basement down a feasible prospect, so we'd built a basement that was not a basement on the first floor with steps leading up to the porch on the main, or second, floor. The goat yard was directly in front of the porch, so I could look straight down into the goat yard and see inside the water bucket.

"The bucket is half full," I said. "I check on their water in the morning and in the evening. I haven't done my evening round yet, but there was plenty of water this morning and there's still water."

"Animals need water all the time," he said. "If the bucket is half full, it's half empty. You should fill it up before it's half empty."

"I haven't done my evening round yet," I repeated. "I'll fill it up then. They're not out of water."

"Animals need water all the time," he repeated. "They'll die without water."

"They have water!" I stared at him, confused. "What is this about? Are you upset about something else?"

"The goats need water all the time. Don't change the subject."

"The goats have water. I'm trying to find out what the subject actually is!"

"Now you're arguing with me."

"I don't want to argue with you. I'm just trying to find out why you're upset about the goats not having water when they have water."

"You're right. Of course. You're always right about everything."

"I don't want to be—"

"You always have to be right. You're perfect, and you think I'm
stupid."

I sat there for a very long pause, then got up, knelt by his chair,
and put my hand on his knee. "I don't care who is right and who
is wrong. I'm not perfect and I don't even want to be. I have never
once had the thought enter my mind that you're stupid. I love you.
I just want us to be happy."

"You're not happy," he said.

"Yes, I am," I insisted. "I'm stressed, a lot, with work and sports
and everything else, but I love it here. I love our farm. I'm happy,
and I just want you to be happy, too. I want us to be happy."

"You're not happy," he repeated. "And you don't care about
me. You want to tell me to leave."

My mind reeled a little bit. I had no idea where any of this was
coming from, and I was completely lost.

"I don't want to tell you to leave!"

"Yes, you do," he said. "You'd have another man in here in
a week. That's all I am to you, a man to do the work around the
farm. You don't need me to build fences. You can find somebody
else. You don't even like me."

I stood, backing off. I had no idea what to say. I was insulted,
hurt, and mostly just stunned.

"I don't want anyone else," I said softly. My voice cracked. "I
don't understand what any of this is about."

"That's because you're selfish," he said. "All you care about is
yourself."

I didn't know how to reason with him. What happened to him
coming home to me at night so we could sit on the porch and hold
hands? I felt hot tears streaking down my face.

"All I really want right now is for you to hold me," I whispered
roughly.

He smoked his pipe, unmoved.

I felt scared. I didn't know this man. I knew the other man, the one who told me beautiful dreams of our sweet life together. I brushed at my wet cheeks, speechless. I went down to fill the goats' bucket, then out to check on the chicken house before going inside to finish fixing dinner. It was already late, and the kids were hungry after their practices. They took their plates to their rooms while I tried to hide my emotional state. I told 52 that dinner was ready, but he didn't come in. I wasn't hungry and didn't care about eating. I wrapped up the leftovers and went to bed alone.

In the morning, he gave me an extratender hug after he filled his coffee cup and told me that he loved me. As I watched his pickup roll down the driveway on the way to his office, I wondered which man was coming home.

CHAPTER 6

Georgia called me on a regular basis to ask me what I was doing. It was almost like I was still living at the Slanted Little House, and in fact, I was there every weekday as I took the kids each morning to get on the school bus. Sometimes I'd go over to Georgia's house to see her, especially if I'd just canned something and had a jar for her. Sometimes I took her to the eye doctor, and she always loved a good funeral outing.

She rarely drove herself anywhere, which was just as well since the little gas station in town had closed. Georgia didn't know how to pump gas.

I didn't know there were still places in the world where you didn't have to know how to pump gas. I hadn't seen a full-service gas station since I was a kid. My own children had never seen a full-service gas station.

I took her to Spencer one morning for a funeral. She wore a hat that made her look as if she were prepared to motor across the English countryside. We went to lunch after the funeral.

She said, "I was the only one there wearing a hat."

At seventy-eight, she walked in the foreign land of people younger than her, a land she didn't quite understand. On the other end of the spectrum were my children, also in need of a guide in this foreign rural land that was in some ways a throwback to decades earlier. I was the in-between, the guide, the sandwich generation between Georgia's childhood without TV and my children's childhoods with YouTube videos on their cell phones. (I frequently reminded my kids that when I was their ages, we only had four TV channels and we had to get up to change them.)

When we first moved to the Slanted Little House, the full-service gas station in Walton was still open. The little old man would come out and pump your gas. No card slots at the pumps. The pumps themselves looked like they were transported from the 1970s in a time machine. These were the gas pumps I remembered from my childhood, the only pumps Georgia has ever known, and pumps my children had never seen in their former suburban lives. In case you're wondering where all those old-fashioned pumps went—they're in the country.

The first time my kids came with me to get gas, they were baffled when I didn't jump out of the car. We sat there for a minute and finally one of them said, "Aren't you going to get gas?" I said, "Yes." The little old man came out and pumped my gas. My children nearly fell over with shock. "What is he doing?" "Why is he doing that?"

I loved that little old gas station and the little old man. He always called me "honey" and if I wanted a bottle of water and a candy bar, he'd bring that out to the car for me, too, along with anything else I might desire.

Georgia got her gas at the little old gas station from the little old man for years and years. When the gas station closed, Mark had to take up filling her gas tank for her. After we had lunch following the funeral outing, and before we left the "big" town of Spencer, we stopped by the modern self-service gas station. I got out, pumped the gas, and got back in the car.

Georgia said, "Aren't you going to pay?"

I said, "I already paid."

She stared at me, not unlike my children stared at me when I didn't get out of the car to pump the gas myself the first time they came with me to the little old gas station. I explained, "I put my debit card in the slot and I paid at the pump."

Georgia said, "Oh my. I didn't know you could do that."

I said, "You need to get the bank to give you a debit card."

She said, "Oh no, no, no!"

In spite of her reluctance to take on newfangled technology, there wasn't much else she thought she couldn't do.

On rare days when nobody had sports practice after school, I also went to the Slanted Little House in the afternoon to get the kids from the bus. Ross was driving and could get himself home, but I had to pick up Weston and Morgan. I'd drive the two-plus miles over the dirt-rock road to the hard road and around a couple bends to the Slanted Little House.

One day, there was a pretty black cow in the road. I knew who the cow belonged to, and it wasn't an unusual sight. I got to the Slanted Little House. Weston stepped off the bus, but there was no Morgan.

I went to Georgia's house to call the school. She'd missed the bus.

Then I made the mistake of telling Georgia that one of Lonnie's cows was in the road.

I said, "You want to call Lonnie and tell him that one of his cows is in the road? I have to go get Morgan."

Lonnie mowed her back pasture for hay every year, so I knew Georgia had his number. I'd called Lonnie a time or two before to let him know when his cows were in the road. The last time, he'd said, "I'll go see when my TV show is over."

Georgia headed for the phone, and I headed back to my car. Before I could even pull out, she was outside loading up her car with my cousin's son, Madison, in the driver's seat.

I rolled down my window. "What are you doing?"

Georgia said, "Lonnie didn't answer the phone. I'm going to get the cow."

"No, you're not. You can't get a cow."

Georgia replied, "Yes, I can."

I said, "Maybe you should go to Lonnie's house first. See if you can find him outside somewhere."

At the pace she let Madison drive, it would take her fifteen minutes just to drive a mile up the road to Lonnie's house. I headed for the school to pick up Morgan and drove back at a fast clip, feeling slightly panicked, imagining Georgia wrangling a cow.

I told the kids, "We have to go help Georgia get a cow."

Weston said, "I can't get a cow."

"Neither can I. And neither can Georgia. But at the very least, we need to stop her from jumping on its back and riding it over the hill."

By the time we got back to the place where the cow had been in the road, Georgia and Madison were parked to the side in the weeds.

I jumped out. "Where's the cow? I raced back here to stop you from jumping on its back and riding it over the hill."

Georgia said, "Oh, it went back in on its own."

I said, "Exactly. That's why Lonnie doesn't interrupt his TV shows. And when Mark gets home, I'm telling on you."

Georgia said, "Well," and that day, it meant that she didn't give a hoot what I told anybody. She'd chase all the cows she wanted, and she knew I was just about as crazy as she was anyway, though I think she secretly enjoyed my imaginary scenarios in which she was riding cows over the hill.

My new daily life on the farm wavered between the fantastical and the harsh reality when it came to livestock.

I gave up milking Clover before winter, beaten by the struggle. I was disappointed with myself. What kind of farmer was I? But I was relieved at the same time. I baked Clover a batch of molasses cookies and told her we'd talk about milking another time.

She said, "I win!" Seriously, I swear it.

The chickens had started laying in the fall, but eggs were scarce as the weather turned cold, and many times the ones I found were frozen and broken. It was snowing by November and I was terrified of our steep driveway, which was even scarier than the road. Winter driving lessons with my cousin didn't help. I took to parking my SUV at the bottom of the driveway, which meant hiking up and down the hill every morning to take the kids to the school bus, only to repeat it all again in the afternoon. To get to the bus, I had to drive the icy, rocky road, past sheer drop-offs that had me clenching my fingers over the steering wheel. Sometimes I had to send the kids to stay at my cousin's house because I couldn't get down the road at all.

Sometimes I made a mistake, starting down the road when it was icier than I could handle, or bad weather would start up after I was already out. We'd have to get home somehow, and somehow meant driving down the road.

Once you started down the road, there was no choice but to keep going. On these occasions, I would inch along, my fingers numb from my death grip on the wheel.

"Mom, it'll be okay."

Morgan was my little cheerleader. If I'd been in her place, I would have had my hands covering my eyes.

I would move the vehicle another inch and tell myself that we weren't dead yet.

Then I'd steel my nerves to move the next inch. The road would be completely covered in snow and ice, and that kind of back road never received salt or scraping by county trucks. There were no guardrails to stop you if you started sliding.

In those conditions, it could take me forty-five minutes to drive the two and a half miles to our farm. By the time we arrived, I'd be shaking and crying.

Starting that first winter, whenever possible in that kind of weather, I relied on 52 for almost everything. The first snow usually came by Thanksgiving, and it could snow off and on until late March—when the mud season started, running through April and into May before summer came to dry things up. The thick, deep mud on the road was as scary as the ice, if not more. 52 brought home the groceries and the mail, and sometimes the kids. He didn't seem to mind doing these things, but I felt isolated and dependent on a man who seemed increasingly hostile otherwise and seemed to mind everything else.

He minded my noise, the kids' noise, any kind of noise. Footsteps running on the stairs, the kids banging around downstairs in horseplay, the sound of pots and pans in the kitchen, doors shutting too hard, and most especially my conversation, which he frequently cut off to tell me I was talking too much or too loudly, that I was repeating myself or telling stories that were too long, and that I didn't care about him and that I wanted to be right about everything. I began to recognize a pattern, which started with him picking on one thing or another, followed by a routine in which he told me I thought I was perfect and he was stupid. Any disagreement I made to those statements was labeled an excuse or an argument. This frequently ended with him telling me that I wanted to tell him to leave.

I found myself running around trying to make sure everything was done just right and trying to get the kids to be quiet before he came home. I was tongue-tied when he arrived, afraid I'd say the wrong thing and spark the next diatribe.

I wasn't standing up for myself. I didn't feel very good about it, and I felt a growing frustration with his unreasonable blowups, which were interfering with the happy life we were supposed to be enjoying.

Hello, we were living on a farm! Dream come true! Time to be happy!

We split the farm expenses and bills for the house fifty-fifty, each depositing our half into a joint account from which we paid bills. We both had our own separate bills, too—car insurances and so on, which we paid from our individual personal accounts.

As busy as I was with writing and running around with the kids, he had taken over paying the bills from the joint account. I realized something was wrong when I got a phone call letting me know that our satellite TV service was going to be shut off. I'd just deposited my entire (slightly measly) royalty check from my latest romance novels in the joint account because 52 had said the bills were high and we needed more money.

I hunted down the checkbook for the joint account, which I hadn't looked at in some time, and discovered that the only person who'd been depositing money in the joint account recently had been me. Even with my regular monthly deposit plus my additional royalty check, that wasn't enough to pay all the bills.

We had no money left in the account. He hadn't made his deposit.

I'd wanted to save my royalty check to buy Christmas presents for the kids, but I'd deposited it in the joint account at his insistence. If he'd needed to reduce what he was depositing temporarily for some reason, that wouldn't have been the end of the world, but I felt as if he'd been dishonest with me. When he came home, I confronted him.

He said he didn't know what I was talking about, but when I presented him with the checkbook ledger, he switched gears.

"You're right," he said. "You're always right. You have to always be right."

"Well, in this case," I said, "I *am* right. I've been depositing money in the joint account and you haven't. Why not?"

"You think you're perfect, don't you?"

I was exasperated. I had no patience for his routine about how perfect I thought I was. We were scraping by financially, but it took both of us.

"I'm not having a conversation about who thinks who is perfect! Why didn't you make your deposit in the joint account?"

"Why don't you just admit that you don't even like me?" he demanded. "You don't care about me. All you care about is yourself. You want to tell me to leave."

"Right now," I spit at him, "I don't care if you leave or not."

"Are you telling me to leave?"

All my repressed frustration with his repeated rounds of nonsense attacks over the past several months welled up in me and I said, "Yes, I'm telling you to leave."

He walked down to his truck and drove away.

I felt strong for a minute or two, then I burst into tears. I didn't know if I'd stood up for myself or just stepped into a trap. Hadn't he been taunting me for months now that I wanted to tell him to leave? It hadn't been my idea, but he'd certainly talked me into it. We hadn't even made it through a year on the farm together, and I hadn't bargained for a farm by myself. I needed 52, and it wasn't long before I missed him. Like, about five minutes. I missed the old 52, the man I'd known before we moved to the farm.

Traffic was increasing on my website, and I couldn't afford the higher hosting fees. Even as I found myself suddenly alone on the farm, the economy took a nosedive and advertising—which was how I got a paycheck—dropped with it. Readers pitched in with donations to help support the site's costs. They also sent letters and e-mails and left comments on my blog to encourage me, telling me how much my writings about the farm meant to them. I was farming inspiration, if little else. Many of them were struggling as much as I was, or more.

One day I went to Georgia's house. I'd promised her I'd help her bake seventy-five mini holiday pumpkin breads. She'd started without me because she was impatient and it had started snowing that morning. Everybody knew I was scared to drive in the snow, so she thought I wasn't coming.

She made pumpkin bread every year for the little church in town. They made up big gift baskets to distribute to the elderly in the community. Georgia had a hard time handling the work of seventy-five mini holiday pumpkin breads because she was one of the elderly herself who should have been getting a basket—but she didn't like that idea. She wanted to be one of the younguns fixing goodies for the baskets, not one of the "old people" getting one. Only she couldn't quite do it because, well, she was elderly. So she called me and told me she'd "help" me make those mini pumpkin breads if I'd come over.

She fussed around a lot while she was "helping" me because she wanted to be sure I did things right and usually I didn't. She had the recipe clipped on her fridge and the clip was right over the part where it said how much ground cloves to put in. It was supposed to be 1/2 teaspoon, but I couldn't see the first part of that and I thought it said 2 teaspoons. Georgia almost had a fainting spell when she found out I'd been putting in 2 teaspoons.

I made her do a taste test on one of the breads baked from the batter with too much ground cloves.

She said, "Well," which meant she liked it and all was forgiven.

In between baking rounds, I wandered over to the Slanted Little House. I stood in the sitting room with the gas fire and remembered how the kids and I used to gather round its heat as we shivered through the winters. On snow days, the children fought for who got to sleep closest to it on the floor.

I peeked into Morgan's old bedroom. I'd bought her new bedding at the new house, so her old bed in the Slanted Little House looked the same, as if she might come home from school and jump right onto it. I walked through the old retro '60s-remodeled kitchen. I had rediscovered my love of baking in that kitchen. I hated it and loved it and missed it, and sometimes I wanted to come over and just cook something in it for old times' sake. Sometimes I couldn't find something at my new farmhouse, like my Bundt pan, and I'd realize I must have left it there so I'd have to go over and hunt through the cabinets. It still felt like my kitchen.

I looked out the big window to the meadow. It was always a good place to watch deer graze along the creek at dusk, or children shooting arrows into hay bales, or cats jumping in the tall, tall grass in summertime.

I walked down to the old cellar porch where I didn't have to worry about lighting the gas on the old stove to keep the pipes from freezing now. Mark took care of that since I was gone. No one lived in the house anymore.

I could close my eyes and see Ross, just the year before, bringing his first girlfriend home one day from high school, hear Morgan tell her, "What do you want to know about Ross? I know him really well." And hear Ross say to his new girlfriend, "We're leaving now."

I could see my younger son, Weston, stepping off the bus in front of the Slanted Little House with his football jersey the first year he'd played, and all three of my kids the day they broke a four-foot-long icicle off the cliff across the road and proudly brought it home. There was a framed photo of that day I'd left in the sitting room of the Slanted Little House—Ross and Weston with their neatly clipped crew cuts and Morgan with her flyaway shoulder-length hair she refused to ever pull back, balancing a giant icicle between them, faces beaming.

I could see Morgan, at one and a half, in the washtub when I gave her a bath on one of our visits to the Slanted Little House way back then and see my mother rocking on the front porch, patting Morgan's freshly diapered bottom.

I could see me, age five, out front riding the little red tricycle Great-Aunt Ruby used to keep around for the little kids in the family.

I could even almost see my dad when he was in high school in town and the weather was so bad he'd have to stay the night with his aunt because he couldn't make it back to Stringtown.

And even more distantly, I could almost see my great-grandparents coming from Stringtown—over the hill and through the woods—to visit their daughter Ruby after she married and moved into this house. I could see them in the parlor and on the porch, not just on the wall where they were framed.

I opened my eyes and I could see generations of family in an almost elastic space and time where no matter how far the years stretched, they also pulled back together—here—in this place.

The Slanted Little House had inspired me in the beginning, and it still inspired me. Someday, I dreamed, my house would be an old farmhouse, filled with memories—joy, sadness, hardship, triumph, all that makes up the fabric of a good life. I wanted, desperately, to grab hold of that good life. I wanted 52 to come back to the farm.

CHAPTER 7

The electricity to the well went out. 52 came back to the farm to fix the well for me, and I asked him to stay. We agreed together to see a counselor, and I was thrilled, certain we could find the solution to our problems.

He took the boys to chop down a Christmas tree in the woods above my cousin's barn where there was a lot of pine. The tree we brought home was too tall, too wide, too sparse, but it was free and it was something to pull us all together.

I went along as the tree picker. I spotted a nice white pine.

52 said, "Go over there and shake it."

And I did. Because I'm so naive. 52 was in good humor.

The boys had divided up their duties before we ever walked up the hill. Weston was going to chop down the tree and Ross was going to drag the tree down the hill.

Weston chopped. And chopped. And even tried to push the tree down. At one point, he kicked it.

He got hot and took his jacket off.

"Any time you want to admit that you're a weenie who needs help with his job, I'll help you," Ross told him. Then they chased each other around the tree, fighting over the ax.

"It might have been safer to keep them in the city," I told 52 after I finished screaming.

Luckily, the chasing stopped before there was any blood. Weston gave it one more good heave, then abruptly said, "I'm done." And handed the ax to Ross. I think he just wanted to give up with dignity.

Ross gave the tree the final blow and it fell. He still had to drag the tree off the hill, which he found quite disappointing.

It was a long way down in the cold, snowy woods with the barren trees set against the bright, lowering sun. 52 held my hand as we walked. It felt like a new beginning. Everything was going to be all right.

I decorated the tree with sugar cookie stars, gingerbread men, dried orange slices, and popcorn garlands. I made homemade gifts for friends and family. We were festive and frugal. 52 gave me an antique ring that had come from his father's clock and jewelry shop that had once stood on the town square in the county seat.

I knew, somewhere inside, was that kind and patient man who had won me with his tender tale of the feral cat. He was under a lot of stress. I redoubled my efforts to make a success of my website, afraid the financial pressure of the farm would do us in.

After Christmas, I baked a beautiful loaf of raisin bread for the Ornery Angel. I put together bags of homemade cookies, bourbon balls, peppermint pretzels, and chocolate-dipped spoons. I'd been engaged in battle with the Ornery Angel for months. When I met her on the road, I would wave to her like a good country neighbor, but she wouldn't wave back. She still wouldn't move over, either, leaving me to creep along anytime I was caught behind her on the road. Nobody understood my battle with the Ornery Angel, particularly me, and I was pretty sure the Ornery Angel didn't even know we were doing battle.

I revealed my plan to Morgan.

"Now she will like me!" I said.

"You're doing this so she will like you?"

"No! I'm doing this so she'll move over!"

"That'll never happen."

I explained it all to 52.

"Now she will like me!" I said.

"You're doing this so she will like you?"

"No! I'm doing this so she'll move over!"

52 just shook his head.

Morgan got into the spirit of my plan, at least as far as making a gift to the Ornery Angel and her family. She gathered some things for the Ornery Angel's children. A brand-new jacket that was too small and never worn, a Nintendo DS game (she had earlier given one of the Ornery Angel's children her old Nintendo DS), and a little pink purse for one of the girls.

The Ornery Angel liked Morgan and was always friendly to her, so I had her do the delivery. Morgan marched down the driveway, wearing her Santa hat, and up the road with the big bag of bribery.

The next week was back-to-school week after the holidays. That Tuesday, I got away from the house late and got caught behind the Ornery Angel. We crept along for half a mile and then . . .

She moved over.

And the fact that my bribery succeeded . . . the fact that I did something nice for her for no reason other than selfish gain . . . the fact that I had therefore made no personal development in the preceding months at all . . .

I didn't care.

She moved over! And in the midst of that first hard winter on the farm, that was something to celebrate. I was, kind of, maybe, a little bit, being accepted. And in a back road hollow in the hills of West Virginia, that was hard to accomplish.

Toward the end of winter, we acquired a flock of sheep. A reader had told me about a farmer in Virginia who was closing out his sheep operation and he was giving away the sheep for free. A friend had recently given me a Dorset-Suffolk bottle lamb I'd been raising on the porch with the dogs. We named her Annabelle and I was completely smitten. I treated her like a puppy.

I didn't know anything about sheep, but next thing I knew I was a couple hundred miles away in the back of a pickup truck inside a barn in Virginia holding on to a 250-pound ram by a fistful of his incredibly long, curly wool while four more sheep were being loaded in with him.

One ewe bolted before making it onto the ramp into the truck and escaped the barn. Luckily, she circled back into the barn from the other side where the retiring sheep farmer and 52 shoved her up the ramp into the truck. Every time a sheep was shoved in, the tailgate on the truck would have to be opened and it was my job to keep everybody who was already on the truck in place. Every time the men loaded one and left me alone standing in the bed of the pickup with those woolly mammoths, I was scared the sheep would kill me before they returned with the next one.

We drove off with a sea of wool waving in the bed of the pickup truck—two Jacob ewes, two Cotswold ewes, and one Cotswold ram. We took all we could fit, and we felt like farmers when we pulled in to a gas station to fill up on the way back with a load of sheep on board. It was the type of adventure that drew us together. 52 would be relaxed at such times, and all our troubles would seem to fall away.

Jacobs are dramatic and unique sheep. An "Old World" unimproved breed (meaning not altered or enhanced over the centuries by crossing with other breeds, also referred to as a "primitive" breed), they're considered to be almost goatlike with their slight builds and more playful, agile personalities. They sport anywhere from two to six horns, and they have very thick multicolored wool. I stuck my hand into one of them and the wool swallowed my fingers before I hit skin.

Cotswold is an old English heritage breed that was popular in the Middle Ages for the long, curly fleece. The ewes are also known as good mothers and are very calm. Not to mention massive.

I was excited at the idea of contributing to the continuance of these beautiful heirloom breeds and had high hopes of raising lambs and shearing wool for sale. I wanted to find a Jacob ram and keep two purebred flocks. I had no idea how much sheep eat, or how difficult it would be to keep two separate flocks of anything on one small farm.

Or that eventually I would become so scared of the Cotswold ram that I wouldn't even enter a pasture where he was grazing if I was alone.

All I knew was that I wanted to become more self-sustaining, and a couple of little goats and a handful of chickens weren't going to cut it. All the goats did was eat cookies, and the chickens didn't lay half the time.

The first thing we did was get the sheep sheared. The shearer was seventy-four years old, and when he showed up, the sheep were still wandering around in the field.

That's how much we knew about keeping sheep. We spent the next hour chasing them around in circles between bouts of throwing ourselves at them while the shearer watched with a doubtful eye. Eventually, we decided to herd them behind the goat house. The shearer stood at one end, blocking outlet from the narrow path between the rear of the goat house and the fence with a pallet while 52 and I attempted to direct the sheep into the makeshift chute. We ran the first one in, and I stayed, blocking with my body, while 52 ran back to the other side. The shearer moved out of the way with the pallet, and 52 and I tackled the sheep.

Then all three of us held on to the long, lovely wool ringlets while we pushed and shoved and ordered the sheep into the pen. We had to repeat this procedure for every single one of them.

Even so, the result was fascinating. I'd never seen sheep sheared before. Once we had a sheep in the pen, the shearer flipped it onto its bottom in a martial arts–type move that belied his age and scrawny appearance. I learned that once a sheep was positioned that way, it was helpless. The shearer went to work.

He'd been shearing sheep for fifty years but told us that he'd never sheared a Cotswold before. Back in the day, he used to shear three thousand sheep a year, but most years anymore, he only sheared three hundred. Sheep weren't so common around here these days.

"I used to be able to shear twelve sheep an hour," he said. He kept a running tale of his shearing experience going as he worked.

I watched in awe as the thick wool fell away, leaving much smaller, bald sheep behind.

I think he sheared about two an hour that day, but that included time spent chasing sheep. The Jacob ewes were slightly easier to manage because they had handles (horns) by which they could be dragged to the pen.

By the time we got to the final sheep, I was covered head to toe in mud from flinging myself at sheep, and everyone was exhausted.

The shearer was several minutes into shearing the last one, a Cotswold ewe, when he said, "I ain't never cut off a tit before."

I don't think I expected to ever hear that particular sentence, in any scenario, in my entire life. The shearer finished the job while I ran to the house for medical supplies. The ewe wasn't happy, but she was all right. We paid the shearer, cleaned up the blood, looked at our huge piles of fluffy wool, and wondered, *Now what?*

The next day, I swept off the back porch and we laid out the first fleece, inside (the part that was next to the sheep's skin) down. The inside is already clean. The "outside" is what needs skirting. The outside of wool is dirty—the sheep has been wearing it. Skirting wool means to cut away the debris, any matted parts, and stuck-on poop. Then, with the "outside" still on top, you fold the fleece over and roll it up. This process always keeps the dirtier "outside" separated from the clean inside and leaves the nice, clean inside out so you can see the lovely wool. Then we'd move on to the next. And the next.

We made bags out of old cotton bedsheets and left the tops open. Wool should be stored in something breathable. After skirting comes washing, drying, carding, spinning, and knitting.

I looked at the five huge rolls of wool and wondered, not for the first time, if I'd lost my mind. I didn't have time to make wool processing my new part-time job. "Let's sell it," I suggested.

"Whatever you want to do," 52 said. He'd helped skirt it, but he was done.

I set aside some of the wool for myself to play with when I had time, and I put the rest up for sale to my readers.

We were lucky the shearer ever came back for subsequent shearings (and that he remained alive, because we were never able to find anyone else who knew how to shear).

Meanwhile, 52 had given me a baby jenny (female donkey), and I'd named her Poky. Not long afterward, I was at the hardware counter at the little store talking to Faye. They'd recently developed a spring to run water into their house. After twenty years at their farm and raising three children, they didn't have an outhouse anymore. I was about to leave when Faye said, "You want a donkey?"

I said, "I have a donkey."

She said, "I know you have a donkey. You want another donkey?"

Someone had come in the store recently and mentioned they were looking for a new home for their old jack (male donkey). Their jack was named Jack.

Of course, I took Jack home.

I still had my small herd of Nigerian Dwarf goats, and I'd started a second small herd of Tennessee Fainting goats, too. They were entertaining, but not much more useful than the Nigerians.

We were one year into the farm, and I felt like the lost baby bird that kept running around crying, "Are you my mother?" I kept acquiring animals and experiences, crying, "Are you my farm?"

That spring, we planted like crazy. Berry bushes, fruit trees, grapes, wherever we could find a spot. 52 hauled in compost and expanded the vegetable garden, building a couple of raised beds that were more manageable for me while he tilled the larger regular garden that was so sloped I could hardly stand to work in it.

He started fencing the meadow bottom for the sheep and building sheep shelters. The counseling sessions we'd started in the winter petered out. I still thought we needed to go, though I wasn't sure we were accomplishing anything. Even so, 52 seemed committed to the farm, and our relationship was better at times. Then there were times when it wasn't better, but I redoubled my efforts to be patient. I wanted this good life that we were building on the farm.

My birthday was on a Saturday in April. It was a lovely spring day. The house was clean, the porch swept, the animals munching peacefully in the goat yard, the roosters crowing, brand-new chicks peeping in their brooder, and company on the way. All seemed right in Stringtown Rising Farm world.

At 2 P.M., I found our little wether, Honey, down. I'd let him out of the goat house that morning. He'd eaten, browsed around the yard with Clover and her doeling, Nutmeg. I'd seen him as recently as 1 P.M., behaving normally. An hour later he was down, couldn't get up, and looked as if he might die. And we had no idea why.

Throughout the afternoon, we worked on various theories. Had he sustained some sort of internal injury? (There was no outward sign of injury, broken bones, etc.) We wondered if one of the big sheep, still up in the goat yard while the fencing was being completed in the bottom, had butted him too hard. Honey had a frisky little way of teasing them. Could he have had a stone, suddenly, lodge that quickly and put him down? I administered vinegar, just in case, but there was no real sign that a stone was the cause of his distress. (A stone would usually be prefaced by a period of straining and crying, not cause a goat to immediately go down in such a severe state.) Could he have some other type of infection? What sort of infection would cause him to go down so fast with no clue in advance? His behavior throughout the morning had been fine. There are a couple of fairly uncommon conditions called goat polio and listeriosis that can cause goats to become very sick, but in both cases, there are usually advance symptoms, and moldy hay/feed/silage is usually the cause.

Company arrived on the brink of this crisis and did what they could to help—researching Honey's symptoms on the Internet while we were on the phone for hours. The first two hours were spent desperately pursuing mission impossible. Large animal (farm) vets are few and far between as it is (even in farm country), and on a Saturday afternoon before Easter? If we'd had a cat or a dog or a bird, there were emergency vets available. Not for a goat. In two hours, the closest vet we could find to call us back was in Maryland.

Honey appeared worse every minute. The vet we spoke with in Maryland told us to find some Banamine. Banamine is an anti-inflammatory that is sometimes administered for shock. She told us to call somebody with horses, that anyone with horses would have Banamine. By this time, we had called every vet in the phone book and were facing the panic-inspiring revelation that this was the be-all and end-all of professional assistance we were going to get. As one farmer I spoke to that day said to me, "This is the ugly side of experience." Now I knew why so many farmers were ama-teur veterinarians—they had learned what I learned that weekend. And I also know why so many farmers were so generous in offering help in this type of crisis—they had been in our shoes and knew how frightening it could be.

We spent the next couple of hours on the phone again—this time calling farmers. We started out calling horse farmers. None of them had Banamine. We called goat farmers. We called sheep farmers. We called farmers we knew and we called farmers we didn't know. We'd call one person and they'd give us the phone number of someone else. We called friends of strangers. We had one phone line going all the time calling people and another phone line for people to call back where we had left messages. Ev-eryone had stories about their own animals and advice. We went back and forth checking on Honey, looking at this, trying that. A farmer we'd never met before drove out to our farm and brought penicillin, administered the shot, and left us needles so we could give him more. (The penicillin was in case there was some kind of infection at work.)

But in the end, there was nothing we could do. By Easter morn-ing, Honey was gone.

I had written so many stories on my website about the animals, and especially the goats—but this wasn't a storybook. Honey was our first major loss, and the first head-on collision with the reality of farm life. This was a real farm and these were real animals, and sometimes there was going to be real heartbreak.

Honey was a little goat with seemingly no purpose in life. He didn't have a "job" on the farm. He didn't make wool or provide milk or lay eggs. He was wethered (neutered) so he wouldn't breed. He was, in fact, free, a product of buckling overflow who came as an add-on with Clover and Nutmeg. He was, pure and simple, a farm pet, and he had been a delight. He was sweet, somewhat submissive to the domineering does of his world, but he was a playful little thing. He loved to dance about the goat yard standing up on two feet, and oh my, he was a tease.

I imagined him dancing on two feet with angel wings, way up there, somewhere, in a sky full of cookies. And I wondered, not for the first time, if I was really tough enough to be a farmer, especially when we decided to get pigs, our first animals brought on with the single-minded intention of slaughter.

CHAPTER 8

We put a pet crate in the back of 52's pickup and drove down the road to the Ornery Angel's house one spring weekend afternoon to pick up two piglets. I sat next to him on the truck's bench seat, my hand resting on his jean-clad leg, as we puttered past our sun-dappled meadow bottom. I liked driving around in the truck with 52 on our farm when he was in a good mood. We had the sheep in the bottom now, and I'd ride down the driveway with him to feed them or check on them.

You couldn't even see the meadow bottom from the house, separated as it was by the steep hillside and thick trees, so it felt distant in a way, despite being part of our farm.

"Who's going to take care of the pigs?" I asked.

I was leery about pigs, but eager for the homegrown sausage. I wasn't planning to get emotionally attached, and I was very interested in making as much of our own food as possible. At some point, that meant addressing where meat came from.

"I'll take care of them," he said. He was planning to build a pig pen in the meadow bottom.

This sounded good since I thought the less time I spent with the pigs, the better.

"What do pigs eat anyway?" I knew nothing about pigs. I'd never been near a pig except at a fair.

"Near the end," 52 told me, "you just feed them corn, to fatten them up. Until then, they'll eat just about anything. I can get fruit and vegetables from the farmers' market in Charleston."

"Really? You mean buy fruit and vegetables?" This wasn't sounding very cost-effective.

"Cast-off fruit and vegetables." He explained that he'd talked to some of the vendors at the market. He'd set up a deal to haul off their bruised or nearly spoiled fruit and vegetables. The vendors would get rid of the stuff they couldn't sell, and we would get free food for our pigs.

52 was really good at finding deals and freebies, whether it was salvaged building supplies or free fruit and vegetables. He was always thinking of things that would never occur to me in a million years.

We turned in at the Ornery Angel's driveway. The whole family was waiting for us in the yard—the Ornery Angel, her husband, and their three kids. I'd never been to their house before, so this felt like a huge step in our relationship.

They led us to the rickety, ramshackle pig pen that backed up to the woods beside their house. There was a kind of shedlike enclosure with a wooden-fenced yard in front of it. The most gigantic pig I'd ever seen in my life lay on her side with approximately five billion piglets attached to her five billion teats.

Or maybe like a dozen piglets and a dozen teats, I'm really not sure. I was kind of stunned by the multiplicity of teats and the size of the sow.

The pig got up, shaking off the babies, some of which tried to latch back on to their rambling mama while others scooted under the wooden fence, racing around the yard squealing.

"Those two in there are the ones you can have," the Ornery Angel told 52, pointing. She wasn't really directing conversation at me.

I was busy staring at the sow anyway.

52 and I approached the pig pen. The sow reared up and came at the fence, which was nothing more than weathered wooden rails.

"She can't get out, can she?" I asked nervously.

"She hasn't gotten out. Yet." The Ornery Angel's husband laughed. "If she gets out, I'm shooting her."

One of the piglets that was set aside for us came near the fence. 52 leaned down and swiped it into his hands, barely catching it. It started squealing bloody murder.

The sow blasted into the fence.

I backed way, way up. Maybe it was all a trick. The Ornery Angel had gotten me here to have her pig kill me!

52 stuffed the first piglet into the pet crate in the back of the truck and went back for the second. The piglets were outrageously cute with their curly tails and high-pitched squeals. The mother pig was one of the scariest animals I'd ever seen in my life.

The second piglet required a lot of chasing, which involved a lot more sow crashing into the fence, but we finally rolled away with two pork producers in the back of the truck. The mother pig was still making a ruckus as we drove off.

"I'm glad you're taking care of the pigs," I told 52. "Because when they get like that one? I'm not going anywhere near them."

The piglets were a boy and a girl. We named them Sausage and Patty. After keeping them up top near the house in the goat pen (Clover's former milking parlor), 52 finished the pig pen in the meadow bottom and they moved down.

Next, it was time to call the pig man, and I don't mean somebody who appears in circus sideshows or special effects sequences in the movies. One of the strange things about the country is that you can always find somebody who specializes in whatever gruesome thing you need done. We needed a man who cuts pigs.

By then, we had a farrier for the donkeys, so we asked him if he knew a pig man.

He said, "My cousin cuts pigs."

Of course.

So we called his cousin, who showed up one Saturday afternoon with his wife and teenage daughter. The pig man and 52 dragged Sausage, our male pig, kicking and screaming out of the pig pen. And I do mean screaming.

Once they had the pig out in the field, 52 got out of the way and the daughter stepped into the action, holding Sausage on his back by his hind legs, tipped so his legs stuck straight up in the air. She was obviously an old hand at assisting her father, though the wife apparently didn't want to take part—she stayed in the truck. The pig man took out his knife and made quick work of Sausage's package.

In the country, veterinarians aren't called in to neuter hogs. You do it yourself, or you call a pig man. The main reason male hogs are castrated is because boar meat can have an odor to it, but it also makes for a more mellow pig in general.

Though Sausage wasn't exactly mellow while it was happening.

It was disgusting and oddly fascinating.

The pig man sprayed the "affected area" with antiseptic when he was finished. 52 took custody of Sausage, and the daughter wiped her hands on her jeans.

Then, approaching me, the pig man held out his palm. Sausage's family jewels sat in a fleshy, bloody clump. "Take it up to the house and fry it," he said. "It's a delicacy."

I said, "You can have it!"

They drove off, and 52 returned Sausage to the pen and Patty. I told the pigs good-bye and that I'd see them when it was time to make the pork chop batter. I never felt any attachment to them whatsoever, which made it easy to look forward to the bacon, and also made me feel slightly more like a farmer.

The free "pig" fruits and vegetables from the market rolled in all summer, and the amazing thing was that so much of it was good, or at least good enough. Cut off a bad spot here or a bad spot there, and it was people food, not pig food. The slightest blemish can make produce unsellable, but that wasn't the same thing as inedible. With money tight, I set to work preserving the bounty. 52 pulled up in his truck at the house after coming home with a load from the farmers' market, and I sorted through to take what I wanted before he hauled what I rejected down to the pigs. It was like Christmas every time, just with vegetables instead of presents. Dumpster diving, farmer style.

After experiencing the previous winter where I could barely get out the road, much less to a store and back, I started preparing early for the coming one. I cooked then scraped over one hundred ears of corn to make cream corn in freezer packs. I processed boxes of peppers, hot and sweet, to freeze and dry. I canned tomatoes, green beans, and all kinds of fruit for fillings and jams. Much of what I preserved came from the free farmers' market hauls, and some from our own garden. I dried zucchini and squash (in chips, to rehydrate later for stews and soups, or to grind for vegetable sauces). Herbs were dried by the basketful and stored in jar after jar.

Pressure canning was still new to me—52 had brought home a fifty-year-old pressure canner that worked perfectly, from a co-worker at his office not long after we first moved to the farm, and had taught me to use it—but I'd learned boiling water bath canning at the Slanted Little House.

Georgia still used the kitchen in the Slanted Little House to do her canning, and she stored it all in the old cellar. Low on money, I enjoyed "shopping" in that cellar for our meals when I first moved in, so I suppose it was only fair that she taught me how to replace what I ate.

She followed me into the kitchen one day the first summer I lived there, me lugging a heavy basket from the garden, and said, "What did you say you were going to do with these tomatoes?"

I hadn't said I was going to do anything with the tomatoes. I was hot and tired because she'd just made me pick them. I didn't want to ever look at a tomato again much less stand in a hot kitchen blanching, peeling, slicing, and canning them. I was a writer, and I was always trying to find time to write. Georgia was always trying to find something for me to do.

"You go to the cellar and get some quart jars and a big pot," she said. "I'll sit down here and wait for you."

The back of the Slanted Little House was lined with windows that allowed the hot summer sun to beam in full force. There were no curtains or shades, and most of the windows were painted shut.

The sills were lined with the most enormous collection of knick-knacks I'd ever seen. Whenever I took a hankering to dust them, it took half the day.

I brought up the biggest pot I could find in the cellar, and there was a dead bug in the bottom of it, which meant I had to wash it. There was never a lack of jars—the cellar was full of them. In the old days, canning jars were a typical gift to a new bride. They were prized possessions and tools of survival. Families passed them through generations.

The old cellar hadn't changed a bit since I was a kid. I still found it creepy yet mysteriously alluring.

On the sagging shelves of the old cellar, you could find all sorts of treasures. Ball Ideal jars. Blue "1858" Masons. Atlas Shoulders. Some of them had the old zinc or bail wire lids, though we didn't can in those.

Georgia had been canning all her life, and on that hot summer day and more in the Slanted Little House, with the sunlight beating in those back windows, she passed the baton to me, teaching me to make the garden witchery of Ruby. She sat at the table and gave instructions. If I didn't follow them exactly, she'd get a little testy. Other times, she'd refuse to give me instructions at all.

She'd hover over the pot, then sit down again. I thought she had me do most of the work because she tired easily. She'd grown up on a farm and had done it all.

Peeling tomatoes burned my fingers even in their ice water bath. Georgia fussed around, lining up the jars, ordering measurements of salt and lemon juice. She didn't use a cookbook. Everything she knew was in her head.

If she'd ever had a canning rack, it had disappeared into the murky depths of the cellar. She showed me how to make do and fold dishtowels to set in the pot to keep the jars off the bottom.

When the water was boiling and the lid safely down, I was ready for a glass of wine and a rocking chair on the porch.

I was sure we were saving the rest of the tomatoes for tomorrow. Or never.

Georgia said, "You better start peeling. When these jars come out, we'll put more in."

Then she sat down, one gnarled hand resting on her cane, and eyeballed me. She wore one of her usual at-home ensembles of a faded West Virginia Mountaineers T-shirt, stretch slacks, and a ball cap with her curly white hair poking out on all sides. She looked like a cross between a little old church lady, a gnome, and a homeless bum.

"Can't we wait till tomorrow?"

Her reply was clipped. "No, we can't."

She fully understood that I was lazy, and she was having none of it. You make hay while the sun shines, and you can tomatoes when they're sitting on the counter. No excuses. Or wine.

The tomatoes didn't go on forever, but there was always something else. Apples off the trees. Pears from a neighbor down the road. She taught me to preserve everything she could get her hands on.

I'd be stirring a simmering pot of some kind of jam or butter and make her come take a look. "Is this ready?" Can we put it in the jars? Is this over yet?

She'd give it a look, then sit down and say, "Do you think it's ready?"

"You're supposed to tell me that!"

Sometimes I'd get frustrated with her because she'd describe what it was supposed to look like, then make me figure out the rest on my own.

The next spring I was helping her plant when she called me over to the far side of the garden where she always put the corn. She was planting giant sunflowers for the birds between the hills of corn seed.

She said, "I can't remember if I planted this row already or not. Can you tell me?"

I looked down the row. Yep, corn seeds, with sunflower seeds between. I looked up to meet her stubborn gaze.

That's when I realized how bad her eyesight had become. No

way was she giving up her big garden any more readily than she'd give up canning, even if it meant she needed me to "see" for her.

"Putting food by" (preserving the garden's bounty) wasn't a hobby or something to do to impress people. For Georgia and the long line of women like Ruby who came before her, self-sustainable living was a way of life.

The first time I canned something at the Slanted Little House all by myself, without Georgia in the kitchen by my side, I was thrilled with the sense of accomplishment. I practically danced across the yard to her house to present her with a jar.

She said, "I need a spoon."

I leaped into her kitchen to get her one.

She dug the spoon right in and ate the whole half-pint of black-berry jam in one sitting, then pronounced it satisfactory.

That's what I'm planning to do when I'm in my seventies. Eat entire half-pints of jam whenever I want.

Once I learned to can, of course, I wanted to learn so much more. What else could I do? If self-sustainable living is an addiction, canning is a gateway drug. Next thing you know, you're dehydrating, pickling, fermenting, and milking a cow. Or at least that's what happened to me.

Morgan came in one day and found me standing in the pantry at our new house, staring at the wall of shelves lined with jars from canning up our freebie bounty. She said, "You like to look at that, don't you?"

I said, "Yes, it gives me a sense of satisfaction for all the work I've done. Like I enjoy looking at you. It gives me a sense of satisfaction for all the work I've put into you."

She said, "What work?"

Children are so ungrateful!

All my preserving efforts weren't just for us, of course—I was planning ahead for holiday gifts, too. We still didn't have much money, and frugal was the motto by which we lived. I made homemade candles and was even mixing my own homemade laundry detergent. I was constantly coming up with new ideas for things to try homemade. It helped the budget and, of course, gave me plenty of material for my website.

52 was a willing participant in every new experiment, trying out anything I'd make, though our relationship continued to be rough and I couldn't understand why. I recognized the pattern of his diatribes, but I never figured out how to stop myself from stepping into the trap. Evening after evening would be just fine, then the next thing I knew, things were going to hell in a hand-basket and I didn't know how we'd gotten there.

It didn't take much.

"Have you fed the dogs today?" he asked one evening when he came home. We had Coco, our Great Pyr, and by then we had Boomer, a little terrier mix stray Ross had picked up behind Mc-Donald's one night after work, and our "farm" shih tzu, Dookie. (I called him a "farm" shih tzu because he was always a mess. He was an elderly dog 52 had given to Morgan when we still lived at the Slanted Little House.)

"I fed them this morning," I said. We were sitting on the front porch, the dogs gathered about his feet in greeting.

"They need to eat twice a day. They're hungry."

"I'm going to feed them tonight," I said. "I just haven't fed them yet."

"Dogs need to eat twice a day."

"I'm going to feed them. I was busy."

I didn't know why it was a big deal anyway. The dogs didn't look like they were starving, and they were going to get their dinner in due order.

"Stop making excuses," he said.

"I'm not making excuses!"

"Now you're arguing. You always have to argue."

There. Stepped right into it, didn't I. I never saw it coming!

I stood. "I'll feed them right now."

"You think you're perfect, don't you?" he demanded.

A heavy weight sank in my stomach. I was so tired of this routine. I was baffled by his pattern of attack. I thought I was pretty obviously not perfect, though this didn't bother me. I wasn't even interested in being perfect and had certainly never claimed to be.

"I don't think I'm perfect," I said.

"Of course you do. You're perfect, and I'm not."

"Nobody's perfect."

"You're right. You're always right. You have to always be right," he said.

I rolled my eyes. I couldn't help it. Once he got started, it was like he was reading a script. The same one, over and over.

"I see you rolling your eyes," he spit out. "I know what you're thinking. You think I'm stupid."

I heaved a sigh, standing there wondering whether I should get some dog food or if he would accuse me of running away if I walked into the house. Since he'd come back after the episode the previous winter, I'd been careful to never let our conversations escalate. I was willing, repeatedly, to just walk away when he got started, but often he'd then accuse me of running away. I didn't know what else to do. We'd stopped seeing the counselor, and he'd resisted going back. I didn't want the kids to overhear what was going on, and most of all, I was afraid if the conversation ever escalated, I'd end up telling him to get out.

I'd promised him I'd never tell him to leave again, and I meant to keep my word.

"I have never once thought you were stupid," I told him. "I think you're a very smart person."

"No, you don't. You think I'm a stupid little boy."

"When have I ever said you are a stupid little boy?" I was flabbergasted. The "little boy" part was new, though it wasn't unusual for him to occasionally add something new to his routine. It seemed to be getting longer all the time, with new attacks or assertions of what he "knew" I was thinking. "Where are you getting this stuff?"

We'd had many conversations in which he'd told me stories

about his family. His mother was a schoolteacher and was known as a hard one. I knew he'd lived in the shadow of his brilliant older sister and that his mother had been a demanding parent, difficult to please. His father was known around town, by the reports of people who remembered him, as a detached and distant man. His mother had been the force in the family, or at least that was how it had been expressed to me, mostly when 52 wasn't present and people were saying what they really thought about his parents. His mother and father had died in a car crash years earlier, so of course I had never met them.

I was starting to put a few things together, though.

Someone who'd been a student of his mother's shared with me that she'd told him he'd never succeed in life and should plan on working at a gas station. He'd all but failed her class under the esteem beating, but he had gone on to be quite successful in life.

"Did your mother call you a stupid little boy?" I asked suddenly.

Maybe I took him by surprise. He didn't answer, but he didn't deny it either, which was answer enough.

I walked into the house quietly, almost forgetting about the dog food.

I'd stepped into something far deeper than I'd realized.

CHAPTER 9

Ross helped me load the .22, and I lifted the gun and fired, killing the raccoon we'd trapped during the night. 52 had already left for work, and I wanted to get the job done quickly. The raccoon rattling around in the cage waiting to be dispatched was unsettling, to say the least. Not that shooting it wasn't unsettling, too.

"Wow," I said. I felt strange. I'd just killed an animal. I felt good and bad all at the same time. "Do you think you could cut off the tail for me?"

I couldn't believe I'd just shot a raccoon and now I was asking my son to cut off the tail. I'd had a series of losses in the chicken house, including a hen dragged bit by bloody feather through a crack in the door to a nesting box while sitting on eggs. After Ross accomplished the deed, I got a hammer and nailed the tail to one of the posts on the front porch.

Somebody give me my redneck union card. I have arrived.

Ross was eighteen now, confident and competent. He'd taken to the back roads West Virginia lifestyle more than any of my kids. He loved to go "mudding" with his friends in pickup trucks (driving off road), camp out, and sometimes get into a little trouble. He loved to work and didn't want to go to college, which worried me. He'd gotten a taste of construction work helping the builder with our new house, then took a construction job after high school. I'd always envisioned my kids going to college, and I had to remind myself to not put him in a box, the way I'd felt growing up, placing expectations on him that were not his own. On the upside, cutting a tail off a raccoon was right up his alley.

I'd never killed an animal before in my entire life. I was beginning to believe I was capable of more than I thought, though I still felt as if I was floundering on the farm. I'd started free-ranging my mature chickens from my first-year hatching so I'd have room to move in new younger ones after they came out of the brooder. I had come to dislike keeping chickens penned. I wanted my chickens to live as natural a life as possible. Chickens love to peck in the grass, scramble through the woods, perch on fence posts, roll in garden plots, and poop on the porch. However, they never did go to the road. It was too far down the hill.

I didn't really need more chickens, but I regularly acquired them anyway. I was possibly a chicken addict.

Eddie, the clerk at the little store in town, showed us his process for picking chicks when we went to pick out what we hoped would be more future egg producers. His method went something like this: Pick 'em up, turn 'em over, and if they draw their legs up to their body, they're female. If they stretch their legs out, they're male. If one leg draws up and the other leg stretches out, put it back and try another.

When that happened, Eddie would say, "That one's no good."

I continued to incubate my own chicken eggs, along with buying chicks at the little store. I loved to watch chicks hatch, so incubating was a necessary component in my addiction. Of course, hatching out chicks means taking what you get, and often that means roosters, so picking up hens from sexed batches at the store was good for rounding out my flock with a majority in the female department. I could only stand so many roosters. Plus, I wanted some immediate chick satisfaction. While I was waiting on a hatching, I could fulfill my chick yearnings by picking up a dozen day-olds.

I had one rooster, Mean Rooster, who scared me to death. He was one of the free rangers, and he'd stalk me. This progressed to pecking at me and sometimes flying up at my back as I was walking. I took to carrying a broom with me when I walked around the farm.

One of the first times he flew at my back to attack me, before I'd started carrying a broom, was a Saturday morning. 52 was home, leaning over the porch rail, watching me as I walked down to let the chickens out of the house for the morning.

Mean Rooster started following me. I walked faster. He flew up at me, jumping on my back. I shoved him off, turning in a circle and half dancing, screaming for help as Mean Rooster flapped around me, darting in and out trying to peck me as I tried to escape.

52 didn't move off the porch, just stood there, watching. In fact, he seemed downright entertained.

"Why didn't you help me?" I demanded when I finally got back to the porch, safe from Mean Rooster.

"What did you expect me to do?" he asked.

"Help me! I was calling you!"

"I'm not going to come just because you call me," he said. "You were being hysterical."

Maybe, but I would have felt better if he'd come down. It hadn't been a serious incident, but it left me with an uneasy feeling even as I plowed dead ahead with our life on the farm.

Georgia reminded me regularly that, a year after moving out, I still had a few things at the Slanted Little House. I needed to collect the last of my things, clean up the Slanted Little House, and finish unpacking at the new house.

When I drove over to drop the kids off for the bus, I stayed to work, packing up stray items, and cleaning up the mess we'd left behind. I'd promised Georgia I'd make it sparkly, and aside from that, I owed it to the Slanted Little House, which now sat uninhabited as it had before I'd arrived, to leave it in pristine condition.

"Be patient," I begged Georgia when she'd remind me that I hadn't cleaned the house yet. "And don't touch anything. I'll do it!" It was past time.

I worked on the old kitchen first. It was probably my favorite room in the house—not because it was a great kitchen, but because I had rediscovered my neglected love of baking in the two and a half years I spent there, and it was where I learned to can with Georgia.

One day when I lived there, Georgia walked into the kitchen and said, "I took care of that possum."

Raccoons and possums are common country pests. They unload your trash cans, kill your chickens, eat your dog's food, and even break into people's houses. A possum had been skulking around my cousin's house of late.

I said, "How'd you do that?"

She said, "I hit it over the head with a shovel."

Georgia was full of surprises. And so many of my surprising conversations with her took place in that kitchen.

I wiped down everything in the room, dusted the glass, put back my great-aunt Ruby's knickknacks that I'd taken down to put up mine while I lived there. It was Ruby's kitchen again.

Except, to me, it would always be mine.

Next, I swept the front room and dusted all the old photographs. Georgia watched, supervising, then went to the cellar and dragged out a sled.

"Sweep all the dust bunnies onto here," she instructed. Then she told me to dump them on the garden.

I asked her why we were dumping dust bunnies on the garden, eager to absorb her drops of knowledge. *Speak to me, Yoda.* She stared at me for a long moment, then said, "I don't know. I just feel like it."

Oh.

Georgia was a character and a half, as was her friend Faye. Every week the Spencer newspaper spotlighted a citizen they caught on the street, sort of the "every man" piece in the weekly county paper.

One week, it was Faye.

They had a routine list of questions for the spotlight. The hapless newspaper editor who fell into Faye's clutches on the sidewalk of the town square could have had no idea what he was getting into, but he found out soon enough. He asked Faye if she wanted to be in the spotlight.

Faye said, "I told him, do you see this sun shining on me? I am already in the spotlight."

I whipped out my copy of the paper and perused her answers to the routine questions.

Occupation: Hardware clerk.

My commentary: Could Faye work anywhere else but at the little store in Walton? Of course not. And of course she worked in the hardware section.

Hobby: Drawing.

My commentary: Faye is an amazing, accomplished artist. I've seen several of her paintings hanging in Georgia's house.

Favorite food: Steak.

My commentary: Could we imagine any different?

Favorite TV show: *The Golden Girls*.

My commentary: I think she meant the alternate universe version. *The Golden Girls Clear Brush*.

Favorite author: Agatha Christie.

I choked on that answer. "Faye! What is wrong with you?"

Faye said, "What?"

"Why didn't you say me?"

Faye said, "I've never read one of your books."

I said, "That is not the point! You could have said me anyway! I'm taking you out of my will!"

"You don't have any money."

Person most admired: David Hedges.

My commentary: David Hedges is the editor of the newspaper. Faye had the driest sense of humor in town.

Faye said, "I told him there was no way they'd put that answer in the paper."

Pet peeve: When something she is expecting is not in the county paper.

I said, "Smart mouth."

Which was why she got along so well with Georgia.

It took me a couple weeks off and on, but I finally got things sparkly enough over at the Slanted Little House that I turned my attention back to my new house with a clean conscience. I unpacked a box that held my grandmother's china. The pattern, French Rose 1264 and imported from Japan, was in delicate shades of pink and gray with a platinum edging. I thought the dishes were beautiful, though I hadn't always thought that much of them.

The dishes came from my grandmother on my mother's side. I could remember eating on that china at my grandmother's little house in Oklahoma. My grandmother was a frugal farm woman, and she didn't have a lot of excess. This was her fine china for holidays and special occasions. It was an extensive set, including an assortment of serving dishes and various-sized plates in somewhat incomprehensibly changing numbers. There were eighteen teacups and saucers, and eighteen dinner plates, but twelve of most other pieces. Some pieces were hard to decipher. Along with the dinner plates, there were also plates in a small size and a medium size. Maybe one was a dessert plate and one a luncheon plate. Or perhaps a salad plate.

I'd had the dishes for about fifteen years. I initially didn't like them that much, but I took them because I thought my mother wanted me to take them. I put them away in a cupboard and never used them. Then I moved and put them away in a new cupboard. Then I moved again and put them in a box. And never took them out.

The box ended up on my porch at the farm, and eventually I started thinking about those dishes. I especially thought about the dishes when the chickens started laying eggs in the box on top of the dishes. Sometimes the cats sat in the box on top of the dishes. The box was open at the top. The dishes weren't that well packed.

I brought the box inside and decided I would wash the dishes and put them away. In fact, I had an urge to use them. I had never been a "china person" in a lot of ways. China always felt too formal to me, but this china had a softer, gentler feel to it than most. The pattern was quiet and minimal. My grandmother lived a simple life in a simple home. It fit that her china was also simple.

I'd developed a fascination with old skills and ideas and things, and possibly I was becoming more sentimental even as I hardened as a farmer. My mother always called my grandmother "Mama"—and when my mother died, I knew I'd never hear someone refer to my grandmother as Mama again. I knew and remembered my grandmother, but my children didn't. My youngest child wasn't even born when my grandmother died. So after all those years of moving that box around, I wanted those dishes.

However, I had no place to even put them. My cabinets were full of junk.

I reminded myself that our ancestors didn't have all this junk. They couldn't afford it, or they just plain knew better. Living frugally and simply is about more than saving money. It's a lifestyle that permeates your entire home. With that in mind, I unloaded the cabinets, spreading out all the stuff on the floor and even the dining room table.

I boxed up all sorts of various items to give away and cleared out the cabinet enough to make room for my grandmother's dishes. I unwrapped them one by one from newspaper that was shredded in places, probably because mice had been in the box. I washed the dishes all by hand and twice in the dishwasher to sanitize and sanitize again. And then I served dinner to my children on "Mama's dishes."

I explained it all to the kids, and I'm not sure they thought it was as important as I did, but I wanted to give them that connection even if they weren't ready to appreciate it yet. And I was, desperately, seeking that connection for myself. Not just with my grandmother, but with the strength and self-sufficiency of the women of her time.

I wrote frequently on my website about my interest in all things old, and one of my readers sent me a big red World War II–era book titled *Food for Health and National Defense, A West Virginia Cookbook*. The cover noted it came from the West Virginia Department of Agriculture. It appeared to be something that was somewhat handmade, typed on an old-fashioned typewriter, filled with tried-and-true recipes from women across the state plus tacked-in additions of newspaper and magazine clippings—almost like a workbook of a sort. Almost every woman listed her name as Mrs. in conjunction with her husband's first name and last name. No first name for the woman herself.

I decided to try a recipe and settled on one for strawberry cake submitted by Mrs. Brooks Randolph from Lost Creek, West Virginia.

The recipe used six eggs, butter, sugar, strawberry preserves, flour, buttermilk, and a mix of spices, all organized in complete disorder in the ingredients list. Things got even more convoluted in the instructions. I tried to make sense of the recipe, putting the ingredients in rational order and modern terms.

After writing about Mrs. Brooks Randolph and her recipe, noting that after attempting to follow the instructions for her cake, I thought she was "ornery" and needed a spankin', one of my readers sent me the phone number for Mrs. Randolph's nephew.

What would anyone in their right mind do with this phone number?

I picked up the phone and dialed it. (That is not, by the way, the correct answer to the above question.)

Mrs. Randolph's nephew's wife answered the phone.

ME: I'm looking for Mrs. Brooks Randolph.
MRS. RANDOLPH'S NEPHEW'S WIFE: Who?
ME: Mrs. Brooks Randolph.
MRS. RANDOLPH'S NEPHEW'S WIFE: That was my husband's aunt.
ME: Yes! Is she alive?

MRS. RANDOLPH'S NEPHEW'S WIFE: No, she died.

ME: I need to know what she would have thought was a *small* teaspoon.

MRS. RANDOLPH'S NEPHEW'S WIFE: A small spoon?

ME: A small teaspoon. What did she think was a small teaspoon?

MRS. RANDOLPH'S NEPHEW'S WIFE: Oh. I don't know.

ME: Did you ever eat her strawberry cake?

MRS. RANDOLPH'S NEPHEW'S WIFE: Strudel cake?

ME: Strawberry cake.

MRS. RANDOLPH'S NEPHEW'S WIFE: She never made strawberry cake.

ME: Yes, she did! She put it in a cookbook! And she measured in *small* teaspoons. What would she have thought was a small teaspoon?

MRS. RANDOLPH'S NEPHEW'S WIFE: I have her daughter's phone number. Do you want that?

What would anyone in their right mind do with this phone number?

I picked up the phone and dialed it. (That is not, by the way, the correct answer to the above question.)

Mrs. Randolph's daughter answered the phone.

Mrs. Randolph's daughter was eighty-seven.

ME: Are you Mrs. Brooks Randolph's daughter?

MRS. BROOKS RANDOLPH'S DAUGHTER: Yes?

ME: I need to know what she would have thought was a *small* teaspoon?

MRS. BROOKS RANDOLPH'S DAUGHTER: A small spoon?

ME: A small teaspoon.

MRS. BROOKS RANDOLPH'S DAUGHTER: A small teaspoon?

ME: Yes. A small teaspoon. What was a small teaspoon?

MRS. BROOKS RANDOLPH'S DAUGHTER: I don't know.

ME: What about when she made strawberry cake? When she made strawberry cake, what was a small teaspoon?

MRS. BROOKS RANDOLPH'S DAUGHTER: She never made straw-berry cake.

ME: I have a book! She submitted a strawberry cake recipe.

MRS. BROOKS RANDOLPH'S DAUGHTER: She made strawberry shortcake. She never made strawberry cake.

Mrs. Brooks Randolph? Where were you, Mrs. Brooks Randolph? What secret life did you and your strawberry cake and your small teaspoons lead that was hidden from your family?

ME: Okay. Can you just tell me something about your mother? What was she like?

I had to know the deep, dark secrets of this strawberry cake woman.

Give me *something*.

Mrs. Brooks Randolph's daughter said, "Oh, she was funny. She loved the farm and she worked hard at it. She canned and made lard and soap. She enjoyed a joke and she saw fun in things. In the summer when the farm would come in, we'd have all that cooking to do. She never fussed about it. She'd pack baskets to take to the hands on our other farms and she was just a good-natured person, very happy. She loved to cook. She made straw-berry shortcake, but I don't remember any strawberry cake. She was a good cook and always jolly."

Mrs. Brooks Randolph was born in the 1890s. Mr. Randolph was a farmer. She was a "farm mother" as her daughter put it. He died first. She died when she was ninety-two. She moved to town when she couldn't take care of the farm by herself anymore and lived with her daughter. She died of a stroke. And her daughter did *not* have her strawberry shortcake recipe. *I asked.*

I said, "Can you just tell me one more thing?"

Mrs. Brooks Randolph's daughter replied, "Yes?"

"What was Mrs. Randolph's first name?"

"Marie."

Mrs. Brooks Randolph was neither here nor there in any kind of reality for me, but she had been real and she was exactly the sort of self-sufficient farm woman I was trying to be. I canned! And when we butchered the pigs, I was going to make lard.

Except unless you counted the pigs (which I hadn't even handled directly), I felt as if most of the time I wasn't doing much more than running a large petting zoo. I started thinking about a milk cow. It would either make me a farmer or kill me.

CHAPTER 10

One rainy fall day, after slogging through thick mud pushing a wheelbarrow full of cement at his construction job, Ross came home and said he didn't think he wanted to do that for the rest of his life.

Great! Could we talk about college again?

No. He wanted to talk about the military again. He'd been talking about the military for four years. And I'd been crying about it for four years. I'd had a few not-so-friendly run-ins with military recruiters. And I'd bothered the principal of the high school a few times about letting those recruiters into the school. Why, why, why must they let them come there? Leave my little boy alone! Don't they know these are children?

Recruiters would send stuff in the mail and I would throw it out. I'm a mother. I like my child just how he is, with all his arms and legs attached. At one point, Ross asked me to sign him into the military when he was seventeen, when it requires a parent signature.

Are you kidding? My grandmother signed my father's little brother into the Marines when he was seventeen, during World War II, and he was killed on a Pacific Island. So. I don't think so.

But Ross was eighteen now and he had already scheduled an appointment with a navy recruiter to go to Beckley, West Virginia, a couple of hours south, to the military entrance processing station there. I asked him what else he'd done without telling me. Was he married? (No. Whew.) The navy recruiter called the next day and I grilled him. He almost made me feel like it might be okay.

Ross wanted to be a Seabee. Seabees are the construction engineers of the navy, and it fit with his interest in building and doing things with his hands. He had taken the ASVAB (general military entrance exam). Only when he went to Beckley to sign up, there were no positions available in the Seabees. The economy had created a backlog in the military for new enlistees.

Oh, happy day! No more military. If only. There were still two jobs needing enlistees in the navy. That would be Navy SEALs and nukes (the nuclear program). SEALs and nukes were in demand because these are positions that require high qualifications.

I actually had some experience and knowledge about navy nukes. A long time ago, in a galaxy far, far away, I was a navy wife. I was married to a nuclear submariner. He was stationed in Charleston, South Carolina, though he ported out of King's Bay, Georgia. He was, in fact (of course), Ross's father, my ex-husband.

To be a navy nuke is prestigious—and difficult. It requires a six-year enlistment due to the two-year educational training. There are big bonuses and advanced pay grades. It's rigorous and only the smartest of the smart get in there.

Ross threw his Seabees dream out the window, but he was bound and determined to join the navy. He didn't want to be a SEAL, though. He'd do that nuke thing. That'd be fine. The navy recruiter took another glance at his less-than-stellar high school transcripts, which didn't include classes like, say, physics, and told him that he didn't think that was going to work out.

Ross + high school = girls + cars.

Sorry, there wasn't much (or any) time for that studying thing. Or taking real classes.

His ASVAB score wasn't high enough. He'd have to take the separate nuclear test and pass it with flying colors. The navy recruiter advised against it. Maybe a job requiring less qualification would come up. Ross decided he'd take the nuke test.

He went home and asked his eleventh-grade football-playing

little brother, Weston, to explain physics to him. Another job in the navy, requiring less qualification, did come up. The recruiter called. Ross refused it. He went back to Beckley and took the nuke test.

And passed it.

Only he didn't pass it very high, so if he was going to get in the nuke program, he was going to have to go back yet again and retake the ASVAB and earn a very high score to qualify.

The navy recruiter said he'd never had anyone retake the ASVAB and improve their score. At all. Much less by a significant margin, which was what Ross needed to do.

He thought Ross was wasting his time. He gave him two weeks to prepare.

I cried a little bit more, then I bought Ross a study book. Ross decided to learn everything there was to know about physics in two weeks. (Teenagers are so funny.) And I decided that if he could really make it into the navy's nuclear program, I was okay. It was safe. He'd be living in a submarine and sleeping on a shelf. I've been inside a navy submarine. I was a navy wife.

Ross took the study book in hand and said, "I don't know how to study. I can't remember the last time I studied."

I replied, "Well, it wasn't in high school, was it?"

He went back to Beckley and retook the ASVAB. He scored so high that, if he'd done that the first time around, he wouldn't have even had to take the separate nuke test.

He was scheduled for boot camp in Great Lakes, Illinois, the following spring, and two years of nuclear school in Charleston, South Carolina, to be followed by four years of sea duty. There was a total six-year commitment. He volunteered for submarines.

I was proud of him, in spite of my fears. He had broken up with his high school girlfriend just before making the decision to join the navy, and after signing his enlistment papers, he decided to go live with his dad in Texas until his boot camp ship date.

A few evenings before he was set to leave for Texas, he came up to the house and said he'd just passed the Ornery Angel's husband on the road. "He said he was dying," Ross said. "Did you know that?"

"He's not dying," 52 told him.

The man had a penchant for telling neighbors he was dying of one disease or another as a joke. (Not telling people it was a joke was the joke, apparently.)

Frank, our neighbor who lived directly across the ford, spent a lot of time cutting and stacking wood for the Ornery Angel and her children for winter. He liked to be outside, working, and he tried to help out the Ornery Angel when he saw her husband wasn't getting wood cut for her. Frank would also always buy anything any of my kids or the Ornery Angel's kids were selling for school. He bought a volleyball hoodie from Morgan one time. She went to deliver it to him and happened on him naked inside his house when she went to the door.

She refused to ever go to Frank's house again, and eventually, Frank (who hadn't seen Morgan that day when she'd gone to his door) asked about his hoodie and 52 had to deliver it.

By this time, winter was coming on. My first little bird had flown the nest, but I was still preparing for a household of four on a remote farm. It was scary, too, but also exciting in a way. Winter was a challenge, and I loved challenges. Winter also meant it was finally time for Sausage and Patty to meet their maker.

I didn't feel at all bad about butchering something we'd raised. I didn't like the pigs. My cousin came over to do the deed, and I mostly avoided the scene, though I was driving home after picking up the kids from the bus and saw the pig hanging in the meadow bottom to bleed out. Or whatever it is you do with a pig after it's dead.

We'd traded the other pig for half a cow, which was already in our freezer, and we took our freshly slaughtered pig to the house of a friend who knew how to butcher. The butchering process took hours and was disgusting, but I was trying to learn to knit so I kept busy and out of the bloody stuff. I couldn't wait to get home and start frying pork chops and making lard.

We were closer to being real farmers than ever. My pantry was stocked to the rafters with home-preserved food, and we had freezers full of meat. 52 had bought a generator so we'd be ready for power outages, and he came up with a used woodstove that he installed on the main floor of the house.

Not that I knew how to start a fire.

52 chopped up fallen trees from the woods and taught me how to light a fire.

ME: I'm scared of fire.

52: That's handy.

After practicing numerous times, I finally got a fire started all by myself. Then 52 went to work, leaving me a supply of logs and kindling on the porch. About two hours later, the fire died. I couldn't get it started again.

I added logs and kindling. I added paper. It kept dying. I e-mailed 52 in a panic. "The fire keeps dying!"

He told me to get more kindling.

ME: But I'm out of kindling!

52: You have forty acres of kindling.

Oh.

On the upside, I felt like a pioneer when I went out to collect kindling. Unfortunately, it was snowy, and stuff out there was wet. Eventually, I managed to collect enough semidry kindling to get the fire started again. I struggled with it all day. And the next day. And for the next several weeks, but finally I got better at it. We were trying to save money on our electric and propane bills. Wood was free. I was the one who was home all day, so it was up to me to keep the fire going.

And to restart it if I let it die.

52 had told everyone at his office that we had chickens, and people unloaded empty egg cartons on him until I had a large stash. Many of these were cardboard egg cartons, which made a great base for homemade fire starters. Since I remained slightly clumsy in my fire-starting abilities, I could use all the help I could get.

I melted down and recycled the bottoms of old container candles to make new candles, so I always had a lot of candle wax. I had friends and relatives giving me their used candles, too.

In perhaps my strangest collection, I had everyone saving their dryer lint for me.

I tucked a ball of dryer lint in each cup of a cardboard egg carton, then poured melted candle wax into the cup, over the dryer lint. To use as fire starters, I'd just tear the cups apart. One cup was usually enough to get the fire started, but two or three was better. I could make fire anytime I wanted! Although I still struggled with keeping a fire going, at least I could restart it, and we would be warm that winter no matter what.

I was over at Georgia's house collecting her dryer lint one day when she wanted to show me her new refrigerator, which was quite lovely, but what I fell in love with were the old jars she had moved around in the whole process of getting the new fridge installed. The jars had been on top of her old fridge and I'd never noticed them before. Her new fridge was bigger and taller, so she was still figuring out how and where she was going to put back the jars.

She had them all lined up on a table in her living room. I examined them eagerly, forever and always fascinated with old canning jars. Some of them had old dried *stuff* in them that might have been ten or twenty or fifty years old. She didn't know what it was.

I told her she better not eat that! You never knew what Georgia might do.

The jars had the old bail wire and rubber rings, which are so adorably quaint and antiquated. They came with reusable glass lids. All you changed out was the rubber seal ring.

Georgia showed me how they worked.

I said, "You're lucky you're alive. They don't let you can in jars like that anymore."

She said, "They might not approve, but I could can in anything I want to."

Rascal.

I reminded her that she didn't can anymore anyway—unless I canned with her. If she tried, I'd take those jars away from her. You know, for safekeeping.

She reminded me that we had bad weather coming and I'd better get ready. Georgia was always on top of the weather forecast.

Power outages, virtually unheard of in my suburban childhood and later adulthood, are more common in a state like West Virginia. The icy trees and mostly overhead power lines, combined with the rough and remote terrain of much of the state, make extended power outages an expected part of winter.

We found, after moving to one of the most remote areas, that we seemed to always be among the last to get our power restored. It was a comfort going into that winter to know we had a generator. The next day, I woke to a poststorm Saturday morning of snow and darkness. No power.

The world is very still when nothing is running. You forget how still it can be. No low hum from the refrigerator. No television. No central heat to kick on if the fire in the woodstove dies out.

There was noise outside. Branches cracking under the weight of snow. Roosters crowing from roosts they refused to leave. Light thumps against the goat house floor and walls as animals rearranged themselves, nestling together to share body heat.

The phone line was still working, so I could use the old-fashioned nonelectric phone to call the power company and report our outage. No panic. We were second-year farmers. We were smarter than first-year farmers! We had a generator. We had wood piled up, and we had a woodstove. We had food laid in for an army, much of it home preserved over the long, wonderful summer and autumn months of bounty.

Knowing the storm was coming, I had simmered a big pot of

beans the night before. I took out the pot of beans and set it on top of the woodstove to heat it up. There were still hot coals in the bed of the woodstove. I struggled a little to start a fire in the cold, cold house.

Winter was difficult, but it was also like the final exam. Without it, how would we prove to ourselves that we had, indeed, become self-sufficient? There was a certain satisfaction in winter's hardships. We spent our months of plenty preparing for that very moment. The moment we could stick out our tongues at winter and say, HA.

In today's sophisticated world, self-sufficiency is in many ways not entirely necessary. In most urban and suburban areas, you can expect power to be restored in a reasonable period of time. Even if it's not restored quickly, you can expect the streets to be plowed so you can go across town to someone else's house who has power, or even to the public library. You can find a restaurant with power and buy your dinner. In truly dire circumstances, there are even shelters. There's a collective joint sufficiency to fall back on. In the most rural of places, there's no such thing as road plows, and you can expect to be last on the priority list for power restoration. And from a remote farm, there is no going anywhere for anything.

For some reason, there are those of us who leave the collective cocoon of public care, determined to test our grit against the challenge of individual self-sufficiency. Maybe it's stubbornness. Maybe it's arrogance. Maybe it's the desire to meet and defeat challenge. Other people jump out of airplanes. Some climb sheer mountain faces. Still others race cars. It's all about testing some deep place inside that the comfortable, secure world today won't make you test otherwise. For me, it was surviving winter on a remote farm. That was my airplane, my mountain, my race car.

My test.

At least that was what I told myself as I sat in the still, early morn dark after finding the telephone and the power company's number by the light of candles I had made myself. I was cold, still having trouble getting things going in the woodstove. I poked at the fire, made it finally flame bright.

And I felt like a total hero.

We had a foot of snow. The woods around our farmhouse creaked and groaned under the wintry weight, branches, even entire trees, crashing to the ground. There wasn't any mystery as to what had happened to the power lines. The power company said they'd have electricity back by midnight, but as the outage mounted into tens of thousands of homes, the message changed.

By the end of the day, they were saying midnight the next day. And then the next and the next. We lost phone service eventually, too, and we didn't have cell service at the farm. Using generator power, I was able to set a post on my blog and send my column to the newspaper, but we had to conserve gas for the generator, so using the generator for satellite Internet service was limited. Our driveway was impassably covered, as was the road—which was also blocked by numerous fallen trees. 52, Weston, Morgan, and I were snowed in. There was no way out. And I was on vacation! I couldn't work on my website every day as usual.

I puttered around the house. I cleaned. I repacked and reorganized all the boxes of extra Christmas ornaments. I cooked. We had beans and corn bread the first day, heated on the woodstove. We were also still able to use our gas cooktop in the kitchen (lit with a match) as well as our gas grill on the back porch. We had chili and pork chops with fried potatoes, and even homemade pizza on the grill. The chickens suddenly set to work in the freezing temperatures, and we had bacon and eggs in the mornings.

I read books. I knitted. 52 moved the generator lines around and kept wood coming into the house for the stove. Weston and Morgan played board games and cards, had fights with swimming noodles, and built snowmen.

The generator was a pull-start model, and I couldn't start it myself. No matter how many times I practiced and tried, I couldn't do it. I had no control over the generator, which bothered me immensely. I had to ask permission from 52 for everything that was plugged in, and if the generator died, I couldn't restart it.

We moved the generator around as needed and wanted and allowed. We ran the coffeemaker and the radio, the refrigerator and freezers. We ran the blower on the woodstove, keeping the house warm.

In the evenings, we watched a couple hours of TV and ran the Christmas tree lights and a few lamps.

The worst part of a power outage in the country is not having water. The well ran on electric and required 220 volts. We didn't have a generator that would run the well, but we had water tanks at the house to hold extra water. We rationed carefully. Showers were out.

Baking was out, too, since the generator couldn't run the electric oven. And it was Christmas. I had to survive a holiday without baking. The power outage, which extended to a week, began just as I was preparing to launch full force into holiday baking.

Anyone who has been without power for an extended period knows—it's a different world. Your life takes on a surreal perspective. Even with a generator, it's not "normal" life. You take care of your food stores and your animals. Survival mode takes over. Certain accustomed basics go by the wayside as if they never existed. Standards change. True necessities rise from the rest. And you find ways to make things happen that are special to you.

I was determined to not let the weeklong power outage defeat me. I experimented with some alternative baking. I honed the art of wiping out and scraping out mixing bowls to reuse because I couldn't do dishes under our water rationing plan. I tried to bake biscuits in the woodstove, but it wasn't cut out for baking. I could simmer beans or chili or a coffeepot on top, but baking inside it meant burning.

I made a second attempt on the gas grill, which worked out much better, only I baked the biscuits in a glass pie pan, due to the dearth of clean dishes, and the glass pan exploded, taking the biscuits down with it as it shattered.

I did manage to bake homemade pizza on the gas grill, and even a cake. Christmas Eve dinner, without an oven, was ham, corn, green beans, and no biscuits, with cake for dessert—by candlelight. On Christmas morning, we had eggs, bacon, and crullers fried on the stovetop.

In a seeming Christmas miracle, on our seventh day without power, the electricity came on just as I finished frying the crullers. It stayed on for about an hour. We spent the hour restarting the well pump and getting water up to the house. Weston and Morgan immediately took showers. I got the dishwasher loaded—but didn't have time to push the button to wash them before the power went out again. I hadn't gotten a shower. I cried.

The electricity came back on that evening and our winter test was finally over.

We passed.

Except for the crying.

And that was just me.

A few days later, we made it off the farm to a post-Christmas get-together at my cousin's house. I brought Georgia half-pints of blackberry jam and orange marmalade, some homemade candy, a "Chickens in the Road" calendar, and a coconut-oatmeal rum pie. She loved treats, and she didn't bake anymore.

For my cousin, I had made some drunken rum cookie logs, with Georgia's recipe, and a big batch of my homemade pepperoni rolls.

My cousin told me to close my eyes, and he brought out a surprise for me. He put something in my lap. I could hear a clink of glass that sounded familiar. I said, "Did you get me some canning jars?"

And then I opened my eyes. Oh, yes, he and Georgia had given me some canning jars. But not just any canning jars.

Three of Georgia's vintage jars with the bail wire lids! A pint, a quart, and a half-gallon jar. I was thrilled, and as usual, went straight home to write about it on my website.

By this time, I'd built a community on my website and had opened a message board forum. 52 periodically and with growing frequency asked my readers questions about milk cows.

He was going to buy me a cow, I just knew it.

I was excited, scared, and worried.

We were broke.

Didn't cows, like, need a lot of food? And pasture?

But I wanted a cow, so I pretended like I didn't notice.

I stopped saying I wanted a cow.

Let the chips fall. Either he'd get me a cow, or he wouldn't.

This was not a very good method for financial health, but it was my way of ducking responsibility. I knew when 52 got it in his head that he was going to get me something, most of the time, he did. Even if it was ridiculous. I hadn't exactly succeeded at goat milking with flying colors. Was I seriously going to milk a cow?

But I wasn't scared enough to say I didn't want one. I just stopped saying I did want one, though I'd started experimenting with home-made cheese again, using store-bought milk. I'd successfully made a farmhouse cheddar, and I'd tried Monterey Jack. 52 had made me a homemade cheese press so that I could make hard cheeses. We were jumping over the cliff before we even had the cow.

Meanwhile 52 kept asking questions on the forum about milk cows.

This should pretty well explain how we got into so much trouble every time we turned around. And all the while, we were still running a pretty bumpy road relationship-wise. The gap between us had widened as I talked to him less and less. Conversation with him often included being cut off, snapped at, and told I was too loud. When I tried to talk to him about our problem with communication, he was emotionally distant and cold. I didn't know where the man I'd met had gone. We worked well together when there was a project around the farm to be tackled, or a power outage to survive, but he didn't like talking to me otherwise. He was very friendly and talkative with other people, but as soon as we were alone, he wanted nothing but quiet. Any but the most succinct conversation with me annoyed him, and yet here he was still wanting to give me a cow. It was as if he loved and hated me at the same time, and I was completely confused.

One time early in our relationship, he had taken me to visit
the old farm where his great-grandparents had lived. Someone
else lived there then, but that didn't stop us from taking a peek
inside when we found no one was home. He wanted to show the
house to me, and there was a childish sense of excitement about
daring each other to go in. We didn't look around long, afraid the
ninety-year-old owner might return, but just inside the door, I
pulled 52 to me and kissed him for the first time.

I knew he wouldn't trespass so much as to kiss me. His reaction
was almost embarrassed yet happy at the same time, which was endearing.

We went back outside and sat down on the porch and he told
me about his great-grandparents and his love for the land and
a dream he'd cherished to someday come back to a farm. We sat
close together and held hands. I loved nothing more than to listen
to him talk in his deep voice—and to talk to him. Then it all went
away, and he became the last person to whom I could talk.

I had begun to feel like his whipping boy, the one specially
picked out in the world to be the focus of his wrath, and I didn't
know what to do about it. The farm was my whole life.

I couldn't have the farm without him.

And he knew that.

CHAPTER 11

West Virginia winters were brutal—but beautiful. I loved them as much as I feared them. I'd always wanted to live some place where it snowed. There was something both inherently peaceful and innocently magical about it.

Our farm turned into a winter wonderland. Snow tumbled on fence posts and slid down rails. No matter the upheavals in my personal life, it was impossible not to love my life on the farm.

I loved the soft crunch of the snow beneath my boots. I didn't even mind going out to do chores. In fact, the chores got me out of the house, where I might have stayed huddled away by the fire otherwise. It felt good to get outside and breathe the crisp air. But winter did make life difficult—more than it should have.

I thought they had it right in the old days when everything was close to home. One-room schoolhouses in every tiny community, little white steepled churches around every bend in the road, mom-and-pop storefronts on farms. What you couldn't get nearby or didn't have stocked away, you didn't really need.

You walked everywhere you needed to go or took your horse and buggy. Doctors made house calls.

My father went to school in a one-room schoolhouse just across the river from our farm. He grew up about a mile down the road. My grandmother was the teacher. On snowy mornings, I could almost see them walking down the road in their coats and mittens.

They didn't have to worry about getting to school. It was no trouble to walk down the road.

My great-grandfather kept a little store by the road on his farm, also just across the river. Anyone who needed anything could walk there, too.

The church was in the meadow bottom on our farm. No excuses for missing Sunday services when it was snowing. You could walk.

I longed for those days in the isolation of winter on our farm. But in these days we are so very, very sophisticated with our superstores (twenty miles away), our centralized schools (twenty miles away), and our high-powered vehicles (that sometimes can't get twenty miles away).

We were all so much more self-sufficient when we arranged our lives so we could just walk everywhere we needed to go.

We can't do that now because we are too advanced.

Our first weeklong power outage that winter, leading up to Christmas, was good practice for all the times it went out again. The first foot of snow melted, flooding the river, just in time for a second foot of snow to fall. Even if one was courageous enough to try to make it out on the road, the river was too high to ford and everything was iced over in the other direction.

We all carried piles of wood and kindling up to the house. Water and generator gas was rationed again.

I walked through the house at night carrying my homemade hand-dipped tapers for light and felt like Jane Eyre.

I cooked bean and egg burritos on homemade tortillas for breakfast, and we made coffee. The hum of the generator was a constant accompaniment to life, background noise to the slow beat that the world seems to take on when electricity goes away. I practiced my knitting and walked down to the meadow bottom with 52 when it was time to check on the sheep. Since we still had no barn, we kept stacks of hay at the bottom under weighted tarps. Between the sheep, donkeys, and goats, we needed a couple hundred bales of hay that winter. We had no place to put it, so we couldn't stock up much ahead of time.

The sheep were always eager for their daily bale. They were two-ton balls of heavy fluff. The Cotswold wool was long and curly. I had an idea to try my hand at spinning since I was learning to knit, though I wasn't sure I had the patience for it. I wanted to try more new things than I could possibly handle.

52 and I usually got along well during power outages. It was a survival challenge. We always did best when we were engaged in an activity, be it a hardship, a new DIY skill, or a new animal.

Whatever new thing I wanted to try, 52 would say, "All right," and help me find the stuff. I'd been wanting to try soap making for a long time, and he called every hardware store in the city until he found one that carried lye.

First I contemplated making my own lye. If I was going to make homemade soap, shouldn't I start with the lye? Lye is made from wood ash. I had a woodstove! Upon researching this idea, I decided it was one of my more harebrained ones. Our great-grandmas made their own lye by leaching wood ashes, resulting in uneven levels of strength. This is where homemade soap got the bad rap for being harsh. Commercial lye available today is of a standardized strength, which makes nonharsh soap a reliable accomplishment. Lye used for soap making is the kind sold in crystal form, which specifies that it is 100 percent lye (sodium hydroxide).

Along with their homemade lye, our great-grandmas also used rainwater (boiled) for purity. Today, most people use distilled water. I almost felt like I was cheating when I used distilled water instead of collecting water in the rain and boiling it. But I'd already given up the idea of making homemade lye, and modern convenience is a slippery slope.

Learning to make soap became my project from late winter to early spring as I researched how-tos, collected ingredients on days we could get out, and built up to getting past my fear of handling lye.

Lye is a poison. It's corrosive, fatal if swallowed, and harmful if inhaled. It will burn the skin if it comes into contact with it, and it reacts to water, acids, and other materials (such as aluminum).

Many people today don't realize that all real soap is made with lye. This is because lye is a scary word, so it appears on labels as sodium hydroxide. Many commercial personal cleansing bars that appear to be soap aren't soaps at all but synthetic detergents made without lye. (If it doesn't say soap, it's not soap, it's a detergent bar.)

Soap is created by combining fat with lye. The fat can be all sorts of things—lard, tallow, shea or other butters, and all sorts of oils—many of which you can find in your kitchen. There are two ways to make soap.

In hot process, the entire saponification process takes place over a heat source. This is how our great-grandmas did it. In cold process, the saponification process takes place away from the heat source. (Saponification is the chemical process that occurs when fats/oils are combined with lye.) External heat is only used in the cold process method to melt the fats/oils before being combined with the lye.

Although cold process can produce a smoother, prettier soap, I was most attracted to the hot process method. It would take me the closest to an old-fashioned experience, and I preferred the more rustic result. Cindy Pierce, a friend I'd met through the forum on my website, coached me on how to make hot process soap in an enamel Crock-Pot and showed me how to calculate recipes.

Our great-grandmas would have used an iron kettle over an outdoor fire, but a slow cooker sounded close enough to me. (A stainless steel pot over the stove would also work. Do not use materials such as aluminum, tin, or copper because they react with lye.)

I already had a Crock-Pot and the rest of the typical kitchenware required, such as bowls, spoons, spatulas, measuring cups, and a digital kitchen scale. I bought a stick blender because I'm lazier than great-grandma and didn't want to do all that stirring by hand.

I also bought safety goggles and heavy gloves for handling the

⇑ The Slanted Little House.

⇒ Newborn and still wobbly, my Glory Bee.

← Clover and Nutmeg, mother/daughter love.

← Curly-wooled Cotswold sheep, left, with an exotic Jac[ob] sheep, right.

⇒ Nutmeg's first baby.

⇓ My chickens love me. Or they think I have food.

PHOTO: JERRY WATERS

⇑ Walking my
Glory Bee at
Sassafras Farm.

⇐ My two horses
at Sassafras Farm.
Zip, left, and
Shortcake, right.

PHOTO: JERRY WATERS

⇑ Woman attacked by horse and donkey, film at 11.

PHOTO: JERRY WATERS

⇑ Cracker candy—
eat yours before you
tell the kids.

⇒ Summer
Vegetable
Pie.

PHOTO: JERRY WATERS

⇐ The state food
of West Virginia,
Pepperoni Rolls.

⇑ Old-Fashioned
Apple Dumplings.

PHOTO: JERRY WATERS

⇒ Sweet Potato Pie.

PHOTO: JERRY WATERS

⇐ My holiday
favorite,
Drunken Rum
Cookie Logs.

⇒ Slicing homemade Lavender-Basil Soap.

⇐ Dried wildflowers turn pint jars into works of art.

⇑ Beulah Petunia on her way to the bull, wearing her flower.

⇒ My dear Georgia waiting for lunch at Stringtown Rising.

⇑ Annabelle's puppy. I mean, lamb.

⇐ The river ford in summer. Stringtown Rising is just on the other side.

⇑ Clover the Christmas Queen.

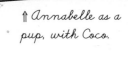

⇑ Annabelle as a
pup, with Coco.

⇐ Hand-dipped tapers lit on the
table at Stringtown Rising.

⇐ Cookies at the gate! The gang's all here.

⇓ Our house at Stringtown Rising Farm.

⇒ A wheel of my homemade farm-fresh cheddar cheese.

⇐ An old-timey favorite, Corn Cob Jelly.

⇑ It's 5:00 somewhere.

⇒ I'm stylin' in my chore boots every day.

← It's a
monkey
lamb!

← Fresh sliced
Grandmother Bread.

⇑ Fresh eggs straight from the staff, my chickens.

⇐ The dirt-rock road Stringtown Rising, beautiful in the fall.

⇒ Coco at the gate at snowy Stringtown Rising Farm.

⇓ The steep, snow-covered driveway at Stringtown Rising. You can't make me go anywhere!

⇑ *Clover wearing a tiara, as well she should be.*

⇐ *Rooster meditating on the porch at Stringtown Rising.*

⇒ *One big happy duck family.*

⇐ Beulah Petunia at her milk stand at Stringtown Rising

⇒ Old-Time Burnt Sugar Cake.

PHOTO: JERRY WATERS

⇑ Make your own vanilla extract with whole vanilla beans.

PHOTO: JERRY WATERS

⇒ *Molasses Cookies with farm-fresh milk.*

⇒ *My homemade container candles.*

⇑ *Beulah Petunia nursing a newborn Glory Bee.*

⇐ The big red barn at Sassafras Farm

⇒ My bottle baby lamb all grown up.

⇐ My little white farmhouse Sassafras Farm. I love it!

lye, and pH strips for testing the soap. I saved up cardboard dairy quart containers to use as soap molds. I'd talked about making soap for months by this time, and no one was more surprised than me when I actually did it. I made sure 52 was home in case I blew myself up.

And, of course, it turned out to be a lot easier than I'd built it up to be in my mind. (See Hot Process Soap, page 280.) First I decided on a recipe. (You can find online soap calculators available for free. A recipe should always be calculated with a soap calculator if you're making up your own recipes, or use a professionally vetted recipe.)

I was in love right away with the magic of hot process soap. Our great-grandmas knew what they were doing. I tried the cold process method, but quickly abandoned it. The cold process method requires taking the temperatures of the lye mixture and fats/oils before combining them, then pouring the soap immediately into the mold after trace. You have to "incubate" the soap by wrapping the molds in towels to keep the mixture warm while it continues the saponification process away from a heat source, and you have to wait weeks for the soap to cure. With the hot process method, the soap is soap as soon as you finish cooking it.

It was nearly spring, and I was heady with my soapy accomplishment. The driveway was thick with mud from the melted snow. Even so, most days, 52 would manage to get his truck up the slippery road. I'd go back down with him to feed the sheep.

One evening, one of the Jacob ewes didn't come to the fence for the daily feed delivery. The next morning, I walked down to the bottom to look for her in the daylight, starting to worry. I saw two little black things gamboling about on shaky legs in the far pasture. I raced back to the house for my camera. By the time I went back down to the meadow bottom and hiked out into the pasture, they were in one of the sheep shelters.

I was so excited that I didn't even notice for a few minutes that this wasn't the ewe that had been missing the night before. I heard a tiny, plaintive *baa baa* from somewhere behind me and turned to find another baby on the bank across the creek. Three babies!

Then I saw what that baby was running toward—the missing ewe and another baby! Four babies!

Each Jacob ewe had had two lambs. The babies were all nursing and healthy. When I went down later to check on them again, the babies came right to me and let me pet them and pick them up.

We'd had the sheep for a year at this point, and these were our first lambs. Initially, we'd had the Jacobs and Cotswolds separated, but they kept managing to bust down fences and get back together. We got tired of chasing and separating them over and over, and we didn't have a Jacob ram. After consulting some experienced sheep farmers as well as a farm vet, we put the Jacobs and Cotswolds together, assured that the Jacobs should be able to deliver babies from the mister. An added plus was the promise of some interesting fiber with the combination of the Jacobs' naturally variegated wool and the long, crimpy curls of the Cotswolds. Months went by and no babies had appeared. Sheep are woolly, so it's hard to tell what's going on in there . . . until something frolics across the meadow.

The sheep needed more pasture than we had, and they were expensive to keep in hay. They escaped often and had to be corralled back in the gates (usually by me, by myself, because I was home). We'd had little luck selling wool, but maybe this new combination of fibers would serve us better, and we could also sell the lambs. Finally, the sheep might start paying for themselves.

That evening, 52 and I went down together to feed the sheep. A sturdy little wool-baby in my arms, I tipped up on my feet and kissed him.

I felt starry-eyed. "This is amazing," I whispered. "Look what we made."

Other than chicks, the lambs were our first babies born on the farm.

"I think the sheep made them," he said.

"We were involved!"

I wanted to know if they were boys or girls. I tried to check in the headlights of his truck splaying bright against the darkened meadow.

52 checked. Three were girls and one was a boy.

They looked like monkeys more than lambs with their dark faces.

"We have a monkey farm," I said.

"You can have a monkey farm if you want," he said. "But I'm not getting you a monkey."

"You would," I said, "if I wanted one."

He set down the lamb he'd been checking and pulled a little baggie of pipe tobacco out of his pocket. He looked at me over the end of his pipe as he lit the tobacco, not commenting.

"But you're in luck," I said. "I don't want a monkey."

I laughed, teasing him, but we both knew it was true. We'd have giraffes, elephants, and zebras if I wanted them.

Every day, but especially on days like that one, I felt as if we could just start over—and everything between us would be wonderful again.

We waded out through the snow one late winter Saturday for a trip to Spencer. 52 had business at the county clerk's office, and I just wanted to get off the farm for a few hours. Between snow and mud, I wasn't driving yet, and I liked the courthouse. There is nothing quite like small-town courthouses and small-town county clerks. They know everything and everybody, and they even remember you personally—because they remember everything and everybody.

Charlie White, the Roane County clerk, was the cousin of our pig man and the brother of our farrier, Tim, which is not surprising because in small-town West Virginia, there are always multiple levels of connection. I did, however, often wonder what it was like when buttoned-down Charlie sat down at the Thanksgiving table with his cousin who cut pig balls and his brother who wrangled donkeys. I always had a hard time imagining the three of them together. Genteel Charlie, Randy (the pig man), who could advise you on the best way to fry up fresh-cut balls, and Tim, who was . . . Tim.

Donkeys, at least mine, are generally calm, happy-go-lucky, cooperative creatures—unless you want them to go somewhere in particular. Then they act like mules. They love people, and get along well with most other farm animals, unless they find them specifically annoying. Like, say, a small dog. They pass their days in serene acceptance of their superiority and dignity.

Until the farrier comes to visit. And then they don't feel superior or dignified at all. In fact, they get a little irritated.

Donkeys are smart animals, and they get to know their farrier. Jack had had a long relationship with Tim. He was Jack's farrier before he came to our farm. They were old friends. Poky was still getting acquainted with Tim and getting used to the hoof-trimming routine. The first time Tim trimmed her, she wrestled him to the ground.

He told her, "You ain't gonna win!"

He shouted that phrase frequently while hoof trimming.

When he finished, we'd give him $50 and a beer. He always had his wife and little boy with him. One time, I asked him if he was going to teach his little boy to be a farrier.

Tim said, "No way!"

He wanted his son to be educated and get a nice job instead of making money getting kicked by horses.

He said, "Would you like it?"

Then, to demonstrate, I suppose, he kicked me in the shin.

I wondered if that ever happened at the Thanksgiving table when Tim and Randy and Charlie sat down.

Frequently, it seemed, Tim changed his phone number for reasons I never understood. When that happened, I'd call the courthouse and tell Charlie I needed to get hold of his brother.

Charlie would call their mother, because he couldn't keep up with his brother's phone numbers either, and then eventually Tim would call me to make an appointment.

With my long family history in the county, I'd been to the courthouse often to look up old wills and deeds, out of curiosity. I loved looking at old hand-scripted documents. They wrote so prettily back then. While 52 was taking care of his business, Charlie and I got to talking about the deterioration in handwriting in America. We decided, with absolutely no scientific studies to back us up, that handwriting deteriorated after the invention of the typewriter and was then completely destroyed by the computer. Charlie told me that he had a really old manual typewriter in the back room where they kept the documents.

Oh my! Now you're talking. Something for me to inspect. I leaped out of my seat, whipped my camera out of my purse, and headed toward the document room on my own, which left Charlie with no real option but to follow. (I don't think he minded.)

I hadn't seen an old manual typewriter in a long time. This was the kind of typewriter my father had. I can remember typing up stories on it when I was a child. As a little girl, I had a dollhouse and lots of tiny glass animals. They lived in the dollhouse instead of doll people. They had very complicated, soap operaish lives. I wrote stories and stories and stories about my glass animals. The king was a little glass bear. The queen was a cat. The cat, by the way, was bigger than the bear. (I can't explain that. Don't make me.) I had this bizarre urge to hug that old typewriter. It brought back all sorts of sentimental memories.

I wondered if kids today would know what to do with that typewriter? Most have probably never even heard of a carriage return.

And then I said, "I must see the pretty handwriting!" Not that I hadn't seen it before, but I was inspired to gaze upon it again. To marvel at the elegant hand-scripting of our forebears, who would have been as confounded as teenagers today by that gorgeous old manual typewriter. They didn't need no stinkin' typewriter. They knew how to write by hand. Life was slower, and people took their time.

Charlie pulled out one of the oldest books in the courthouse for me. He pointed out how they used every bit of the paper back then, right up to the edges. The frugality of our ancestors, in every little way, is a constant wonder when looking back at them from today's world.

Encouraged by my enthusiasm for the precious old books, Charlie showed me his favorite oddity. In 1863, West Virginia seceded from Virginia and became a separate state, joining the Union in the Civil War. (Bit of trivia: West Virginia is the only state that was formed because of the Civil War.) There were never very many slaves in this area compared to other parts of the South. (Situated below the Mason-Dixon line, West Virginia is generally considered part of the South, and pre–Civil War, of course, was part of the state of Virginia.) This isn't really plantation country, and much of what became West Virginia was populated by poor farmers trying to scratch out a living in the mountains. There were some individuals, however, who could afford slaves. Charlie showed me a bill of sale, from 1857, documenting the transfer of two slaves in what was then Roane County, Virginia. One was a twenty-two-year-old man. His name was Ben. There was also a girl, "say nine months" as the bill of sale put it.

They were sold together for $1,000. That was a lot of money in 1857.

There was something quite surreal about touching the original, ink-drawn pages of a transaction in human beings.

Ben and that baby girl weren't slaves for long. They soon found themselves living in a free state. I'd love to know what became of that little girl. But courthouse records never tell the whole story, only parts, glimpses of lives that are difficult to imagine today.

Before going back to the farm, we stopped in at the Salvation Army thrift store across the street. Thrift stores are a good thing, but all I could think about that day was how frugal our ancestors were—down to writing to the edges of the paper—while we are so wasteful today. A thrift store is filled with the cast-off excess of our not-so-frugal modern society. I wanted to be a more frugal person, living as self-sustainable a lifestyle as possible.

I knew a cow would be the epitome of self-sustainability—if I could actually milk it—and my birthday was coming.

CHAPTER 12

We drove across the West Virginia/Ohio border to a farm where there were four cows for sale—a Brown Swiss bull and three Jersey cows. Two of the Jerseys were mature milkers, and one was still a heifer. I was there to pick from the girls.

If 52 had any reservations about getting a cow, he didn't say so.

"What about hay?" I asked as we crossed the river into Ohio. "How much hay do cows need a year?"

I was worried about the cost of a cow, whether we could afford to keep one. Buying a cow was one thing. Taking care of one was another. I'd already discovered when we'd hastily acquired sheep that the amount of pasture we had available at Stringtown Rising was seriously deficient. Now we were going to add a cow?

"A hundred bales a winter for one cow," he told me.

We'd only needed around two hundred bales for all our donkeys, sheep, and goats combined the previous winter. We didn't have any place to store even that much hay.

"Can we afford that? What about feed? How much pasture does a cow need? I don't have a milk stand! What if I can't milk her?"

"Do you want a cow?"

We were probably within thirty miles of the farm with the cows for sale. I'd waited till now to panic?

"Yes."

"Happy birthday."

It was a ridiculous conversation anyway. We both knew we were going to get a cow.

The gesture itself was romantic. 52 often gifted me with things that were out of the norm, not something you'd find in a magazine gift guide. An elderberry bush. A vintage KitchenAid stand mixer. A box of day-old goslings. He was thoughtful at keying in on just the things I wanted but wouldn't buy for myself.

In between those gestures, his behavior toward me seemed to be growing increasingly angry and sometimes irrational. I was his second chance, just as he was mine. He told me he wanted our relationship to work, but he wouldn't discuss our problems.

He pressured me to make more money, but he blew up at me about the time I spent working. I kept hoping he'd be less stressed if I could take the financial pressure off, so I continued to work hard to grow my website. We were still on shaky financial ground from building the house.

Taking on the responsibility of a cow wouldn't help with the financial pressure, but it was almost like a couple in trouble deciding to have a baby. We threw ourselves in headfirst, off on another adventure in self-sustainable living. Moments like these brought us together.

And eventually pulled us apart, but we weren't good at looking ahead.

We arrived at the farm to look over the cows. I thought the heifer was gorgeous, but she'd never been pregnant, never been milked. Probably not the best choice for an inexperienced person who'd never had a cow before. Or even spent much time up close to one. I didn't need a cow that required training. What if she was a kicker? And she wasn't even in milk, of course.

The younger mature Jersey was pretty, too. I thought she might be just right except she didn't have a good udder. Not that I would know, but the man selling the cows pointed it out.

And then there was the old cow. She was priced at a bargain. She was a career girl with a good udder, but she wasn't a beauty queen like the others. She looked rode hard and put up wet. She'd been worked in a dairy operation. She was a professional cow. One of us had to know what we were doing, and it wasn't going to be me, so she seemed like the best choice despite the fact that she was, well, almost ugly. I'd never seen a more bony cow in my life. Add to that, she had a limp.

I reached under and gave her a quick test. She just stood there, placidly staring back at me as milk squirted from her long teats, relieving my lingering not-so-good feelings since my experience milking Clover. I looked up at 52.

"I like this one," I said.

So did he. She was the cheapest one, at $500.

She'd been with the Brown Swiss bull for four months, so she might be bred.

The man said, "I can't feel a calf when I punch her, though, so she might not be."

He showed me how he punched her to feel for a calf. I tried punching her. It was a complete mystery to me how anyone could tell if there was a calf in there or not. And she was so skinny, I was afraid of killing her by punching her.

"If she's not bred," the man said, "just milk her as long as she has milk, then she'll make good hamburger."

I looked into those humongous placid cow eyes. She needed me. She was old, ugly, bony, and she had a limp. Without me, she'd be hamburger.

A week later, we went back to get her.

We backed the truck up to a big pile of gravel, and they led my new cow up the pile, using the feed to entice her to move, and then onto the truck. The man selling the cow had a bunch of kids, and the whole family got involved with the pushing and shoving.

I wondered, if it took half a dozen people to shove her on, how were we going to get her off? I asked them if they wanted to come to West Virginia with us. They said no. And right about then they leaped into action as a family again, chasing down a calf that made a break for it while we were all paying attention to putting the cow on the truck.

It's always entertaining when a farm animal gets out—if it's not yours.

I helped block the calf from going on down the road and herded her to the gate. They thanked me for helping. I said, "No big deal. I herded a ram this morning before I got here." Sentences like that made me feel like a farmer. Our sheep were constantly escaping and wandering down the road.

Once we got back to our farm, 52 backed the truck up to the creek bank. We got the cow turned around inside the truck, and it only took a little pulling to encourage her to come right off. She walked around our meadow bottom like a giant in Lilliput. I started milking her the next morning.

Her previous owners had been getting up to two gallons a milking from her, sometimes a gallon and a half, and they had her trained to milk once a day. I'd never heard of milking a cow once a day, but I liked it. I brought home three-quarters of a gallon the first time. I stared and stared at the milk in my refrigerator. And took it out and examined it. And put it back. And took it out. And photographed it like it was artwork.

My cow and I, we made that. I named her Beulah Petunia and became besotted with her.

Morgan declared she was having nothing to do with the fresh cow milk. I told her I wasn't buying any more milk from the store, so she'd have to drink water for the rest of her life. She insisted she would buy her own milk. Of course, she had no way to get to the store, and she liked milk. She came home from school the next day and declared, "I'm drinking this milk!" And filled up a big tall glass and drank it down.

It was typical of her short resistance to farm life. She'd say no to anything new and different, then quickly jump in. The boys were older when we moved to the country, and their resistance usually lasted a little while longer, though Ross had eventually embraced West Virginia and would try anything with bravado and move on as if he'd been doing it all his life. Between work and his girlfriend, he'd never been much involved with the farm, but he helped out with anything I asked of him. His boot camp ship date was nearing, and when he came home from Texas, he didn't think twice about drinking my fresh milk.

Weston was the most resistant to farm living, and it was a bone of contention between 52 and me that I wouldn't push Weston to take on more chores around the farm. It had been my choice to move to a farm, and I didn't see the kids as laborers in fulfilling my dream. I encouraged 52 to develop more of a relationship with Weston so that Weston might enjoy doing projects with him, but he said Weston didn't like him and he wasn't going to ask him to do anything.

"Weston is a child and you're an adult," I pointed out. "You have to take the lead." This got me nowhere, and the sense that he and I, and I and the kids, were two families living in the same house grew.

I started out milking Beulah Petunia inside a sheep shelter in the meadow bottom. The first couple of days, I just had her tied to a post in the shelter. That didn't work very well because she could move around quite a bit. Side to side. Back and forth. Once she'd run out of her feed, she'd get even more restless. I couldn't blame her. I wasn't an experienced milkmaid, and it took me forever to hand-milk her. Within a few days, 52 had built a stanchion with a headlock inside the shelter, which was similar to a goat milk stand except the cow walked into it rather than climbing up on a stand. A feed bin at the far end encouraged the cow to stroll right in, put her head between the boards, and start eating. The two boards were then pushed in place to hold the neck, with a pin to lock them until the milking was done. Beulah Petunia couldn't get her head out of the headlock until I released her, though one day she did walk off with the entire milk stand still locked around her neck.

After that episode, 52 secured the stand to the posts of the shelter.

Since I milked her in the meadow bottom, I'd take the milk back to the car where I'd sit on an overturned bucket in the middle of the dirt road and pour it into quart jars to take up to the house. I didn't have a tight-fitting lid for my make-do milk pail and unless I poured it into jars with screw-on lids, I'd spill the milk lurching up our rocky driveway in my vehicle. Back in my kitchen, I'd filter it and pour it into an oversized bowl in the fridge to set the cream.

It was a production, but nothing I'd done on a farm to that point—hatching chicks, collecting eggs, raising and milking goats, raising and chasing sheep—had made that primal connec tion for me with farming that a cow did. A cow was an experience— work and hardship and challenge. Everything I'd been looking for when I'd come to the country.

My life had been sheltered, spoiled, too easy. When I came to the country, I'd been looking for some kind of connection with life that was visceral, purposeful, even sometimes dirty, but most especially difficult. I'd left my box behind, but I was still trying to find out who I was outside of it. I felt weak for all the years I'd lived up to everyone else's expectations. I set new expectations for myself, many of them difficult, looking for some intangible sense of strength.

I was driven by that deep-seated need to test myself—in a situation that was both harsh and quaint. A cow was a perfect vehicle to that end.

In the first few weeks, the physical exhaustion of milking, and handling all the milk, nearly beat me into the ground. It took me an hour and a half the first day just to get three-quarters of a gallon. Two weeks later, I looked up one day to realize I was milking twice that amount in a third of the time.

My fingers and arms and back were stronger. I had more stamina.

I learned to make butter from heavy cream using a quart jar to shake the cream until it thickened. 52 often got involved. He'd shake the jar, then I'd finish up with washing the butter and pressing it out. We had buttermilk biscuits and buttermilk pancakes. I'd bake fresh bread and bring him a warm slice with a pat of the newly made butter.

Difficulties I'd had before with making cheese were forgotten as I started making cheese left and right, improving as I gained experience. I experimented with all sorts of different hard and soft cheeses.

My milk pitchers were overflowing. I was feeding my family out of that skinny, limping, ugly cow. I loved her and that wonderful spring. We'd been at Stringtown Rising for two years. Our farm finally seemed to make sense and have purpose. We had chickens laying eggs, a cow providing all our dairy, and lambs bouncing around our meadow bottom. The ramps I'd planted the first year were coming up on our hillside for the second year in a row, and they were spreading. We had fruit trees, berry bushes, and grape-vines, and our livestock were flourishing. The farm was bursting with life.

But spring also meant flooding rains, and some days, it was almost like winter again and I was stuck. The rain would come in pouring blasts. The goats would hide in their shelter. The chick-ens would hide in their coop. The dogs slept on the porch. And I'd be scared to drive because of the deep mud and high water.

Georgia called me one stormy afternoon to tell me the water was up to the trees behind her house.

"You better not go anywhere!" she ordered. She worried about anything and everything and called me on a regular basis to make sure I wasn't getting into trouble.

"I have kids to pick up from the bus!" Weston and Morgan would be getting off the bus at the Slanted Little House, where I picked them up every day since the school bus didn't come down our road.

I headed down my driveway. I could see trouble before I was all the way down. The river was flooded, rushing wildly, out of its banks.

There was water running down the road.

The bridge over the creek on our driveway was stopped up with branches and brush and a tire that had washed down the creek from who knows where.

The water was flooding out over the driveway and into the road and part of the sheep's field. The creek running alongside the sheep's field was full to the banks.

I rolled down my window to stare at the creek, checking the crossing in the field. The water was loud, high and running hard.

The first creek in the road was the deepest, and it was full and running fast, too. I chickened out, backing up to a place where I could turn around and go home.

I called Georgia and made her day by telling her she was right. The kids would have to spend the night at my cousin's house, and I wasn't going anywhere. Even if the water was down enough in a few hours for 52 to make it home, he wouldn't bring the kids, not when the water was high. If it rained again overnight, they would miss school the next day if they came home, so it was safer for them to stay put in civilization.

I missed my kids the most on those unexpected days when they couldn't come home. School was almost out, and Weston and Morgan would be leaving for summer in Texas with their dad. Ross would be leaving soon for boot camp.

I wasn't one of those mothers who had cried at the kindergarten door. I was one of those mothers who skipped back out to the parking lot full of plans for what I could do all day now that the kids were at school. Not that I didn't love them, but I had stuff to do!

It was different watching them grow up and leave the nest.

The next week, I delivered Ross to the navy recruitment office in Charleston. He packed up his room, leaving everything, even his beloved cell phone. He went with nothing but the clothes on his back and his wallet. His clothes would be taken from him and either donated or sent home at his expense. He wore clothes he didn't care about and told them to donate them. He walked in the door of the recruitment building, made a sharp turn, saluted, and said, "First Recruit Ross McMinn, reporting for duty." They sat him down and had him sign a bunch of papers. I stood, watching him, feeling suddenly superfluous as his mother. I kissed him good-bye and cried, leaving before I could embarrass him too badly.

I wrote him a letter every single day. I didn't expect to get many letters back, but he surprised me.

I saved all his letters. Carried them around in my purse. Read them over and over, cherishing my favorite parts and all the fascinating details of the mysterious life behind boot camp walls.

"The day I got here," Ross wrote me, "we came in around 2100 and they yelled and screamed and cussed us out all night. We were all pretty much shell-shocked. The way they acted is kinda funny to me now. When we finally got to the compartment, it was 0430. They let us sleep for 5 minutes then got us up again."

I got so many shots, I lost count. I couldn't sit down for three days after the butt shot.

I wish I could take a shower by myself for more than 2 minutes, have my cell phone, sleep in, have my truck, eat McDonald's, and get a day off. I miss you.

Boot camp is stressful. It's not like on TV. I mean it is, but on TV all they do is work out and do drills and train. They don't show you that you have to take tests and prepare for inspections. We have to make our own time to study, like cutting into our 6 hours of sleep and eating with one hand and holding our book in the other. We get from 0700 to 1300 on Sundays to do what we want, but that's also the only time we have to shine our boots and iron our clothes. I've been sneaking in writing after "Taps."

We lost one guy because he punched another recruit. Two

guys quit and one guy from the division across the hall deserted, just ran away in the middle of the night.

I can now make a flotation device out of a set of coveralls while I'm in the water and start wearing them in about 3 seconds.

I hurt my foot but I haven't told anyone because I'll miss training, so during the PFA I did 75 pushups in 2 minutes (only needed 46), 79 sit-ups (only needed like 50) then I ran a mile and a half on one foot in 12:40.

Mail call is the most exciting part of my day.

We just got told at 1400 we are all gonna get beat because one of the guys decided to sneak a cookie into his rack and got caught so now we all gotta pay for it. If we are lucky, they'll let us watch fireworks today, but the way this day has started, I doubt it.

His next letter read:

We didn't get to watch fireworks yesterday. We just marched.

And then:

I've decided I hate marching.

He made me feel like a good mother for all my daily writing

We've all been talking about back home. Everybody's homesick. We have so much to study, we always have a book in our hands. Keep writing me. I'm always excited about mail. Most of the guys don't get any and they're always jealous.

I just did the math to see how much they're paying me since
I'm on the clock 24 hours a day, and it's roughly $1.80 per
hour.

Everybody here is already just counting the days to graduation.

The dates on his letters were always way, way behind from when
I received them. When he left for boot camp, I promised him that
I would come to his graduation. In the first few weeks he was there,
my mother decided she would fly from Texas to meet me there and
we'd attend his graduation together. She was eighty-one and not in
very good health, but she was determined to make the trip. I wrote
Ross that his grandmother would be coming, along with me and
the kids.

Weston and Morgan were in Texas for the summer by then, and
52 and I were having our usual summer to ourselves. Our neighbor across the river, Frank, was letting us fence the five acres ad-
joining our farm that he owned on our side of the river for more
pasture for the sheep. One of 52's projects that summer was getting the new field ready. One lazy mid-July evening when I'd finished all my work and had dinner simmering on the stove, I walked
down to the bottom to hang out with him. I walked along the river-
bank taking pictures, then sat on the tractor talking to him while
he strung electric fence wire.

He was in a good mood, which was the best time to talk to him
because then he didn't find me so annoying. The oddest thing
about our relationship at this point was that we hadn't been intimate since the previous fall. We shared the same bedroom, but
we were like ships passing in the night. I kept farmer hours, up as
early as five and to bed before ten, often by nine. On weekends,
he didn't get up till nine, and any day, he didn't go to bed—or even
come into the house—until after midnight.

I wasn't sure what to think about our lack of physical intimacy,
but whenever we got along and had an enjoyable evening, I thought

we could just start over again and everything would be all right. The tirades would disappear and we'd go back to being lovers and best friends. The old 52 was back!

"Do you think you could come to bed early tonight?" I asked him.

He gave a shrug and a half smile. "Maybe."

I don't know what time he came to bed, but it was long after I did. The phone rang in the middle of the night.

It was Morgan calling me from Texas.

The phone had woken 52, too. He asked me if anything was wrong.

I said, "My mother is in the hospital. She had a seizure or stroke or something, I don't know." My voice broke. "She's brain-dead."

He was silent for a long beat then he said, "I'm sorry," and rolled back over to sleep again.

CHAPTER 13

Whether or not to tell Ross that his grandmother had died was one of the most difficult decisions of my life. I contacted his recruiter to understand the options and found that if I asked that Ross be told about his grandmother, there was no guarantee he would be allowed to leave for the funeral. Usually, leave was only granted for the death of an immediate family member, and grandparents weren't considered immediate family by the military.

Boot camp was stressful enough, and to find out that his grandmother had died in the middle of it would be even more stressful for Ross, especially if he wasn't allowed to leave for the funeral. Withholding the information was a painful choice, too.

I wrote Ross and told him that his grandmother wouldn't be able to come to his graduation, after all. I didn't tell him that she'd died. I borrowed a thousand dollars from my cousin and flew to Texas for her funeral.

My mother and I had had a difficult relationship in her last several years. My parents had had a hard time accepting my divorce and were befuddled by my adoration of farm life. But through it all, my mother remained a sweet mother, always trying her best even when she didn't know what to do or say. All my life, she had been my biggest fan. She never said a critical word to me, no matter what.

She loved romance novels and gave me my first romance book to read. After I became a published romance novelist, I took her

with me to book signings and Romance Writers of America conferences and Harlequin parties. Nora Roberts was one of her favorite authors, and I enjoyed being able to introduce her to Nora
at a Harlequin party in Dallas one year.

She didn't really know how to use a computer, but she got one
so she could see my blog every day. She could hardly figure out
how to send an e-mail (and frequently sent me blank e-mails or
e-mails cut off in the middle of a sentence because she couldn't
remember where to click), but she knew how to get to my website.
Every day.

Some of my most vivid memories of her from childhood were
how she would wiggle her hips with a natural exuberance about
herself that she couldn't contain. Even in church. She'd wiggle
right down the aisle. She loved jewelry and makeup and fash-
ion, and most of all, she enjoyed keeping herself fit and looking good. She was born Norma Jean Prescott on a dust-bowl farm
in Depression-era Oklahoma, but she embraced modern city life
with both arms in her identity as a successful preacher's wife. She
loved to entertain, and she enjoyed fine things without placing
them above what was real. She had taste and a soft heart.

My mother was sixteen when she met my father on a double
date. They weren't dating each other. Pretty soon, though, they
were. I suspect there was some hip wiggling involved. My father
was stationed at a base in Oklahoma following his missions in
World War II, and that's how a farm boy from West Virginia met
a farm girl in Oklahoma. They eloped when she was still sixteen,
and he took her away from the flatlands to the hills of West Virginia where she learned to make Grandmother Bread from my
father's mother—and one day taught it to me. I was her youngest
child, and her favorite. Or so she always told me. And if she ever
told anyone different, I didn't want to hear about it.

Most of all, she loved her grandchildren. Morgan was her only
granddaughter, and she enjoyed showering her with girly things
and taking her to lunch and shopping and the beauty salon. When
Morgan was eighteen months old, my mother commissioned a

porcelain doll made in Morgan's image and dressed it in one of Morgan's baby dresses. She loved all her many grandsons just as much, but she only had one granddaughter and they had an extraordinarily close relationship. Even after we moved away from Texas, Morgan continued to spend a great deal of time with her every summer. Morgan was with her when she was taken to the hospital, and she was heartbroken at the funeral, bursting into sobs.

Usually, Weston and Morgan would have stayed a few more weeks in Texas before coming home, but after the funeral, they made the trip back with me.

I was glad to get home to West Virginia and its lush green woods, enfolding hills, gurgling streams, and simple comforts. It was where I belonged.

I'd missed 52, too, and he said he'd missed me.

As usual, I thought we were on the verge of everything being perfectly fantastic, but within a few days, I was proved wrong.

My financial prospects had recently improved. I'd had to borrow money from my cousin to make the unexpected trip for my mother's funeral, but in the near future, I expected to see an earnings increase. I'd signed with a new advertising network to handle the advertising on my website, and I had good reason to expect a rise in income. I didn't think I was about to be rich, but I was pretty sure I would soon be able to pay my cousin back, keep up with bills more comfortably, and hopefully take some pressure off 52 by taking over some of the farm bills completely.

As soon as I got home from my trip with the kids, 52 started complaining about the electric bill again, set off every time they left on a light or ran the dryer too long.

"As soon as I can, I'll take over the electric bill," I told him.

"Hurry up," he said. "You need to pay more of the bills."

"I'm paying my half of the bills, and as soon as I can, I'll pay more than half." I had kids living in the house and he didn't, so

I didn't mind paying more than half. When we'd moved in, we'd agreed to split everything fifty-fifty, but I'd realized a long time before that he resented that arrangement. I'd decided early on that as soon as I could afford to pay more, I would.

"You've never paid half," he said.

I blinked. "I've paid half every month except for a few months after the economy dived and I had almost no income," I reminded him. I didn't remind him of the time he hadn't paid his share at all. I didn't like to ever bring up the events surrounding the time I told him to leave the farm. What I'd been upset about that time wasn't so much that he hadn't made his deposit to the account but that he hadn't been up front with me about it. He was secretive about money in general, which baffled me on a regular basis. I told him how much money I was making every month, and the times I'd been short, I'd told him in advance.

I'd put more money into the farm in the beginning because I had a settlement from my divorce, and I'd taken out more personal credit to finish the house because home improvement stores were willing to give more credit to me than they were to him. My income fluctuated, so I'd told him at the time that the up-front cash I had to put into the farm between my divorce settlement and the extra credit debt was to make up for times I might be short month to month, but he quickly dismissed the money I'd put in up front as if it had never happened. But he'd also helped me in several ways, for which I was grateful. He'd helped me pay for my website hosting when my traffic grew faster than the income to support it, and he'd helped me buy a new computer. He often gave me unexpected or generous gifts (like a cow). Overall, I thought we were pretty even, but I didn't really care. I just wanted us to be happy, and I was willing to pay for it if that was what it took.

"You've never paid half," he repeated.

I stared at him, dumbfounded as to why he would say that I hadn't been contributing my share. I'd paid half every month without fail for a long time. In fact, I paid it in a single check that I wrote directly to him once a month, so how could he deny it? He was still handling the bills for the farm, so I wrote one check to him and he paid the bills.

"What are you doing?" I asked. "Why would you even try to say that? All I have to do is get out my checkbook to show you that's incorrect."

"Why don't you do that? Prove you're right. You have to be right and I have to be wrong."

"I am right!" I didn't usually have any patience for his right/wrong thing, but this time, it mattered. I cared, deeply, about being financially self-supporting. "And if you'll just let me, I'll pay more than half as soon as I can. I'm starting to make more money. You know that. I thought that would make you happy! I told you all along that I was going to make a success of my business and then everything would be okay. This is what I've been working for—for us!"

"You think I'm supposed to be happy because your business is successful?"

"Yes!"

"Well," he said, "I'm not."

We were sitting on the porch. It was getting dark. Dinner was in the oven. The chickens needed to be put up. Beulah Petunia needed her evening feed. The goats were bleating, hungry too.

I didn't care about any of it at the moment. 52 sat in his rocking chair on the porch puffing at his pipe, not looking at me.

"Why? Why would you not be happy that my business is successful?"

He jerked his gaze to me suddenly. "How do you think that makes me feel? Do you think I don't feel inferior to you?"

"You feel inferior to me?" All I could do was stupidly repeat what he'd said. I was floored. He'd told me that he had always felt insecure in general, all his life, but the idea that he would feel inferior to me, that somehow I could make him feel that way, hurt.

"Your readers just love you," he said. "They love you! Everybody loves you. Why wouldn't I feel inferior?"

"My readers don't even know me personally," I said, trying to reason with him. "Not really. They love my work, not me, and that's a good thing. That's how I make money, by people liking what I write. I'm a writer. If people don't like what I write, I can't make a living." I stared at him. "Are you"—I couldn't believe it—"jealous?"

"Yes, I'm jealous."

I didn't know what to say to that—or what to do about it. I was shocked that he'd admitted it.

"I'm not going to fail so you can feel better about yourself."

"As soon as you make enough money, you're going to tell me to leave," he said. "You'll hire people to do everything I do. You won't need me anymore."

"That's insulting."

"It's true. That's what you want. It's what you're planning."

"It's not, but I'm not the one who can convince you of that," I told him. "You have to convince yourself."

The next day, I sent him a list from my bank records of how much I'd contributed to the farm bills every month since we'd moved to the farm. It was the only objective issue, and the only one I could solve with factual evidence.

The rest was an emotional morass, and I was lost.

"You're pushing me away," I told him in an e-mail. "Is that what you want?"

He came home from work and hugged me, telling me that he loved me. I knew that everything would be fine again. Until the next time.

My relationship with my cow was much simpler, and I loved milking. A cow is a teacher of patience, and I thought that was what 52 needed, my patience. I was, generally, an impatient person. 52 had milked her while I was in Texas. I was glad to be back to it. Milking a cow is a meditative event. It was completely unlike my experience fighting with Clover.

I learned to sit still long enough in the mornings to listen to the birds—because I was sitting at my cow's udder and couldn't go anywhere else. I learned every movement of her tail and her hooves and her head as I grew accustomed to predicting her movements in protecting my milk bucket. I was one with a cow. The cow was in no hurry, which meant neither could I be. When I'd moved to West Virginia, I didn't even know the difference between a bale of straw and a bale of hay. Now I was milking a cow. I was drunk on farm life. I could have milk, cheese, butter, and cream even if I couldn't get to the store. I felt empowered by my self-sufficiency. I was also really exhausted.

I got an idea that I could help the Ornery Angel—and give myself a day or two a week off at the same time. One day when I came across her on the road going in the opposite direction, I rolled down my window and said, "Do you know how to milk a cow?"

This wasn't a serious question because of course she knew how to milk a cow.

She said, "No, I've never milked a cow."

I was shocked because I had assumed she was the epitome of the wise, tough country woman who knew how to do everything. She did, however, want to learn to milk a cow and take home free milk, so she came over the next morning. She talked about her kids, her husband, her parents, and her job "sitting" with elderly people, and I taught her how to milk a cow and make butter.

Then someone told me that sharing milk from a family cow was illegal in West Virginia, and I was never able to let her milk again. We weren't quite friends, but we'd come a long way (or at least I had). We were neighborly, and she talked to me like I was an accepted (or at least tolerated) member of our little rural community. She called or came up when the lambs were out to let me know they were in the road, which happened frequently, and her daughters came up on a regular basis to visit Morgan or, when school was in session, to sell me whatever the latest thing was they were selling at school.

One day they walked in when I was fixing dinner.

The oldest girl was a couple of years younger than Morgan. She said, "What are you cooking?"

I said, "Fried chicken."

She said, "Which one and what did it do?"

It took me a few seconds to get that.

"It's not one of my chickens!" I told her. "It's chicken from the store!"

"Oh," she said. "That's always when my mom fries chicken. One of them makes her mad and then that's what we have for dinner."

Every time I felt like I'd gone real country, something or someone reminded me that I was really only scratching the surface.

One time, a deer fell over dead outside the Ornery Angel's trailer. She thought something was wrong with it, or I'm sure she would have fixed it for supper. We came across her driving out the road with the dead deer in her truck, looking for a better eternal resting spot for it than her yard. It was the type of gruesome activity she'd take on by herself, which would impress me because if even a chicken fell over dead in the chicken house, I'd wait for 52 to come home to dispose of it. The Ornery Angel was like an alien from another planet, and I always wished I could be more like her. I could milk a cow, but I was still nowhere near as self-reliant and tough as she.

I wasn't sure I'd be able to keep milking my cow, though. By this point, I was becoming very concerned as to whether or not Beulah Petunia had been bred when we brought her home from Ohio.

Some months previous, a veterinarian from the USDA had come out to our farm to enroll our livestock in the federal scrapie program. Scrapie is a fatal degenerative disease in sheep, and (more rarely) goats, which is evidenced by signs such as excessive rubbing and scratching, lack of coordination, and tremors. It's a disease of the central nervous system. The federal government operates a program to identify and track sheep and goats through assigning flock or herd numbers to individual farmers and providing free genetic testing. Dr. Casto, the USDA vet, became quite

interested when he found out about our animals as we had such
unusual breeds. He was particularly interested in our Jacob sheep
and Fainting goats. Often, they just assign a flock and/or herd
number over the phone, but he said, "I want to come out and see
those critters." He was generous with his time and expertise and
gave us a free examination of all the sheep and goats.

Around the time I was becoming insatiably curious as to
whether or not Beulah Petunia was in the family way, Dr. Casto
made a follow-up visit to test more of our sheep.

I couldn't let him leave without saying, "Do you know how to
tell if a cow is pregnant?"

He laughed and said, of course, he did, but he didn't have any
long gloves with him, sorry! (He didn't look sorry.)

His assistant said, "I have some in my truck!"

Dr. Casto told his assistant he was fired!

Poor Dr. Casto. He wasn't even getting paid for this.

His assistant went back to his truck for the gloves while I raced
off to corral my cow. The most common method for determining
whether or not a cow is pregnant is called rectal palpation. This
explains the shoulder-length gloves.

I locked Beulah Petunia into her milk stand while Dr. Casto
put on the gloves. Holding her tail out of the way with one hand,
he went in with the other. And in. And in. And pulled out some
fecal matter to get it out of the way.

And then he'd had all he could take and he taught his assistant
a lesson for bringing those gloves with him. Dr. Casto told him to
get another pair.

"I haven't done this in a long time," Dr. Casto said. "You do it."

His assistant got behind Beulah Petunia and went in.

He looked back at me with as much of a grin as a man can have
who has his entire arm inside of a cow.

"Oh, yeah," he said. "There's a calf in there."

When Beulah Petunia was due was another question. They
could only guess. We'd gotten her in April, and she'd been with
the bull for four months at that time. Cows are pregnant for nine

months. It was late summer, and she could be due any day for all we knew. Ross's boot camp graduation was coming up. I'd be gone for a week, so either 52 would have to milk her again for me or I could go ahead and dry her off. Cows should be dried off a month or two before they give birth in order to give their bodies a chance to refortify before calving and starting the milking cycle all over again. I decided to dry her off before I left, but I had the faucet on and no idea how to turn it off.

I took Georgia to visit her sister and brother for lunch one day. Her brother Nelson used to milk five cows every day before he went to school, and he'd worked with cows all his life.

ME: I don't know how to get my cow dried off.
NELSON: Stop milking her.
ME: But I'm worried she'll get sick.
NELSON: Stop milking her.
ME: But don't I have to—
NELSON: Stop milking her.
ME: But—
NELSON: Stop milking her.

It could be that I made everything too complicated.

I went home and stopped milking Beulah Petunia, but I still drove down to the meadow bottom every day to check on her. One morning, she wasn't there and I found a section of fence down. I contemplated panicking.

What do you do if your cow is missing? Who do you call? Do you drive up and down the road looking for your cow? What if you don't find it on the road? Do you put up flyers in the local stores? Do you call the sheriff? "Hello, I want to report a missing cow."

If I were Lonnie, the old farmer who cut my cousin's hay, I might go back to the house, watch a couple TV shows, and wait for the cow to show up on her own. But I didn't have a couple hundred cows like Lonnie. I had one cow, and she was pregnant. We weren't sure exactly when she was due to deliver, but it was soon.

Our farm was hilly and surrounded by more hills and thick woods. Beulah Petunia wasn't that agile. She spent most of her spare time sitting on the creek bank chewing her cud. How much ambition could she have to go anywhere? I called for her just like when I was going to milk her.

I heard something in the woods.

It was just a chicken, scratching in the underbrush on the hill.

I was never going to see my cow again. I was ready to throw myself on the ground and sob. If I could find a spot that didn't have any cow, sheep, or donkey doo-doo.

Then I heard something else . . . Something . . . that was not a chicken.

Beulah Petunia!

She stood between trees on an old logging track that ran along the far side of the creek outside the fence line, up against our hillside. Sort of like a child who runs away and only goes to the backyard.

I snapped the lead on her halter and pushed, pulled, and dragged her back, moving her into another field and shutting the gate on the field with the damaged fence.

No sooner did I get back to the house and sit down on the porch to relax after all that pushing, pulling, dragging, and panicking than I heard something suspiciously like a baby goat in the goat yard. Clover had recently delivered twins, and she and her babies were supposed to be confined to a pen.

I ran down the porch steps, into the goat yard, and tackled the baby. Then I fought off four goats and two donkeys who wanted to come into the goat pen with me when I put it back. I sat down on the porch again and waited for the next disaster. I didn't have to wait long. We'd acquired guineas and ducks by then and one of the guineas had gotten into the garden. It was running back and forth, desperately, because it couldn't find the gate to get back out.

Minor animal "emergencies" were par for the course. Most were of the "Three Stooges" variety, but farming can be a dangerous occupation, and it's even more dangerous if you don't know what you're doing. 52 had grown up in town, but he had some previous farm experience from a few years when he and his former wife had lived on a farm. They hadn't developed their farm to the extent that we had at Stringtown Rising with so many different kinds of animals, but he had more experience than me. I had no experience at all.

We went down to the meadow bottom one night to move the sheep. We planned to move them to the next field over and shut the gate between the fields. 52 worked in the city, so often it would be late in the evening when we did things that required both of us on a weekday. I had a can of feed and I went into the field while 52 stayed at the first gate, where he would give them feed and keep them there while I had time to get to the second. I was to take the can of feed through the field to the next gate and lure the sheep after me once I had it open. I could never remember later why we were doing it exactly this way since there were about ten thousand things wrong with this plan, but it was probably my idea.

We'd driven down to the meadow bottom in his little car. His truck was in the shop. His headlights were beamed on the first gate. By the time I got into the middle of the field, I was walking in pitch black. I had a sense of the general direction of the other gate, and I just kept walking. I heard the thunder of sheep behind me and I turned.

Mr. Cotswold came at me full force, ramming me in the lower abdomen.

I reeled in pain.

The field around me was covered in darkness. I could see the light of the car beaming on the gate at the end of the field. I screamed for 52.

He didn't answer, and I couldn't see him.

I couldn't see where the ram had gone either.

I was scared to move, not sure where the ram was, but I was scared to keep standing still, too. I cried for help, over and over. I was terrified of being alone in the field, in the dark, with the ram. I had nothing to use to protect myself if he came at me again.

Finally, I gave up on help and stumbled in the direction of the road to find the fence line, afraid with every step that Mr. Cotswold was going to come up behind me. I was closer to the gate I'd been heading for than the gate I'd come from, so I followed the fence along the road, then down the field until I came to the second gate. From there, I followed the fence back up the other side and on to a gate that let out onto the road.

I walked back up the road in the dark to the car.

52 stood at the gate.

I said, "Why didn't you come to me? I was calling for you!"

He said, "I don't like demands."

I said, "He rammed me! He hurt me! I was afraid he was going to kill me! Didn't you hear me calling for help?"

"You sounded hysterical. I'm not going to come just because you're hysterical."

The coldness in his voice left me stunned. His words echoed his response the time Mean Rooster had been attacking me. That incident hadn't been serious, but this was different and his reaction was the same.

"Of course I was hysterical! I was terrified!" I wanted to go back to the house.

He told me he wasn't finished with some other things he had to do, and we'd go back to the house when he was done.

I was hurting too much to hike up the driveway, and it was too dark anyway. I sat in the car, shaking.

I'd made a terrible mistake to walk into a field with a ram in the dark with a can of feed. But it wasn't the only mistake I'd made.

I was hip-deep in a farm with 52, and I didn't trust him anymore.

CHAPTER 14

I drove to Great Lakes, Illinois, with Weston and Morgan for Ross's boot camp graduation. The navy puts on an amazing show in an enormous hall with music and the graduating divisions marching in formation. I could hardly wait to pick Ross out from the sea of white uniforms. He could hardly wait to ask for his contact lenses, which he had not been allowed to wear during boot camp.

He had a weekend of liberty, and I had a whole list of potential entertainment, but he didn't want to do much besides hang out in the hotel room with his family. I had to tell him about his grandmother. As difficult as that was, I could see how much he had grown up during boot camp.

I was a little bit sad that boot camp was over, because I knew that would be the end of the wonderful letters.

On the last evening, he cried when I drove him back to the base. He was heading to Charleston, South Carolina, for nearly two years of nuclear power school training before being assigned to a submarine, and we were heading home to prepare for another school year and another hard winter. The annual Party on the Farm was coming up, too, and I went into cleaning mode. Every fall, I had a big party and invited any readers who could attend. But the farm was a mess. 52 was a hoarder, and I had a hard time convincing him to ever get rid of anything—but I could throw away my own things at will and did.

I'd started throwing things out the year before when I'd made room for my grandmother's dishes, but I wasn't done. I tackled my closet that fall, which was packed with clothes I hadn't worn in years. I lived on a farm. I wore jeans and T-shirts or sweatshirts every day. A closetful of dresses from a former life was doing me no good and taking up space I needed for more functional storage.

I made the first pass through my closet and came up with a mountainous pile. Only the closet looked almost the same. (How was that possible?) I took a break, reflected on the meaning of life and all this excess clothing that I never wore. I had fancy dresses from when I used to go to writing conferences and the accompanying dinners and parties. I didn't do that anymore. I took a second pass at the closet. And a third.

Then I let Morgan pick out whatever she wanted for herself from the piles. She took four or five items. I found her pickiness very inspiring. I thought about Ross, carrying everything he owned away in a seabag.

I made another pass at the closet, and another. Weston's girlfriend came over, and she took a couple of pretty dresses that she liked.

Morgan was a real helper. She made fun of almost every piece of clothing. ("That looks like something an American Girl doll would wear!") She helped bag up the clothes and said "No!" when I backpedaled and considered keeping something.

In the end, I threw out almost every single item of clothing in the closet. I didn't want to live that way anymore—surrounded by purposeless excess. I had almost no clothes left, and I couldn't have been happier about it.

I encouraged 52 to tackle his own purposeless excess, but I got nowhere. I got the kids to help me clean up outside, making piles of crap in the driveway and the yard for 52 to examine. Most of the junk outside belonged to him, or at least was claimed as under his control. I could understand stacks of extra building supplies— leftover supplies from one project often found use in the next— but there were used furniture pieces (often in disrepair) that no one wanted in the house, broken tools, rotted construction materials, and various other odds and ends and items that were truly junk. Remains of hay and chicken poop complemented the scene as it was impossible to clean around all that crap, and most of it was piled up around the foundation of the house, making our house look like the centerpiece to a junkyard.

52 came home and pulled most of the junk out of the piles and put it back in keeper stacks around the house, but at least I got the chicken poop and old straw raked out while it was moved.

I had this vision of a storybook farm, where everything would be cute and tidy, and walking around the house and farm would be like turning a page to see the next colorful, enchanting picture. But 52 liked junk, and he was possessive of it.

We were at odds on our ideals of simple, minimalist living. My concept involved keeping what was functional and cherished. Everything should have a purpose. I organized all my crafting supplies, soap making, candle making, and so on. I had pots and pans and supplies for cheese making, and I could barely pass up a cooking gadget. I loved to cook! If it was decorative or sentimental, it was chosen carefully for meaning, and the excess was tossed, even when it was difficult. I didn't need every birthday card my grandmother ever sent me, for example. I kept one, the sweetest one, to remember my grandmother's handwriting and got rid of the rest. I was ruthless.

52's concept of simple, minimalist living entailed keeping everything, because you never knew what you might need that might save you a dollar ten years from now. I was all for spending a dollar later if necessary rather than keeping twenty piles of junk all over the farm (and mostly around the house). I tried to talk him into paring down to a few piles of good, solid materials and neatly tucking them somewhere out of sight on our forty acres. You'd think there was room. I got nowhere, and his excess wasn't just limited to materials.

He did much of the grocery shopping since he was in the city every day. If he brought home a package of chicken, he'd bring home twenty, just because it was on sale. Sometimes this was great, and I understood the concept of buying on sale, but even with four freezers by this point, we were squeezed for space, and I was running out of room to keep home-canned goods, too. I asked him for canning jars one year and for the next three years, he brought home jars from ads in the paper—some free, some cheap, some with old food still inside them out of people's attics they'd inherited from their grandmas. I had use for pint jars and jam-size jars since I often gave away jellies and jams and needed to regularly replace those jars, but he mostly brought home used quart jars. By the time I had over three hundred quart jars, I was ready to take quart jars and throw them over the hill—and he wouldn't stop bringing home more jars. We had boxes and boxes of quart jars stacked in the house.

One year, a church in Charleston handed out over forty thousand pounds of sweet potatoes they got from a farm in South Carolina where they were going to be plowed under if someone didn't haul them off. They shipped them back to West Virginia and gave them away free to anyone who'd take them. 52 brought home a couple hundred pounds of sweet potatoes. Of course.

I made mashed sweet potato pie, sweet potato fries, sweet potato casserole, sweet potato bread, and sweet potato muffins. Then I was in the mood to throw sweet potatoes at 52's head, so I called Georgia.

She said, "Oh my, that's a lot of sweet potatoes." Luckily, though, she wanted some, so I happily took the excess to her house. She went on a mission to pass them out to her church ladies and friends and shut-ins. She had Weston and Morgan unload them right into the trunk of her car for easy delivery.

That evening, we were planning to head out to a visitation for my first cousin once removed who had passed away at ninety-one. Georgia said, "Do you think we can bring sweet potatoes to the visitation?"

I said, "I think we're supposed to bring flowers."

Georgia said, "We don't have flowers. We have sweet potatoes."

And sure enough, when we pulled in to pick her up (Georgia would never miss a visitation outing), there she was with a bag of sweet potatoes in each hand. Morgan, who insisted on coming along (she would never miss a social event), ran around asking everyone at the visitation if they wanted sweet potatoes while Georgia handed them out at the door like funeral wake party favors. Morgan wore her darkest blue T-shirt in honor of the somber occasion and put it on inside out because she didn't think it was appropriate to have any print on her shirt at a funeral visitation.

I said, "But it's appropriate to ask everyone if they would like a sweet potato?"

I should have brought quart jars.

I filled as many of the excess jars with home-canned green beans as I could stand. The kids didn't like green beans any more than they liked sweet potatoes, and they were harder to disguise. I loved green beans, but I couldn't eat them all by myself and, for some reason, 52 barely ate, at least not at home. I finally came to the conclusion that he barely picked at the meals I prepared because I loved to cook—which was a pretty good commentary on the contrary state of our relationship, and yet we just kept truckin'.

I stayed close to home as much as possible, waiting for Beulah Petunia to calve. I didn't want to miss it.

But it was pear time, and Georgia had pears. She'd gotten them from a friend who had a pear tree. She couldn't see well enough to read directions anymore, and she couldn't bear up to all the cutting and stirring involved in the preparation for canning something either.

She called me to tell me about her pear bounty.

"What should we do with the pears?" she asked.

This was Georgia's way of telling me she wanted me to help her. I told her I'd check my recipes and find something. A few days later I gave her the choice between pear jam and pear butter.

Another day or two later she decided on pear butter. Every time I talked to her, I said, "How are the pears looking?"

"They aren't ready yet." Of course, Georgia couldn't see very well, so by the time I got there on the day she told me it was time, half the pears were rotten and unusable, but we got enough out of them to make one batch of pear butter.

The kitchen at the Slanted Little House was, as usual, filled to the rafters with all sorts of things, except what you might be looking for. When I moved in there, the shelves and drawers were packed with old dishes and odd implements, and things literally fell out of the cabinets when you opened them. I spent the first few months there packing up a lot of things, adding organizational shelving and drawer inserts, and bringing in my own things in order to make the kitchen functional, semiconvenient, and pseudomodern. I moved it all out when I left, and I moved the old things back in.

Georgia and I scrambled around and came up with the things we needed. We cut the pears and weighed them.

I said, "We need a big pot."

Georgia said, "I suppose there's one in the cellar."

Yeah, along with the spiders, bats, and trolls. I went to the cellar and came back with what looked like a witch's cauldron in which to cook the pears. I scrubbed the dead bugs off the bottom.

Cooking at the Slanted Little House—to think I'd missed it!

With the pears cooked and softened enough to mash, I measured in the ingredients for the pear butter recipe and set the pot to simmering. The fragrance of orange peel, nutmeg, and sweet fruit filled the old house. Dead bugs and all, I loved that house.

We canned the pear butter in the big canning pot on the gas stove in the cellar porch, the stove I would light on those freezing cold winter nights when I lived there.

Sometimes I wondered what my life would have been like if I'd never left the Slanted Little House. My cousin wasn't set up for livestock, and he didn't particularly want to have them. I knew I'd made a big mistake partnering in the farm with 52, but I couldn't ever regret the farm itself. It had become my life, and I loved it. Waiting for a calf felt like the biggest event ever.

It wasn't long before Beulah Petunia calved, though as much as I'd tried to keep an eye on her, I still missed the big moment. We had checked on her a couple times the morning she calved, then we'd each gone out for the day. I was worried about leaving, but I had an appointment. Her udder had blown up to a point that it looked as if it might explode, so I knew her calving time had to be near. She'd been standing at the gate by the road when I drove out that day. She was still standing near the gate by the road when I came back. About an hour later, I checked on her again, and she had moved to the back of the pasture. We'd closed off the far field so she couldn't hide out. Next check she'd moved across the creek. An hour later, she was standing there with a calf.

We brought her water with molasses to refortify her system after the birth. Molasses—for the sugar and iron—mixed with water is a standby cure-all for animals any time they are dehydrated, sick, just had a baby, or just about anything else. She drank two bucket-fuls, then we stood there watching her lick the calf. The baby was already trying to stand, rooting for its food source. It was dark, and I was never good at sexing baby animals, but I thought it was a girl.

Next morning, I looked again and was sure it was a boy. Which brought to mind baby calf names like Darn It, Auction Block, and Hamburger Helper. I had no idea how old Beulah Petunia was, but she was no spring chicken. I'd been hoping for a girl to raise up as a future milker.

I called Skip. Skip lived across the river and a mile down the road in the old house where my father grew up.

I said, "Skip! I have a calf and I'm a dingbat. Could you come over and tell me if it's a boy or a girl?"

Skip said, sure, he'd be down after a while.

I went to the meadow bottom to wait for him. Skip came across the river in his beat-up truck. He was a small, wiry man, full of energy and country know-how. He'd come from the Northeast years ago, looking for cheap land and freedom. He'd been working with cows all his life.

He looked at the calf from behind, then he flipped it over and said, "What you were looking at was its umbilical cord. It's a girl. You can even see the little udder."

He pointed out the tiny pink teats. Well, duh.

I had my little Jersey–Brown Swiss future milker.

One day a few months earlier, the Ornery Angel's two little girls had ridden by on their bicycles on the road in front of our farm. They asked what our cow's name was. I said, "Beulah Petunia." They giggled and giggled. Every cow needs a name that makes people smile. I decided this baby needed two, just like her mama.

I named her Glory Bee, and as winter approached, I was back to milking my cow.

Winters were never easy at Stringtown Rising. The winter before, we'd had a foot of snow three separate times and lost power for a week—over Christmas. It was record snowfall. The third winter wasn't much better. I wasn't a courageous driver in snow and ice. I still depended on 52 for nearly everything, which was why I couldn't see my life on the farm without him even as my life with him became more and more intolerable.

In the winter, he was the one who picked up the mail and took out the mail, took away the trash, drove the kids out of the holler and brought the kids home, and brought groceries and feed for the animals. I kept the woodstove burning so we could save money on electricity and propane, but he chopped down the trees and split the wood.

I continued to be close to my cousin and his wife, Sheryl, and Georgia. Sheryl, in particular, became a sounding board to my private troubles with 52 and helped keep me sane, along with my friend, Cindy, who had also started helping me with my ever-expanding website. She had all the technical skills I lacked, and she became a confidante, too. She lived in Michigan, but with the Internet, it was almost as good as if she were next door.

Weston was a senior in high school. He spent a great deal of that winter staying at his girlfriend's house in town. She was an adorable girl, a year behind him in school, and she was a vegan. In my kitchen of fresh milk and butter and cheese, she was yet another challenge when she visited. Weston was a finalist in the National Merit Scholarship competition and was planning to attend West Virginia University in Morgantown. My new part-time job was scouring the Earth for more scholarship opportunities and making sure everything got filled out and sent in on time.

He'd had a more difficult time transitioning to West Virginia socially than my other kids. He was more introspective and loved spending time on the computer when he wasn't playing football. He'd gradually developed a small circle of very close friends, so close that they all planned to go together to WVU.

Morgan spent a lot of time in the winter at Mark and Sheryl's house unless 52 brought her home—or she walked. Sometimes if the kids were at my cousin's and got impatient to come home, they'd walk the three miles over the hill, in the snow. They'd walk out sometimes, too. They enjoyed telling people it was uphill both ways, and it was true. Our dirt-rock road never saw plow service or salt, and the icy narrow route over the hill with steep drop-offs and no guardrails terrified me more every winter, not less. Luckily, Mark and Sheryl loved having the kids anytime, but I was afraid they'd have to adopt them if I separated from 52.

I thought constantly about separating from 52.

I was still holding on to my doomed idea that if I made enough money to take the financial pressure off him, his behavior toward me would change. I realized all along that money couldn't buy happiness, of course, but it could certainly relieve stress. By then, I was making enough money from my website to start taking over the household bills. One at a time, I took over each bill, no longer splitting them as we had in the past, until the only bills he was participating in with me were the mortgage and the second mortgage. The mortgages were so high, there was no way I could pay them alone. I took as much pressure off him as I could.

Nothing changed. I still saw occasional glimpses of that man who had told me the story of the feral cat he'd tamed with kindness, but he never came back for good—and I gradually accepted that he probably never would.

We still worked well on activities involving the farm. I never got over the incident with Mr. Cotswold, but most of the time, it was doing things together on the farm that drew us together, at least for brief periods of time. There were always new plans we were making for the farm, projects to be tackled, animals to move up, animals to move down, the birth of a lamb or a goat, or the death of one. We had terrible luck with lambs. One day, 52 was down in the meadow bottom to do some work, and one of the latest crop of lambs was eating on a bale of hay.

The lamb walked away from the hay and dropped to the ground. 52 tried to stand it up. The lamb was dead, that sudden, for no apparent cause. 52 came back up to the house, stunned.

If you want to get in touch with life and death, get a farm. It's beautiful and brutal all at once. Like the hen that I found dead one morning, fallen between the slats on a pallet gate. Or the half-grown chicken that somehow got mashed between the side of the feeder box and the wall of the chicken house. One time I was taking a nice little break in the evening sitting in front of the chicken yard watching the ducks and chickens and guineas, and a guinea killed a chicken. Right in front of me. In the blink of an eye. No notice.

There's a saying in farming: if you're going to have livestock, you're going to have deadstock.

It's true. Animals are sturdy but fragile creatures at the same time. Sheep could be particularly difficult. A saying about sheep is: as soon as sheep are born, they start looking for a way to die.

The animals were also always looking for a way to escape. I

had Jack, our donkey, running down the road to the river one day when he got away from me. I had sheep running down the road to the river. I had goats running down the road to the river. Even Beulah Petunia got out one day. You can't build a fence or gate that animals can't figure out how to outwit every once in a while.

Not everything that happens on a farm is fun and sweet. Some of it is difficult or sad. And if you care about your animals, it's hard. Mean Rooster was so mean, I was afraid every day he'd peck out my eyeballs or rip out my jugular, and yet I cried when I found him dead after one of the other roosters killed him.

But no matter what happens, you get up the next day and do the best you can with what you have all over again. I loved farm life even with all its hardships, and I loved my job writing about the farm, too. It was limitless and filled with new challenges of its own every day.

I wrote "children's stories" with talking animals. I wrote sentimental essays about life in rural Appalachia or memoir-type pieces about my family history in West Virginia. I created recipes and wrote about food. I designed craft ideas or tried out old-time skills. I was working if I was making bread. I was working if I was putting hats on Clover or giving Poky a licorice treat or trying to find where my hens were hiding their eggs. I was working if I was taking a drive, looking for a new old outhouse to see if it had two seats or three. I was working if I was learning to knit or dye wool. I was working if I was cutting wildflowers on the creek bank. When I was finished, I would write about it all.

And I enjoyed it so much, it never felt like work. I was following my passion, for writing, and for life on a farm, and there was a deep sense of rightness to it. I was doing exactly what I was supposed to be doing.

Readers responded. Traffic doubled and tripled, then doubled and tripled again. People left comments, sent e-mails and letters, letting me know how I was changing their lives, inspiring them to follow their dreams, try new things, or at least bake a loaf of bread. They told me that my daily posts were the highlight of their day and that my writing made them happy.

In the darkest days at Stringtown Rising, it was my readers who inspired me and kept me going. Making up recipes and stories for them took me away from my own life, at least in my mind. Hidden behind all the funny or informative or poetic posts I wrote on my website about life on the farm, I was hiding the terrible secret of my deepening unhappiness. I was afraid that 52 and I were not going to make it, and if I didn't figure out how to make it without him, I was going to lose not just my farm and my dream but my business, because it was directly tied to the land.

I was trapped in a web of my own design, and I couldn't see any way out.

CHAPTER 15

I kept a secret list.

It was the list of things I needed to operate the farm on my own. It included things like a push-button start generator so I could manage power outages, insulated hoses so I wouldn't have to carry heavy buckets of water from inside the house to the animals when it was freezing, a proper milking parlor so I could quit milking in the mud, and some kind of massive feed and hay storage so I could stock up for the animals before winter. I knew that to take care of the farm by myself, I had to streamline chores and make things easier. I was going to kill myself with physical labor otherwise because the farm was so poorly laid out.

It was a squeeze to keep a hundred bales of hay at the house. Because of the way the main floor of the house had been raised to the second floor during construction, there was covered storage space under the wraparound porch. We kept hay there, and 52 kept a lot of junk there, but if I was going to keep more hay, a building would have to be constructed to hold it. I knew myself well enough to know that I would never get hay up to the fields around the house, where most of the animals wintered, unless it was brought up before bad weather hit and the driveway turned to ice and sludge.

But where would such a building go, and how much would it cost? What about feed? Feed tended to go moldy if it was kept too long, even in dry storage. 52 brought fresh feed every week. I could possibly hire someone to deliver feed, a man who would drive up the driveway with it when it was icy and not be terrified, but that would cost money, too.

Every issue relating to managing the farm by myself involved money in one way or another. The one thing I couldn't change about the farm was the difficult geography. Overcoming the difficult geography required money or physical labor or both.

Even once the hay was stored up at the house, it wasn't easy to get it to the animals. The land was a narrow strip, with the house taking up a good deal of the space. The house backed up to a hillside. In front of the house was the fenced goat yard. Wooded pasture had been fenced for Beulah Petunia on the far side of the house so that I wouldn't have to milk her in the meadow bottom anymore. There was no way I was going to get milk up and down the driveway in the winter. To get hay to her, I had to throw it over the fence into a small pen that had been fenced under the porch. The gates to the pen were made from pallets and had long since stopped operating because of hay and poop buildup. After I tossed the hay bale over the fence into the pen, I had to go around and back through the goat yard to get to the pen. Then I tossed the bale over the other (nonworking) pen gate into the side yard. Once I got back around there, I would roll the bale end over end to get it to Beulah Petunia.

Hay bales are heavy, weighing fifty to seventy-five pounds.

I did this every morning. A cow eats a bale of hay per day in the winter. I wanted to hire someone to dig out—with the tractor—the pen and repair the pen gates, but 52 was opposed to hiring anyone to do anything. We were supposed to do everything ourselves. I couldn't do this myself, though, and he never did it, either. I was afraid of how mad he'd be if I hired someone over his objections, so I tried to call moving the hay by hand over gates good exercise. I called 52 something else, but only in my mind.

If I had the farm on my own, I was going to hire someone to fix it. Immediately. 52 had suggested repeatedly that it was what I was planning to do after I got rid of him, hire a man to do the farm labor. Often I wondered if he just wanted out and was trying to give me instructions.

I transferred all the household bills into my name and set up online accounts to pay them so it could all be done online. 52 didn't question this reorganization since I was paying all the bills anyway. I needed to solve the problem of getting to the post office in the winter, since mail was not picked up or delivered on our road. I still couldn't figure out how to solve the hay and feed problem, though.

Since I'd taken over the bills, the only money I gave 52 anymore was for the weekly feed. I wrote him a check once a month for the feed, and he picked it up weekly at the little store in town on his way home from work, sometimes more often if I ran out. I e-mailed him at work one day to let him know that Beulah Petunia was almost out of sweet feed. I needed him to stop for feed that evening.

He e-mailed me back and told me he didn't have any money for feed.

I said, "I just gave you a check for feed two days ago!"

He told me the money was gone.

I had already filled up Beulah Petunia's feed bucket, getting ready to milk her. She was standing by the gate, waiting expectantly. I didn't know where the feed money had gone, and 52 wasn't explaining other than to say he'd spent it on a personal bill of his own. No matter how much I took over, paying for more and more of the costs of running the farm, his money troubles never seemed to improve. The more I paid for, the more he complained about having no money.

Beulah Petunia mooed angrily at the gate to her pasture.

I walked outside, leaving the bucket of feed behind. I had no idea when I would be able to get more feed. I'd given 52 all the money for feed for the month, and it was gone. There was snow on the ground under a crisp, cold sky. I told my cow I was sorry. I stared up at that deep blue winter sky, my face wet, tears freezing on my skin, urgency burning inside me. I had to figure out a way to run this farm by myself. I couldn't trust 52.

Several days later, 52 showed up with some feed. He told me he'd sold some of his father's gold. Occasionally if he needed money, he would sell gold he'd inherited from his father's clock and jewelry shop. I was unsympathetic to his plight of having to sell gold for cow feed.

I opened an account at the little store in town. 52 could pick up feed as needed, and I could pay the feed bill all at once by phone at the end of each month. I never gave money to 52 for anything ever again, but I was reminded constantly by the farm itself that I couldn't manage it on my own.

I couldn't even manage a calf.

There are all sorts of reasons to put a halter on a calf, particularly if it's a future milk cow. You want a cow that is tame and friendly, and you need to be able to move her around if and when necessary. You also want to be able to handle a calf as needed for vaccinations or other treatment. Glory Bee started out pretty friendly, and she would still frolic around me and come up to my hand, but she grew skittish when I tried to touch her, which is common with a mama-raised baby. It's the same thing with lambs or baby goats. If they're separated from their mothers and bottle-fed, they're more friendly than if they're left with their mothers. Getting a halter on Glory Bee, and using a lead on her at times, would make me able to handle her more and socialize her to my handling.

I spent hours one day haplessly flinging myself at the calf while she darted away from me.

· ·

WOMAN BEATEN BY BABY COW

A woman, reportedly beaten by a baby cow on a farm in the boonies, declined to comment on the incident, which occurred late Tuesday. Officers arrived at the scene after chickens in the area filed a disturbance call. A goat identified only as "Clover" stated to officers that the woman had been harassing the baby cow before the beating and that she was known for her inability to control animals. "It's embarrassing, really," Clover said. "But at least she makes good cookies."

Officers attempted to question the woman about the reported harassment, but she fled the scene in chore boots. A calf halter was taken into evidence. The case remains under investigation.

I couldn't even catch her, much less put a halter on her. The field where we kept Beulah Petunia was fenced with electric—which did nothing to contain the calf.

I'd tried to catch Glory Bee off and on for weeks when I decided it was time for 52 to take a turn. He got a rope to lasso her like a cowboy.

However, cowboys have horses so they can run as fast as calves, and we didn't have any horses. We also had steep hills and rough terrain, and I don't even think a cowboy on a horse could have caught this calf, though I would have liked to see a cowboy ride circles around the milk stand with Glory Bee, then up the hill and down the hill and under the electric fence.

So many different directions to go. Uphill. Downhill. The hinterlands. She needed to be herded into a pen from a smaller world. The only fencing that would keep her in would be the woven wire in the goat yard. But we'd moved the donkeys up for the winter, so Jack, Poky, and a whole passel of goats stood in the way.

The only thing 52 really had on me with the animals was brute strength, but he was very sensitive to being questioned about one of his plans. Generally, I waited until his plan finished not working before suggesting mine. My plans were often convoluted and nigh upon ridiculous, but they usually worked. I spent a lot of time with the animals, and since I had no brute strength, I relied on my instincts for animal behavior. 52 resented following my plans, but he lacked the instincts I had developed. I tried to manage by myself whenever possible, but in this case, I needed help pulling off the plan because at the end of it, somebody with brute strength was going to have to take control of the wild calf.

Step 1. Put everybody (goats and donkeys both) in the goat house and lock the door.

Step 2. Get Beulah Petunia.

Step 3. Tie her up inside the goat yard and leave the goat yard gate standing wide open.

Step 4. Wait for the baby to go looking for mommy.

Step 5. Slam the gate shut.

Step 6. Run the calf across the yard, away from the gate.

Step 7. Take mommy back out the gate and back to her field.

Step 8. Run back and forth and all over the goat yard until the baby accidentally runs into the confined space of the goat pen.

Step 9. Slam the goat pen gate on her. Corner the wild calf and get a rope on her!

Step 10. Struggle with ill-fitting halter. Give up on halter and lovingly convince angry, bucking calf to walk from the goat yard to the milk stand pen on a rope.

Step 11. Shut the angry, bucking baby in the milk stand pen and finally get the halter on her. (Don't forget to go back and shut the goat yard up again and let everybody out of the goat house.)

Step 12. Start crying when the calf escapes.

Further secure the pen, then repeat steps 1 through 11 above.

Do not, under any circumstances, repeat step 12.

52, of course, was the one holding on to the rope with an angry, bucking baby at the other end. I was afraid she'd get away from me, though someone had to start working to tame her, and I knew that was largely going to fall on me.

Once we had the halter on her, trying to work with her on a lead was like walking a Tasmanian devil, but at least she was under some modicum of control. I started out milk sharing half days with

Beulah Petunia. I'd let Glory Bee milk her in the morning, then I'd get mine in the evening. As Glory Bee continued to grow and didn't need the milk, eventually we traded days. I'd get Beulah Petunia one day, and Glory Bee would get her the next. (This gave me every other day off, which I liked.) Glory Bee remained a giant brat, but I continued to work on my "relationship" with her while keeping her contained in the goat yard, separated from her mama when it wasn't her turn. She was very curious about me, following me everywhere, running along the fence to "follow" me even when I was outside the goat yard. When I went into the goat yard, she'd tag along behind me like a toddler holding on to an invisible apron string.

She was a gorgeous creature, and I was as besotted with her as I was with her mother. Cows sucked me in like no other farm animals I'd experienced. They were an incredible amount of work, but they gave back a hundredfold in so many ways—not just milk, but in honing my confidence and perseverance and patience.

Cows made the farm for me. It wasn't just about the butter, though it was delicious. Cows fed those questions deep inside, questions about myself, that had led me to West Virginia. Milking a cow made me prove myself every single day.

Yet as satisfying as that experience was, I never seemed to arrive at my destination. The cows were part of the journey, but they weren't the answer.

I was living a crazy life, fulfilling in so many ways, but empty at the same time. The best part about it was that it was too busy to let me contemplate for long.

Three of the goats popped out four babies that winter. The last one to give birth, Sprite, one of my Fainters, had been behaving normally all day when 52 and I spotted her standing in the middle of the goat yard making "I'm in pain" noises. We moved her quickly to the goat house, which was blocked off then as the maternity ward. She went to the corner and stood and cried a little bit. She finally sat down, and 52 and I watched as the baby came out.

But then—

Sprite walked away.

The baby flopped and mewled for its mother.

Sprite went to the opposite corner and wouldn't even look upon what had sprung from her flowered loins. Whatever it was, she didn't want it. I took hold of her and turned her around. She turned back. I turned her back around and pushed her a little toward the flopping, crying thing. She climbed up onto a little table in the goat house to get away.

The baby struggled to its feet, still covered in goop. Sprite wouldn't clean it.

I thought—maybe she's having another baby. Maybe she's *busy*.

We'd discovered Fanta, another of the Fainters, the night before, just as she'd had her second baby. It was still covered in goop and she was cleaning it. The first baby was already on its feet, cleaned off and fluffy. Fanta didn't wait till she had the second one to clean off the first one.

Sprite wouldn't even look at her baby, much less go near it. I made her move down off the table. The baby half walked, half flopped toward her, crying. Sprite climbed back up on the table.

Afraid the baby would get chilled as the minutes ticked by, we got a towel and dried the baby off as best we could without, you know, licking it. The other babies came around, nuzzled it, and talked to it. Sprite drank some water and ate some hay. And wouldn't look at her baby. She ran away every time it wobbled up to her.

It was one of the strangest, most unnatural things I'd ever seen, and I had no idea what to do.

We put the baby under Fanta, who was still only twenty-four hours from delivering her twins and would still have colostrum in her milk, and let it suck on her. She was busy eating hay and she had two babies so she wasn't paying attention to who was sucking on her. And that baby wanted a mommy so badly.

When Sprite never showed any sign of delivering a second one, I went inside and found the little goat milk pail from back when I was milking Clover. 52 held Sprite down for me and I milked some colostrum out of her, thinking to put it in a bottle. Then I thought—why not try the baby? I put the baby under her. We had to hold her. She didn't want the baby anywhere near her. We let the baby nurse a good long time to get colostrum. I took the colostrum I'd milked out of her into the pail inside the house to store. We stayed with the baby in the goat house for a long time before leaving it for the night to snuggle in with the other goat mommies and their babies inside the goat house.

The next day, I went down to the goat house alone, backed Sprite into a corner, held on to her with all my might to stop her from running away, and let the baby suck. A baby needs all the colostrum it can get within the first twenty-four hours of birth, and especially within the first twelve. Sprite continued to run away unless she was held in place.

I was sure I'd end up bottle-feeding that baby, but after a week of consistently going down to the goat house multiple times throughout the day and holding Sprite down against her will to nurse, she started nursing her baby voluntarily. While I was still struggling with Glory Bee, convincing Sprite to be a mother was an accomplishment that felt especially good.

Farm life is full of mysteries, with no one right way to do anything. It helped just to know that, at least sometimes, sheer determination could win the day.

Determination was pretty much all I had going for me, though by this time I was starting to feel slightly experienced. I was still no good at driving in the snow, but by that third winter at Stringtown Rising, I'd developed some skills nonetheless. I was good at stocking up, planning ahead for grocery staples and supplies. I was canning and dehydrating and had a full pantry. I had full freezers too. I'd grown adept at keeping the woodstove going. I had chickens for eggs, my cow for milk, butter, and cheese.

Winter in the country is a time for farmers to relax, sit by the fire, sip hot chocolate, and enjoy the rewards of a garden well sown and a harvest stored away. Time to put tired feet up and knit and read books. Time to—

Oh, wait. That was my fantasy! But it was such an endearing dream.

Winter in the country is time to break up water, carry hay, haul firewood, and keep animals sheltered. Time to muck about in the snow and mud, chore boots sinking halfway to China. There was so much work to do in the winter—and it was that much harder because it was cold.

Mornings started out icy and dark. I carried water to the chicken house, then went back for more feed. I lugged the five-gallon bucket of layer pellets to their feeder. The chickens would be so excited that they'd jump into the feeder bin with the feed. I'd push them out and they'd squawk at me. They'd change their minds ten or eleven times about whether or not they wanted to free-range for the day, then I'd move on to the goats. They'd need hay. I used the end of a rake to break up the frozen water in their buckets. Then I carried more water from the house.

I searched for eggs. The chickens loved to hide eggs. I carried food and water to the dogs and the cats. When everyone was fed and watered and where they wanted to be for the day, I'd carry armful after armful of wood up to the house. Every once in a while, if I was tired, I'd secretly turn up the central heat, which we normally kept very low just to keep the house from turning too cold if the fire went out overnight. I was paying the electric bill by myself, but it still made me feel guilty to use it, and I'd be careful to turn it back down and put wood on the fire before 52 came home to find I was "cheating" on the woodstove. I liked living off the land, but sometimes I was just plumb worn out. If he discovered I'd been using the central heat, I knew I'd be in for a ranting, so I didn't want to get caught.

After the wood was in, it was time to milk my cow. I'd reach my freezing fingers eagerly for her big warm udder and think about my past life in suburbia. Mornings spent with a cup of coffee or three, morning talk shows for company, my feet propped up on the coffee table. I was so spoiled!

And yet the cold, crisp air was invigorating. I was forced outside to confront winter head-on. I couldn't hide indoors and wait for it to go away. I didn't need a gym or a Wii Fit. I got my exercise tramping back and forth in heavy boots carrying buckets of feed. I worked out my upper arms breaking up water and lugging firewood or pushing those hay bales over fences to get them to Beulah Petunia. I breathed in the fresh, frozen air, hard earth under my feet, barren branches all around. I knew winter, and winter knew me.

I'd seen old photographs of pioneers who hauled equipment to Stringtown to build gas and oil wells, their mule-driven carts sinking deep in the thick mud. I knew that deep mud. I didn't work nearly as hard as they did, but I felt more of a kinship with them than I did with that girl who used to drink coffee and watch morning TV, even if sometimes I cheated on the woodstove.

No matter how hard the work was on some days, I wouldn't have traded winter in the country for the world—and I hoped I'd never have to.

CHAPTER 16

One of my readers sent me a book called *The Legend of Mammy Jane*. (Subtitle: *An uneducated girl becomes the lady of the manor in Appalachia*.) Readers often sent me gifts, books, or even odd vintage items from their attics that they thought I might enjoy. At first, I didn't like the book much, but I soon became obsessed with it as another peek into the past and connection with one of those pioneer women to whom I so aspired. The book was written by Sibyl Jarvis Pischke about her grandmother, Jane Jarvis, and was set in the pre–Civil War and Civil War period in what would eventually become West Virginia. Jane was a poor but resourceful girl who was working as a "hired girl" by the time she was ten. She was cute and a hard worker, and by the time she was seventeen, a widower with five children made her his wife.

At her first job, taking care of a family during and following a "laying-in" (childbirth), she's barely arrived before she's fixing a complete dinner, cleaning everything in sight, and burying the afterbirth out back. And saying things like, " . . . a man wanted his supper as soon as he washed up." And Jane didn't even say, "Well, you better get started on it, mister!"

After she married and arrived at her new husband's neglected home, she had everything in the house in washtubs, and she was scrubbing the kids in the creek, digging potatoes in the garden, milking the cow, and making new straw mattresses. And that's just what she did before lunch. Not including the biscuits. She got all the kids who were old enough to help, too. Lots of kids/helpers is a plus, but Jane was an undeniable driving force.

The book was interesting for its detailed descriptions of customs and remedies and sayings of the time as well as for the amount of work a pioneer had to do every day to survive, but it was the central figure of Jane, who could work like nobody's business and was the epitome of perseverance, that carried the story. There was no problem, not even war, that Jane couldn't overcome by working harder or making a nut cake.

I'm not sure if I fell in love with Jane, or if I just loved to hate her, but she was definitely fascinating. And there were pieces and parts of her life that resembled mine, too. I lived on a farm! I didn't have enough money! I had a cow and a woodstove! Jane even lived in Calhoun County, which was just the next county over from where I lived in Roane County. I decided to act like Jane for a day. (Except for the part where she treated men as if they were masters of the universe.)

Jane bounded from bed in the wee hours and started the day with breakfast for everybody. She got the woodstove going. Put the biscuits in the oven.

I woke at 6:10. We had to leave to drive to the bus at 6:15. No time for biscuits. I didn't even check the woodstove. Got my boots on and got going. There was some hardship involved, though, so that kind of took the place of the biscuits. The driveway was muddy. And it had snowed. Again. The kids and I had to walk down the driveway in the dark to where I'd left the car at the bottom then drive across the river and out the frosty road to meet the bus. When I came home, I had to walk back up the muddy driveway. In the dark.

I figured predawn hiking in snow and ice beat biscuits any day. I gave myself a check. Or half a check. Jane probably could have hiked the icy, muddy driveway *and* made biscuits.

My kids would have to eat breakfast at school.

Having started the day with an excuse, I worked on improving. I got the woodstove going and started feeling my inner Jane.

Jane always made biscuits before she went out to milk. I'd already missed biscuit time so I made a loaf of bread. I got the dough started and in the bowl to rise.

I was Jane! Check!

Next, out to feed the animals. Dogs, cats. Hay to the goats and donkeys and Glory Bee in the yard.

Hay and water to the goat mommies in the goat house.

Feed to the chickens and ducks. I collected eggs. I only found six.

Jane wouldn't have put up with that. I told the chickens Jane would have tossed them in a frying pan. They didn't care. They knew Jane wasn't there.

Beulah Petunia was mooing angrily and impatiently by this time. Jane's cow was sweet and docile and stood still for milking without any feed. I didn't have Jane's cow. I carried hay and feed to Beulah Petunia, then milked her.

I carried the milk back to the house, checked the fire, punched down the dough and put it in the loaf pan, and took care of the home dairy. Filtered the day's new milk. Skimmed the previous day's set milk. I was Jane! Check!

I had heavy cream in a jar sitting out overnight, ready to make butter. I used my KitchenAid stand mixer, the modern churn. Was that cheating?

Jane used a real churn. Churning butter was one of the few things Jane admitted to not enjoying. She couldn't wait to turn it over to the younguns as soon as one of the girls was old enough to take over the chore. I was so Jane! I made Morgan make butter once! Check!

By this time, I'd baked the bread and had stopped to have a couple slices for lunch with my fresh butter, barely resisting the urge to devour the entire loaf.

Jane didn't have a website, but I did, and she had a whole passel of kids to help, and I didn't, so I eschewed heading outside to dig taters or scrub the curtains in washtubs filled with boiling water. I did some writing instead and tended to some other officey-type business. (I don't think Jane had an office.) I also made ahead some balls of piecrust dough, brewed and chilled some vanilla coffee for homemade Frappucinos for Morgan, washed one and a half dozen eggs (collected over the last few days), and took in and out three loads of dishes from the dishwasher. Jane would have washed all the floors, cut up pumpkins to dry, found a cure for cancer growing in the woods, then milked the cow again. It was time for me to milk the cow again, too, and feed all the animals all over again. Jane would get supper on the table, then sew some diapers out of feed sacks or make new outfits for the children from the curtains. They didn't have meat available all the time, but Jane could whip together a dandy meal with fried squash, potatoes, and corn bread with cream.

I whipped together some fried eggplant, rice with pork and corn, and fresh homemade bread. I didn't hand-sew any baby diapers out of feed sacks, but I did do some crochet. I decided I knew why they sewed so much. They got to *sit down*.

Luckily, I didn't have to go to bed on a straw mattress. At the end of the day, I prepped a pot of soft cheese to set overnight and hang in the morning. I had fresh buttermilk. I'd make biscuits in the morning!

Later in the book, Jane's husband went off to war and she struggled through life with the children by herself, ultimately prospering and becoming known as the lady of the manor and a figure of resourcefulness and courage. She helped others and helped herself. The thread that went through it all was the hard, hard work.

I wasn't a stranger to hard work, which was a large part of what attracted me to Jane's story. She had a strength I was looking for in myself. When I wrote about the book on my website, my readers told me I was their modern Jane. I thought that was an overstatement (they didn't know I cheated on my woodstove sometimes), but I felt a connection with Jane all the same. I knew she had lived in the next county over, but it was only when I actually checked a map that I realized her house was a mere fifteen to twenty miles away from our farm. I also knew, from researching Jane, that her house was still standing.

The enticing proximity led me to forget everything I'd learned about West Virginia since I'd moved there, such as that fifteen to twenty miles translates into approximately fifteen hundred to two thousand miles since there is no straight path to anywhere here unless you are a crow. Going to find Jane's house was precisely one of those nonsensical adventures that 52 and I did so well together. He was charming at such times, completely indulgent of my latest crazy whim, reminding me of why I loved him and making me think we were going to make it.

That alone was worth the trip.

And so, all common sense tossed behind me, I set out upon my adventure, an intrepid explorer, full of bravado in the face of twisting, unmarked, switchback dirt roads and overlapping hills that send you to New York and back trying to get around them. I was going to find Mammy Jane's house! Well, 52 was going to find it while I rode shotgun.

And do what once I got there? I had no clue.

I was sure it would only take a couple of hours, max, to go there and back, unmarked twisting roads notwithstanding.

We set off across the river ford, in the opposite direction from town, and promptly came upon one of Skip's cows in the road.

Dear readers, if there aren't livestock in the road in the story, you aren't reading a story about West Virginia.

Skip was the farmer who came over to sex Glory Bee for me. He owned the house in which my dad grew up along with much of my great-grandfather's old farm across the river. Skip was just a bit farther up the road, past the wandering cow, near his sawmill. We reached him and I rolled down my window. "Skip, your cow is in the road back there."

Skip said, "They're all in the road."

Turned out someone had stolen Skip's fence. Seriously. Someone had stolen his entire fence along the road. He had put up a new fence, and someone had stolen it again. They caught the guy after the second time, but Skip hadn't put up the fence again yet because, you know, he was a bit miffed.

So his cows were wandering more than usual. Skip said he wasn't worried about it. They came home at feeding time.

We continued on, following the road that followed the river. The "hard road" in that direction turned into a dirt road. The river was narrow and shallow and looked like a creek.

About two miles from our farm, the road passed my great-great-grandfather's house. I wondered if my ancestors knew the Mammy Jane family, but back then, fifteen miles was a long way. Especially in West Virginia. And I was about to find out how far fifteen miles still was. It took us about three hours to find the house.

I recognized it right away from a photo I'd seen online in my research. I was there! I'd found it! What to do now? I got out of the car and started taking pictures. 52 suggested that since I was running around taking pictures outside the house, it might be a good idea to knock on the door and introduce myself before somebody started shooting.

I knocked on the back porch door. A little bitty teeny tiny elderly woman came to the door. I told her my name and explained what I was doing and she waved her hand at me and walked off. She came back putting a hearing aid in her ear and I started over. I said, "Are you Irene?" Because I knew that Irene was Mammy Jane's granddaughter and that she owned the house now. She said she was, then turned to take some corn bread out of the oven. The back porch door opened into the kitchen. I half expected her to pour cream over the bread, fry up some squash, and call the younguns. I was standing at Mammy Jane's door!

We chatted for a few minutes about Jane and the book. I thanked her for letting me take pictures of the house and said I had a cow waiting at home for me, so I'd better go.

She said, "Why don't you come in?"

Okay!

I felt guilty for showing up there like that, though, so I just stood right inside the door. By then, 52 had joined me. We chatted for probably another thirty minutes about Jane. I never stepped a foot away from just inside the door. Eventually, I told her again that I had a cow waiting at home for milking, so I'd better go. By this time, it was getting dark.

She said, "Don't you want to see the rest of the house?"

Well, yes! So I finally stepped away from just inside the door, and she took 52 and me through the entire house, room by room, telling us about each one.

I already had an idea from some things I had discovered in researching Jane on the Internet that not everything in the book was accurate. It was, of course, a fictionalized account of Jane's life, so that was to be expected. Irene shared with me a number of fabrications and inaccuracies in the book, and that most of what was true in the story was Jane's character and how she worked. She never learned to read or write, but she conducted business with an iron hand and ran her home with a backbone of steel. She knew how to do anything, could make everything, worked like a dog, and managed money. She was an extraordinarily strong woman in her time. But that, Irene said, just wasn't dramatic enough for a book.

It was good enough for me, and I admired the real Jane as much, if not more, than the fictional character. For me, it was equally satisfying to find out the truth. And I think that was why I was so driven to go in search of Jane. I knew the book was fiction. What I was looking for was the truth.

And then finally I said to Irene again, I have to go, my cow is going to be mad. By then, it was way past dark and considering it had taken us five billion hours to trek the fifteen to twenty miles there, we still had another five billion hours to get home. I thanked her for her time, and she invited me to come back.

I thought often of returning to visit again, but never did. I'd found out what I needed to know about Jane.

It was the truth inside myself for which I was still searching. I felt, more and more, as if my whole life was a lie. I wrote about frugality and simplicity while my days were absorbed with trying to make money so I could somehow take over the farm. I did everything I could think of to expand my readership and develop extra income streams.

I'd started working with New England Cheesemaking, writing posts for them that appeared on both my site and theirs in a traffic-trading partnership. Beulah Petunia was pouring milk from her udder, and I was making a new cheese every month as part of my "cheese challenge" with NEC. Since my first year on the farm I'd been writing a bimonthly column for the *Charleston Daily Mail,* and for a time I wrote a monthly column for a regional publication called *Two Lane Livin'.* I was deep in plans for a Chickens in the Road Retreat—several days of workshops to be held at a large camp facility with a hall for classes and meals and cabins for lodging.

It was going to take money for me to take over the farm.

It was also going to take 52 deciding to leave voluntarily— because I'd promised him I'd never tell him to leave again. Most of the time, he seemed miserable enough that I had reason to hope he might decide on his own to go back to the city.

I really couldn't understand why he stayed there. Except for when we were having an "adventure" that pulled us together temporarily, he appeared to find me intolerable.

When I'd ask him if he was trying to drive me away, he'd say no. When I'd ask him if he wished he could leave, he'd say no. When I'd ask him if he wanted to continue to have a relationship with me, he'd say yes.

I'd say, "Well, then, could you stop yelling at me?"

Apparently, that was a bridge too far, and I felt stuck. He wouldn't offer to go, and I couldn't tell him to leave. And worse, he wouldn't stop ranting at me.

Sometimes I felt guilty for constantly imagining the farm without 52. Then he would start yelling at me, and I knew I had no choice but to imagine another way. I had to survive, and by this point, the emotional beating of his abuse was beginning to crush me. Some days, those cheerful posts on my website were hard to come by. I was sinking into a depression.

Meanwhile, I kept working, trying to earn my way out of my nightmare. Between working and milking and other farm chores, I had a hard time keeping up with the house. Cleaning was the bottom of my priority list, but I liked a tidy house and my time was better spent writing.

I hired a cleaning lady. Secretly.

By this time, I had a lot of secrets, and this one was about to blow up in my face.

CHAPTER 17

With Ross moved out and in the navy, and Weston soon heading off to college, I started renovating the lower floor of the house where they had their bedrooms. I had some ideas about installing a second kitchen downstairs. There was already a sitting room, a bathroom, and two bedrooms down there, with another space that could be a kitchen. I was toying with a plan to host farm stays and workshops at Stringtown Rising.

The downstairs was a mess. The cement block walls made it look like a prison. In the area I hoped to turn into a kitchen, we'd periodically kept brooder chicks, and 52 kept his workbench and a lot of his tools stacked in one corner. Much of the rest of the space was cluttered with stacks of those detested quart jars and other junk, some of it mine, and I was quite eager to dispose of it. I started painting the block walls a cheerful off-white that brightened the space considerably, and I made plans to clean up and redesign the boys' bedrooms. It would make a really nice workshop and farm stay space, separated from the house on its own floor yet part of the house at the same time. If I was ever going to take over paying the mortgage and second mortgage by myself, I needed to come up with another source of income. Taking over the farm on my own felt like a pipe dream, but the fantasy kept me going.

The plans became a bone of contention between 52 and me when I asked him to move things he had stored downstairs to open up space for the kitchen.

Despite his objections, I kept working on the renovations, mostly by myself. Even if we stayed together, we needed the money that could come from utilizing the space.

Sometimes I also toyed with simply moving downstairs myself, making it a separate apartment. It would be a way to move away from 52 without leaving the farm. After all, I couldn't force him to leave, so even if I ever managed to overcome all the other obstacles to taking over the farm on my own, I might never have the chance. If I just moved downstairs, I could get away from all his browbeating. Might as well paint the place and pretty it up.

Maybe down deep 52 recognized that potential, too, because his objections never made sense otherwise, especially after I offered to pay half for a nice outdoor storage building where he could store his workbench and tools. He agreed to put in the other half for the building and move his things, but not without a lot of angry tirades. He ended up with a nice little building, but I don't think he was ever happy about it.

I would have paid for the whole building, but I didn't think that would make him any happier.

At this point, I couldn't think of anything that would make him happy. And he was about to get unhappier.

Debbie had been coming to clean the house for me for three months when he caught me.

He left for work every day at 8 A.M.

Except when he didn't.

Debbie came every other Tuesday at nine.

He'd noticed the house was cleaner and had complimented me several times and thanked me for keeping the house clean. He was, between bouts of anger, very polite.

One Tuesday morning, he woke late and decided not to go to work. Debbie drove up the driveway in her big blue pickup truck.

52 and I were sitting on the porch drinking coffee. I was waiting for the sky to fall.

He said, "Who's that?"

By this time, Debbie was out of her truck holding her mop and pail, ready to start coming up the steps.

I said, "That's Debbie. She's the cleaning lady."

The sky didn't fall, of course, until she left. 52 would never misbehave in front of other people.

When she was gone, he said, "It's ridiculous for you to have a cleaning lady."

I said, "I work hard. I need the help."

"It's a waste of money."

"I pay my half of the mortgage and the second mortgage, and I pay all the bills for the house and the farm," I said. "What I do with my spare money after that is none of your business."

"I need money," he said. "If you have extra money, then give it to me."

"I'm trying to help you. That's why I took over the bills here."

"I need money," he repeated.

"For what?"

"Gas."

"You have all the money that you're not using to pay your half of the bills here," I pointed out.

I tried to not ever mention that I was paying the bills because I knew he was sensitive about it, although he'd been quick to let me do it. I didn't want to rub it in or hold it over his head. All I really wanted was for him to be nice to me, but obviously I couldn't buy that.

Giving him gas money wouldn't make him be nice to me either, and I resented the demand. I worked my tail off to pay all the bills and if I had extra that I could use to hire a cleaning lady to make my life a little bit easier, I wasn't going to stop so I could give that money to him, too.

"Then pay me to clean the house," he said.

I blinked. "Pay you to clean the house?"

"Yes. If you're going to pay someone to clean the house, pay me."

"I'm not going to pay you to clean your own house! You live here! If you want to clean it, go ahead! I'm not going to pay you."

He'd said a lot of outrageous things to me, but this one really took the cake.

"Are you not embarrassed to ask me to pay you to clean the house?" I asked, dumbfounded.

"No," he said. "You should pay me to chop firewood, too."

I thought a lot about hiring a man to do things around the farm, but I wasn't going to hire 52. He owned half the farm. Besides, if 52 ever left and I got a hired man someday, I'd expect him to be nice to me.

I couldn't pay 52 enough to get him to do that.

I said, "I'm not paying you to do anything around here any more than you pay me. You don't get paid to take care of your own place. If you want to clean houses for extra money, put up a flyer at the post office. That's how I found Debbie."

"You're just selfish, you know that?" he said. "You're selfish, selfish, selfish."

He was off and running. I was pretty good at going off myself—into my own world. My latest project was developing a more open crumb, an airy texture with holes, to my breads.

"Your readers think you're so wonderful—"

I'd been experimenting with longer rise times, then I'd worked with the sponge method.

"—but you're not."

I tried adding vital wheat gluten to recipes too. A wetter dough also seemed to help.

"You're selfish, selfish, selfish."

I could plan out entire new recipes while he went on.

And maybe he knew I wasn't really listening. Probably. Especially since I never responded once he got rolling. But the ranting would quadruple if I dared walk out while he was in the midst of a tirade.

At least I made up a lot of good recipe ideas that way. It was also a good time to come up with cute animal stories or ponder a new craft project.

But by the time he wound down and it was safe to get up and

walk away, even though I tried really hard to not listen, I felt like I'd been run over by a couple of out-of-control 18-wheelers.

I was never sure if he truly understood how exhausting the farm was for me. He left for work at 8 A.M. and often didn't get home until after 7 P.M. or later from his job. When he'd built a new milk stand for me near the house, he'd built it at the base of a ravine in the hillside that stretched out above the plateau where the house, goat yard, and upper cow pasture were located. When it rained, water poured down the hillside in that cut in the hill—right into the milk stand. The ground grew muddy in the spring and never dried up because Beulah Petunia's constant stomping in and out of the stand kept it churned up.

Eventually, I couldn't walk to the milk stand because of the mud. One day, one of my boots was sucked right off when I stepped in it. It would take me so long to get through the mud to the stand that Beulah Petunia would attack the feed bucket before I could get in there. Electric fence wire separated the cow pasture from the yard to the side of the house. The milk stand backed up to the ravine and the hillside, making it difficult for Beulah Petunia to get around there, so I started hiking up the steep hillside to the back of the milk stand, carrying the milk pail and a five-gallon bucket full of feed. From there, I'd duck under the electric wire and climb over the back of the milk stand, avoiding the mud.

By the time I milked, then did this all in reverse, with a pail full of milk, I was worn out. And I hadn't even had breakfast yet. But I loved milking, so I kept doing it until it occurred to me to give up the milk stand completely. I started milking Beulah Petunia wherever it was dry, in the side yard, up beside the house, in the goat yard. I never used the milk stand again. Constantly changing milking locations came with its own problems, but at least I wasn't clambering up a steep hillside.

I knew our farm was more difficult than it had to be, but I didn't know how to get to the solution. I would need hired help to make the various construction modifications that the farm desperately required. When I'd asked 52 to make steps in the hillside

so I could get around to the back of the milk stand without so much
fear of falling on the steep, slippery hillside, he'd chopped out a
few shallow steps in the ground. The steps were so shallow, I gave
them up immediately because they were more dangerous than the
hillside itself. I didn't think he understood my problem, but then
he wasn't clambering up the hillside carrying buckets and pails,
and he didn't seem to care that I was. Sometimes I felt sure it was
all designed to drive me away—the ranting, leaving the burden of
the bills to me, neglecting to fix problems on the farm that made
my chores difficult or dangerous. I didn't think he wanted to take
responsibility for walking away, but I didn't put it past him to
make my life so impossible that I would do the walking away for
him. Anyone with half a brain would have given up in my circumstances. I persisted. If he was trying to drive me away, he'd under-
estimated my love for the farm.

He'd also do incredibly nice things for me out of the blue,
which would leave me confused all over again. I couldn't figure
out if he loved me or hated me.

I was thrilled to get out of town for a week. In the spring, I
took Morgan, Weston, and Weston's girlfriend on a trip to South
Carolina to visit Ross while he was in between A school and power
school. I turned Glory Bee in with Beulah Petunia and ran away
from home.

Because I was hopeless this way, I missed 52 while I was gone. I
didn't really want him to leave. What I wanted most of all was for
us to be happy together on the farm, the way we'd dreamed when
we bought it. By the time I got back, I couldn't wait to see him and
tell him all about our trip. I waited for him on the porch.

He came home from work, kissed me, and told me that he'd
missed me.

I launched into a tale from our trip, eager to tell him everything. I got out about two sentences.

52 cut in to say, "I don't want to hear a long story."

I burst into tears.

He hadn't had to listen to me speak for a week, yet within two sentences, his patience with my conversation was exhausted.

He felt badly and told me so, and I believed him. He did feel ashamed for cutting me off and making me cry. I think he even truly missed me.

But that didn't diminish the fact that he couldn't stand to be around me, even if he wished that were different, and worse, he couldn't control his behavior in response.

And it wouldn't be long before he'd be ranting at me about how selfish I was, demanding I give him money, or blowing up if I made too much noise in the kitchen.

We'd been at the farm for three years. Spring was tumbling fast toward summer. After summer came fall, and after fall . . . Before I knew it, I'd be trapped with him for another winter.

If I was ever going to separate from him, it had to be in the summer, by my thinking. By fall it would be late, and by winter, it would be too late. I had to have time to prepare for winter alone on the farm. Only I couldn't figure out how to adequately prepare to manage the farm alone in any season, much less winter.

"Does it make me a terrible person that I live with him, but I spend all my time trying to figure out how to live without him?" I asked Sheryl.

My cousin's wife was used to these philosophical questions about my relationship with 52. She was a good listener, a good hand patter, but she couldn't solve my problem.

"No, it doesn't make you a terrible person," she said. "He could be nicer to you, then it wouldn't be an issue."

"He's not going to be nicer to me."

"Then you have to do what you have to do," she said plainly. "There's no point feeling bad about it. You have to survive. And the way he treats you, he may be thinking the same thing and just doesn't know how to get out of it."

I had no idea what he was thinking, but I'd given him plenty of chances to get out of it. By this time it had been a year and a half since we'd had an intimate relationship, but every time I broached the subject, asking if he wanted our relationship to be over, he told me no. I wasn't sure what his idea of a relationship was, but I thought it had been over for a long time.

We weren't married, and we didn't have sex.

We were co-owners on a farm, period.

Yet no matter how I tried to establish this truth about our relationship, he wouldn't admit it or accept it. I thought maybe if he stopped thinking of me as his girlfriend, he'd treat me like he treated everybody else—politely. Only I couldn't get him to admit I hadn't been his girlfriend for a year and a half.

He kissed me every day before he went to work, and he kissed me when he came home. Half the time he followed that up with an evening ranting session, but he liked following certain rigid structures, and the kiss was part of it. He'd have a fit if I didn't say good night before I went to bed, and good morning when I saw him in the morning. If I said, "I'm going to bed," but forgot to add "good night" at the end of it, he'd even come flip on the light, stand over the bed, and berate me for not saying good night. As a creative person, his regimented behaviors left me baffled, but I tried to comply because I didn't like the consequences if I didn't.

Weston graduated from high school that spring, having achieved his National Merit Scholarship and a full ride to West Virginia University. He and Morgan went away for the summer, and I started sleeping downstairs. I was still fixing it up and working on my downstairs kitchen dream of workshops and farm stays, though I'd run into a few major obstacles with the county health department. We had well water, which was the biggest problem. To give cooking, even cheese making, workshops, or any workshop that involved food or where I wanted to provide a lunch, I had to have a health-department-approved kitchen, and the health department wouldn't approve well water unless I jumped through some complex hoops. I'd have to install an in-line UV water filter, and do tests and make reports regularly. To do the tests, I'd have to get a sanitation certification. There was hurdle after hurdle, and they were all expensive.

The prospects of ever achieving my dream of workshops and farm stays downstairs in our house starting looking pretty dim, but I was determined to persevere. I was a sucker for the pursuit of lost causes and, mostly, desperate. I was also overwhelmed.

The Chickens in the Road Retreat was coming up at the end of the summer, and the preparations were massive. I'd never thrown such a huge event before, lasting several days, and the organization was time-consuming. I'd decided to book-end the retreat with the annual fall Party on the Farm, which would be bigger than ever. I sold spots at the retreat through my website.

My website had come a long way. It had started as a blog about a farm but had grown to much more. The CITR forum was active, and I'd added a separate recipe community, Farm Bell Recipes. I'd been doing the Party on the Farm, inviting readers out for a day of food and demonstrations, since our first year on the farm, but adding the retreat along with it was a big step.

Most of the time, I did okay with my monthly income from advertising, but advertising was a risky and changing business, based on a shaky up-and-down economy. Some months, I still struggled, especially since I'd taken on most of the financial responsibility of the farm. Other months, I made extra money. In any case, I always somehow made ends meet, and Debbie kept coming every other Tuesday.

One month I had enough extra money to splurge on a milking machine. It wasn't very Jane, but it definitely helped me get more done in a day as I was never a very fast hand milker.

I had an idea to create a "duck 'n' buck" yard to house the male goats and halfway—and more safely—free-range the ducks, fencing a field around the pond. I also wanted a barn, and 52 was keen on the idea of building one from pallets. He loved pallets, which he collected for free from stores eager to get rid of them, and he'd used them in several projects on the farm. Enthusiastic about a large pallet project, he started collecting more pallets right away while still finding time to build a fenced herb garden for me with a gate. (The gate was made from a pallet, of course.) The only thing I had against the pallets was that they were never weather protected. After just a few years on the farm, things he'd built with pallets were already beginning to fall apart.

But he enjoyed building things, and he was usually in a good humor when he was involved in a project. Sometimes I still thought we might actually make it. Things were going to miraculously turn around!

Most of the time, though, I knew we wouldn't make it, and my fear of losing the farm grew more intense. I had trouble sleeping at night.

I found myself stretched out on the couch some days, staring at the ceiling, wondering what I was doing with my life, just as I had at the Slanted Little House a few years before. I had convinced myself I could take 52's abuse for the sake of the farm that I loved, but I felt as if I were dying inside. I knew I wasn't perfect, but I didn't deserve his attacks—and I didn't know how to stop them. I rarely responded to them for fear of escalating any given situation. I didn't want the kids to hear any conflict, but my silences only gave him more room to go on. In front of the kids, or anyone else, 52 was the picture of polite perfection.

Occasionally, I couldn't resist the deep-seated urge to tell him where to stick it, and I was afraid that eventually my self-control was going to crack and I was going to tell him to leave.

My life, my business, everything, depended on the farm—and 52's help to survive there. I recognized my own responsibility. For the farm and for my business, I made a pact with the devil every day.

I liked challenge, but living with 52's abuse was becoming more than I could take. Taking on more and more challenges on the farm kept me focused away from my depression and looking forward in positive ways.

I'd created challenge for myself in various ways during my life, including relentlessly attempting to sell books to New York publishers back in my romance days. Now *that's* difficult. I didn't have to do that, but I would have been bored if I hadn't and would have taken up mountain climbing or something. People left farming in droves decades ago, in part because it's difficult. Difficult was, in part, what attracted me to farm life.

Which didn't mean that sometimes it wasn't difficult to embrace the difficulty. But then, if it weren't, I wouldn't have wanted to do it. Similar to people who really do go mountain climbing. Part of the attraction is the risk, and if it wasn't risky, they wouldn't enjoy it as much, even if sometimes they were scared.

If everything about living on a farm were easy, there wouldn't be nearly as much satisfaction in it. And even on the worst day, when that farm was harder than it had to be and I'd had just about all the satisfaction I could stand, I wouldn't have traded one minute of it for anything easier.

I loved that cold, muddy, hard life. And while there are probably as many reasons why people move to the country as there are people, I believe one reason is because there's not enough innate challenge in the world today. It's too civilized and convenient, and in a world filled with convenience, there's an oddly tempting appeal in inconvenience and the challenge of a more difficult life.

There are other paths to pursue to add challenge to one's life, of course. The farming life is just one—a very special one—of those paths, and it is, like all paths of challenge, not about the destination but the journey.

52, for some reason, was part of that journey for me. I thought about my marriage a lot in comparison to my relationship with 52. I'd left my marriage, looking for happiness and the real me I felt I'd lost along the way.

I was losing myself again with 52 even as I found myself in the farm and West Virginia.

How could I be so happy and so miserable all at the same time?

When I divorced, I still thought I needed a man to take care of me. 52 did less and less to take care of me, often leaving me with bags of feed not where they were supposed to be, buckets of water or heavy hay bales to heft, or any other number of things that were left some distance from where they needed to be. Just as he'd gradually decreased his financial contribution to the farm, he began decreasing his physical contribution. He had his moments when he'd still take on a project like my herb garden or the duck 'n' buck yard—as long as I paid for the materials—and he'd happily started collecting pallets for our imaginary pallet barn.

But he was progressively "checking out," and I didn't believe there was ever really going to be a barn.

CHAPTER 18

The duck 'n' buck yard was an immediate dismal failure with the bucks escaping repeatedly. Two of the Nigerian bucks had become a problem. Unlike Mr. Cotswold, they were small enough for me to handle, but they could still be quite aggressive. Eclipse, my oldest Nigerian buck, was particularly hard to manage, as was one of his babies by Clover, Pirate (who was full grown then). I had several other bucks and had sold them all except for Eclipse and Pirate.

Eclipse was jet black, with blue eyes from a recessive gene that was somewhat unusual. He was a gorgeous stud. I'd bought him as a baby from Missy, the same place I'd gotten Clover and Nutmeg, my first goats. Pirate looked just like Eclipse, but with a sword-like marking on his side that had led to his moniker. One of the other bucks I'd had at the time was his twin from the same birthing, Sailor, who had a white top knot like a sailor's cap. Sailor had inherited the blue eyes from Eclipse, but he was gentle and sweet.

Eclipse and Pirate were a constant nuisance, escaping from the buck yard, breaking into the yard with the does and chasing them around until they were hiding under the goat house or risking life and limb jumping up on things to get away from their aggressive suitors. I risked life and limb tackling Eclipse and Pirate (they had horns) to capture them and get them out of the yard. I had decided to keep only Mr. Pibb, my Fainter buck, and if Eclipse and Pirate got to the does, I wouldn't know who was the papa if they were bred and wouldn't be able to properly register the babies or even tell potential buyers what their lineage was, if they were half Fainter (from Mr. Pibb) or pure Nigerian.

The goats didn't go with a very high price, and those two were so aggressive, I didn't think it would be fair to sell them without a warning label. As difficult as it had been to find homes for sweet Sailor and the other bucks, finding homes for a couple of "bad" bucks would be nigh upon impossible. They were worth more as meat to feed my family. I was trying to operate a self-sustaining farm, wasn't I?

Butchering the pigs had seemed easy. I'd had little to do with the pigs. I didn't feel as if I knew them personally. The goats were different. They were full of personality and spunk, and I spent a lot of time with them.

I decided to take Eclipse and Pirate to the butcher.

I asked 52 if he would eat the meat if I had Eclipse and Pirate butchered. He said, "Yes."

But he didn't want to take them to the butcher for me. I knew that I was going to have to take responsibility for what I planned to do. He helped me load the bucks in a crate in the back of my Explorer.

I took off for the butcher, which was over an hour's drive from our farm. Eclipse and Pirate were noisy all the way, making bleats from the back. When I arrived at the butcher shop, the butcher shop man had me back the Explorer up to a sliding door that led to holding pens. The man helped me unload the goats. Eclipse and Pirate locked eyes on me, bleating in fear.

Turning away from them was painful. I walked through the office door of the shop. I sat down at the desk and the attendant said, "How do you want them cut up?"

I thought about running outside and putting Eclipse and Pirate back in the crate in the Explorer.

Then I thought about how aggressive they were, how Eclipse had nearly gored me a few times with his horns when he'd broken into the goat yard and I'd caught him chasing the does, and how difficult it would be to sell them.

"Mostly ground," I said.

A few days later, the meat was ready. Eclipse and Pirate came home in vacuum-sealed plastic packages. There were a few small roasts, but as I'd requested, most of the meat was ground.

I put the meat in the freezer, keeping out a pound of the ground. I cut open the package. It looked pretty much like ground beef, red. I dumped it in a skillet, getting ready to make spaghetti. I turned on the burner, and the meat began to sizzle.

The buck scent hit me. Like with a pig, other types of livestock that are intended for butchering are often neutered (in the case of goats, it's called wethered) so that the meat doesn't take on a smell. I wondered if the meat would be edible.

I also wondered if Eclipse was going to jump right out of the pan. Smelling his scent made me feel as if he were right there on top of the stove.

Using a spatula, I broke up the meat, trying to shake off the feeling that Eclipse was about to leap out of the skillet at me. Gradually, the buck smell faded until it dissipated completely.

By the time the meat was cooked through, I couldn't smell it at all.

Over the weeks and months that followed, I cooked with goat meat often. Goat burgers became one of my favorite things. Goat meat, like lamb, is flavorful. I found it to be delicious. Beef, particularly store-bought beef, is bland in comparison. Whenever anyone asks me what goat meat tastes like, I tell them like a cross between pasture-raised beef and lamb, which is the closest I can come to describing it. Goat meat tastes like goat meat.

I decided to wether and raise all future male goat babies for meat. I loved my female goats, and they had a useful purpose as milkers and breeders, and girl babies were relatively easy to sell, but I knew I'd never see anything again but goat burgers when they popped out a boy, and as difficult as it had been to take Eclipse and

Pirate to the butcher, I felt good about it. I wasn't a vegetarian. I ate meat. A farm meant I had the opportunity to raise my own. Pirate and Eclipse had a good life—and one bad day, which was more than one could say for animals in most factory or mass agri operations where meat from the grocery store originates. Eclipse and Pirate lived natural lives on green grass in the fresh air with petting and cookies. This wasn't anonymous meat wrapped in plastic on a foam tray. I found myself feeling differently about how I cooked and how I ate. Eliminating waste by portioning carefully became more important. To scrape meat off a plate to the dog bowl or in the trash suddenly seemed almost criminal. I had a new respect for my food. Eclipse and Pirate were sustaining my family with their bodies, and I felt a great obligation to honor that in the meals I prepared and how I treated those meals. We're often so nonchalant as a society about tossing leftovers. When we grow our own food, and raise our own meat, it changes how our minds work. I wanted to embrace that change in myself.

I'd looked in the eyes of the meat I was putting on my plate. It was a connection with my food, and a responsibility to it, that felt right and honest.

There was something both hard and beautiful in it, and as with every other step I'd taken toward a more real life, I didn't want to go back.

In moving out the Nigerian bucks, I'd also tightened my goat herd. I'd just kept one buck as my herd sire. Mr. Pibb, my Fainter buck. As whip smart as Nigerians were (which, in the bucks, could translate to aggression), the Fainters were gentle souls, even the buck. I had two Fainter does, which would produce purebred Fainter babies with Mr. Pibb, along with my Nigerian does, who would be giving birth to crossbreeds. I'd discovered that I could register the Fainter-Nigerian crossbreeds as 50 percent myotonic (the gene that makes them "faint" or actually stiffen and sometimes fall over when startled) with the Myotonic Goat Registry (the Fainter association). My streamlined herd would be easier to care for on my own in my imaginary 52-less future. I could keep them together in one field, running the buck with the does full-time.

I needed to cut the sheep flock, too. I'd never gone into a field alone with Mr. Cotswold again, and never without a stick or something for protection even when 52 was with me. I wanted to keep a couple of the ewes, including my "pet" Annabelle, the "puppy" I'd bottle-fed on the porch our first year on the farm. I also planned to keep one of the Cotswold-Jacob cross ewes. They were young, and they'd both recently lambed. I'd keep their babies, too.

52 liked the sheep more than I did. I had to convince him that the ram and older ewes needed to go, but finally one evening he agreed to let me give them away. They were all too old to butcher, so that wasn't even a question.

I put up an ad on Craigslist and by the time 52 woke up the next morning, I had a new home for Mr. Cotswold and the older ewes. I was afraid to give 52 time to change his mind, or time to ponder why I was so bent on getting rid of the more unmanageable or purposeless sheep.

It was like I was constantly dressing up for a party that wasn't happening because I couldn't figure out how to actually manage the farm on my own. But I never missed Mr. Cotswold for a second.

I drove to Spencer one day to meet a friend for lunch, a rare outing for me by that point. I stopped in at the Farm Service Agency afterward, then picked up a few staple groceries at Walmart. I didn't have to do much shopping anymore. We grew or made most of what we needed. On the way home, I swung by Georgia's house. I'd made some apple butter and had a jar for her.

After knocking on her door, as usual, I just walked in. She was sitting in her chair. I brought her a spoon from the kitchen and gave her the jar.

She'd come across some things while sorting papers that she'd set aside for me to look at, and she had them waiting on the table by her chair. She enjoyed my visits and often saved things to show me. One of those things that day was an old newspaper.

It was the December 1, 1960, edition of the county paper. She'd wanted me to see it because it had an article about the hard-won election to the sheriff's office of my great-uncle C.W. "Doc" Dye.

Back then, the paper cost five cents.

The article about my great-uncle was actually kind of boring, but the newspaper was fascinating. The movie showing at the Robey that week was *Elmer Gantry*. There was a big advertisement.

> "BLESS HIM! DAMN HIM! Tens of thousands of believers shouted his praises! Three women damned his soul!" Starring: Burt Lancaster and Jean Simmons. Costarring Shirley Jones.

The Robey disclaimer:

> The Management of the Robey Theatre DOES NOT Recommend This Movie for Anyone under 16.

This must have been before standardized ratings.

The classifieds were pretty interesting, too. There was a listing for a 1947 Dodge sedan. The phone number to inquire was only three numbers. 291.

The headlines were about the recent presidential election. Nixon beat Kennedy in Roane County. The local news was more interesting. A bizarre accident was reported (not to mention the bizarre reporting).

> Miss Penny Stephens, a Dental Hygiene student at West Liberty State College and the daughter of Mr. and Mrs. J. Stewart Stephens of Parkersburg Road, Spencer, suffered painful, but not serious injuries when she fell from an automobile near West Liberty Wednesday of last week. She was on her way here for the Thanksgiving holiday. The car door flew open on a curve and Miss Stephens careened to the roadway. The vehicle was traveling very slowly when the

mishap occurred, but Miss Stephens was bruised nearly all over from her shoulders to her knees.

"I think somebody pushed her, Georgia. Don't you?"

Georgia laughed. This was really why she saved things for me, I think. She'd set things aside, then wait for me to come over and start making up stories.

The county extension agent's column was about apple pie. "What can be a better choice for this season of the year than the tangy goodness of a fresh apple pie?" The column went on to suggest that the secret of perfect pastry is a package of your favorite piecrust mix.

"What is wrong with these people?" I asked Georgia. I was almost ready to throw the paper down. "A piecrust mix? That's shameful!"

"It is?" Georgia said.

"You've never used a piecrust mix in your life."

"Well." She looked a little secretive, making me wonder if she'd been sneaking around with piecrust mixes.

And then I found the personals, and that was no time to throw the paper down. This wasn't "single white female" stuff. This was 1960s personals. Gossip.

> Mr. Ralph Carper of Walton was attending to business affairs in town last Wednesday.

In case Mrs. Carper was wondering where he was.

> Mr. and Mrs. John Dye and son Carson were visiting in Akron, Ohio, this past week with Mr. and Mrs. H. E. Young.

John Dye was one of my dad's cousins.

> Mr. and Mrs. Clay Miller will leave Thursday for a two-week Caribbean cruise.

Bragging! And, oh, for the innocence of December 1960 when this didn't represent an invitation to burglary.

> Mr. and Mrs. Cecil Moss and grandchildren of Newton were shopping in town last Friday.

And on and on, an entire half page of trivial gossip.
"How does this sound?" I said to Georgia.

> Ms. Suzanne McMinn of Walton lunched in Spencer on Friday then attended to some business affairs followed by shopping. Then she ate some pie and went to bed.

"You have pie?" Georgia asked.
"I'm making one when I get home. Then I'm so sending that to the paper."
Georgia said, "Well." Which meant she wished I'd made the pie before I came over.

Glory Bee was eight months old that summer and still not weaned. Sometimes she even managed to break out of the goat yard to get to mommy, who was in the field beyond the house. Beulah Petunia was always glad to see her. They'd take off for the hinterlands of the partially wooded cow pasture, clutching plane tickets in one hoof and hastily packed suitcases in the others.

Glory Bee broke out so frequently, I actually became adept at getting her back to the goat yard by myself, which I considered a big accomplishment. We tried putting her in the bottom pasture, but that made things even worse. She broke out one day and ended up in the Ornery Angel's yard. I figured it was better to keep her closer to the house. If she escaped from the goat yard, at least I knew where she'd go—to her mama. If she broke out from the bottomland, she might go anywhere, including up and down the road.

I was down to milking Beulah Petunia once a day. I'd had a milk cow for over a year. I defined my life in the country into precow and postcow. A cow is a life-altering event, an experience that will push you, even when you're tired, and make you grow. A cow will test your will and take you on a daily adventure. You will handle a thousand-pound animal every day. The most surprising part of it all was that I loved every minute of having a cow. Even as I streamlined and reduced in other areas on the farm, my commitment to my cows never wavered. I was obsessed with getting Beulah Petunia bred.

I explained it all to my cow. She started picking through her wardrobe, polishing her nails, getting her hair done, spraying on perfume.

Or something like that.

I researched cow heat cycles and started studying Beulah Petunia's "flower petals" twice daily, looking for signs. A cow goes into heat approximately every twenty-one days and is in heat for about thirty hours. The peak fertile period is in the middle of this time and is called standing heat. When cows first go into heat, they may not stand for a bull. Which, you know, gives you time to go find one. But you can't wait too long because before you know it they will be out of heat. We would be taking Beulah Petunia across the river to Skip's farm.

There's nothing like getting all up close and personal with a cow and her flower petals. The "petals" are right under certain other parts. Did you know that cows moo from both ends? Really, the things you learn when you start spending quality time with your cow's flower petals.

One morning, Beulah Petunia came up for her feed early. After she'd been milked, instead of disappearing back to the hinterlands as usual, she stayed up at the gate to her field. Bawling. Angry mooing. For like two hours. I thought, *Wow, she sure is being mean today.* Then—lightbulb!

I had forgotten to even check her that day, slacking on my petal patrol. So I grabbed my chore boots and ran out to her. She looked red and swollen in the important parts, and I thought she was in heat.

I e-mailed 52 at work, and he said he'd come home to help me take her to the bull.

Beulah Petunia started going through her dresses, tossing clothes left and right, trying to decide what to wear. By the time 52 got home, she was adorned with a bright pink blossom behind her ear, attached to her halter. Simple. Understated. It said, *I'm happy to be here and this is special*, without also saying, *Overeager and needy*.

Or at least that's what Beulah Petunia and I thought.

Or possibly just me. I was so excited, you would have thought I was the one headed for a date.

It was only one mile to Skip's farm, but it was a long mile. I'd been going to Skip's farm all my life, but I'd never gone there with a cow. Back in my father's day, Skip's farm was part of my great-grandfather's larger farm that went all up and down the road across the river from Stringtown Rising, and my father took me there often when I was a little girl. By the time I was in my twenties, Skip owned it, and together with my father and subsequently my own children when they were little, I'd been visiting Skip for years when we took the "family history" tour on trips to West Virginia.

When we were walking Beulah Petunia over there, I had a moment where I thought back to all the times I'd gone to Skip's farm in the past and how I would never, and I mean never, have imagined that I would one day live across the river and down the road from Skip and be taking my cow to his bull.

One time when we were visiting Skip, my (crazy) father wanted to walk way, way up to a big open meadow on the hill above the house. Skip would always say, sure, go wherever you want, when we came calling. A bull came running in the meadow and we were all clambering down a steep cliff, hanging on to tree trunks not to fall, to the creek far, far below to get away from the bull. And now I was headed there in search of a bull.

While it was a mile by the road from our farm to Skip's, Skip suggested it might be shorter if we took her up the road to the family cemetery, over the hill, and across the river that way.

If it was shorter, it was maybe shorter by nothing. It felt like twenty miles and involved climbing. But then, going a mile anywhere in West Virginia feels like twenty miles. We took her down the driveway, out the road, and up the steep, rough road to the cemetery.

We passed through a sunny field of daisies and into a shady path of enchantment as we crossed the hill. Beulah Petunia kept wanting to stop and eat and eat and eat Skip's tall, tall grass. 52 held her on the lead while I followed behind with a switch to keep her going. I didn't like to swat her, so that was a bad job. I swatted her really gently, and she didn't really care, so sometimes I had to push her on her rump.

We finally came down and out toward the river and found the crossing by Skip's sawmill. We took Beulah Petunia across the river and to the road and on to Skip's paddock. Beulah Petunia bawled and bawled, letting the bull know she had arrived. She was thirsty after all that exercise, and when we let her out of the paddock and into the pasture, she went straight for the creek. From there, she started walking up the creek, into the shaded distance, and then . . . she was gone.

I could hardly stand it. My cow! I didn't want to leave. I wanted to go after her, camp out, watch over her, see the action. But it didn't really seem practical. Beulah Petunia was a big girl. She knew where she was going and she wanted to go there.

The late report that night from Skip was that the bull checked her out but didn't mount her. Had he not seen her flower?

It was my first clue that getting a cow pregnant wasn't going to be that easy.

I left Beulah Petunia over at Skip's farm for two days, and by the end of that time, I was feeling a little frustrated, not sure what was going on or what I should do about it. Even as I was contemplating that conundrum, I was also wondering how I was even going to find my cow on Skip's big farm full of sunny meadows, shaded creeks, nooks and crannies, and . . . cows.

The last time I'd seen Beulah Petunia, she was disappearing into the woods following a creek. I went back, passed through the paddock and into the field above the creek, looked up at the hill where I knew lay a huge open meadow full of tall, tall grass . . . and called her name, feeling a little hopeless. I figured I was about to take an (arduous!) hike all over Skip's farm looking for my cow—who was in serious need of milking.

I heard a cow answer me. I thought it was her, but—I didn't have a bunch of cows. Maybe they all sounded the same. I called her again, twice, and—

She came right out to the edge of that sunny meadow, looked down at me, and started coming.

I couldn't believe it. I'd arrived at this big farm and called my cow. And here she came!

She plodded in her slow, sure, methodical way, straight for me, off the hilltop and down the bank.

My cow!

She loved me.

Or she thought I might have some goodies.

Anyway, she came!

And she was still wearing her flower!

I didn't know anything about her *other* flower. Using a bucket, I hand-milked her on the spot. The ground was uneven and she stepped in the bucket, but she seemed happy to be relieved. The next evening, we went back with the milking machine and a generator set up on the back of 52's truck to run the vacuum pump by the paddock. I shifted her around to an evening milking schedule since that was when 52 could help me by bringing his truck with the milking machine on it.

A few evenings later, when I went to Skip's farm to milk her, she had company: Skip's Black Angus—Gelbvieh cross bull. There was a lot of nuzzling going on.

I was a bit freaked out. How was I going to milk? The bull, whose name was Adam, seemed a little concerned we were going to take away his Eve, and he went to work. Which freaked me out even more and I had to watch. And take photos. And go home and enlarge the photos so I could see if he was *getting in there*. He *was*.

52 ran the bull out of the paddock so I could milk, which I could barely accomplish after being blinded by the salacious activity. The bull waited up on the hill until Beulah Petunia was once again available.

The next day, thinking she was surely bred, I brought Skip a loaf of homemade bread and a jar of apple butter and took Beulah Petunia home. This time, 52 drove me to Skip's and I took my cow by her lead and walked her home on the road, instead of over the hill, with 52 following behind me in his truck.

Walking down a country road leading a cow was one of those events that made me feel like a little girl playing dress-up in farmer clothes, or maybe as if I were wandering on foot through a children's storybook. Beulah Petunia *clip-clopped* down the road by my side, the sun shining down, the air filled with birdsong. It was a mile to the river ford. Across the ford, she could hear Glory Bee mooing from the top of the hill, and she knew she was home.

I marked the calendar and started the clock.

Three weeks later, she was in heat again. It was the summer of Beulah Petunia and Skip's bull, and we spent a lot of time going back and forth across the ford, not just with the cow, but taking feed to the cow and milking the cow, trying to get her bred.

Our farm was near the river ford, and back in the day, the ford was the center of society here. This tiny spot of civilization in the heart of Appalachia, remote and mostly deserted now, was once a busy teeny tropolis of oil and gas activity that brought money and people to this sideways mountain foothills farmland. Back when my great-great-grandfather first came here, there was no one and nothing. By the time his son, my great-grandfather, was growing up (late 1800s), the boom had arrived. My great-grandfather's house was across the river ford from our farm. He owned over eight hundred acres up and down the halfway paved road across the river. Our dirt road formed a T with that road at the ford.

We were the dirt-rock starving tail falling down from the

half-paved top of that T. The river ford was the connection, then
and now. The ford was still the center of Stringtown. There just
weren't so many people there anymore.

We'd drive across the ford every night to go see Beulah Petunia. I'd scratch her and pet her and remind her that she was my
cow, and half the time when we got back to the ford, someone from
the 'hood was on its banks and we'd stop to shoot the breeze for
an hour.

I loved our 'hood of Stringtown. It was full of family-style
squabbling and family-style help. We were out in the middle of
nowhere, and yet we had a 'hood, centered on the ford, as it had
always been for a hundred years and more. And for a hundred
years and more, not everyone has gotten along, but when someone needed help, the 'hood was there. Every single one of them
had helped us at one time or another, and when we could, we had
helped them. On either side of the property belonging to the
farther members of our 'hood (Sonny on one side, Skip on the
other), you had to drive quite a way to reach the next home. There,
centered on the river ford, was our little community. The ones in
easy walking—or even yelling—distance if you needed help.

And I don't care what they'd say if you asked them ahead of
time, but when the chips were down, even if it was Frank who was
in trouble, every single one of them would be there if they were
called. Country life in that remote holler was just strange and
wonderful that way.

CHAPTER 19

Meanwhile back at the farm, I found raspberries.

When we built the house, a lot of ground was disrupted. I'd looked and looked, hoping for wild blackberries and raspberries, but didn't find any. That summer, while I was trying to get Beulah Petunia bred, I found both—and lots of them. There was a huge patch of blackberries back behind the house, on the hillside between the house and the cow pasture. I found more small patches of wild raspberries every day, up and down the driveway and even up by the house. Once I started looking, they popped up everywhere.

Over the past few years, desperate for my own berries, we'd planted a number of bushes—blackberry (the thornless kind), blueberries, elderberries, and raspberries. I was hoping to get a few berries that summer off those plants—if the chickens didn't get them first.

I was especially excited about the wild raspberries because I wasn't expecting them at all. Wild blackberries were more common around those parts than raspberries, so it felt like magic.

But then, Stringtown Rising was magic in so many ways. Whip poor-wills were rare, too, but we had them and had the rare pleasure of listening to them every spring. Now we had raspberries, too.

I became every bit as obsessed with the berries as I was with Beulah Petunia's love life. Every day, I'd check on my newly discovered magic berries.

I collected them as they ripened for fear the birds would get them if I waited till they were all ripe. It was me against the birds. Every once in a while, I'd find a ripe one that had been half eaten and I knew they'd gotten there before me, but most of the time I'd pull off the plump, juicy berries first. I'd go out collecting every day. It became a little daily ritual, my walk around the farm to all my spots. While I was walking, I'd look for new spots—and sometimes I found them. I found more raspberry patches than I ever imagined the day I found what I thought was just one patch by the driveway. I found more along the driveway, then I found them up by the house, below the driveway, and across the road.

I grew better at finding them along the sunny edges of the woods, and also better at identifying the new canes shooting up first-year growth. I knew where more raspberries would be the next year.

I also grew bolder as my obsession grew. I collected raspberries high. I collected raspberries low. No ripe berry was left behind. I leaped to raspberries along cliffs. I clambered up banks and dived into underbrush and through trees. You had to get down in there because sometimes the berries were hiding.

I'd hear the phone ringing back at the house and I didn't care. I was collecting raspberries.

One of my favorite patches was a huge sprawling patch of both raspberries and blackberries below the driveway, between the driveway and Frank's field. There was about a six-foot steep bank dropping off from the driveway down to a run that drained into the creek. On the other side of the run, the ground sloped down to the fence and the field beyond. I walked along the fence, risking life and limb to reach across the ditch to the berries growing along the steep bank.

The sheep thought it would be funny if I fell in. Or not notice, because sheep don't care much about people. Unless you are carrying a feed bucket.

The flora was exploding on our farm that year. Before the disruption of our construction three years earlier, there had been a previous disruption by loggers when the farm was selectively timbered a few years before we bought it. Our driveway was built by the loggers, and the location of the house was a large cleared area once used as a staging ground by the loggers who spread and graded it, widening the area, which provided space for our garden and goat yard in front of the house. The wide cleared swaths out past the duck 'n' buck yard and out through the cow pasture were originally logging roads.

Because of the loggers, the hillside behind the house was also disrupted quite a bit before we got there and added to the general disruption with our construction. The forest was bursting back. The land was recovering, and it was gorgeous—and filled with berries.

When I'd get all the way down the driveway in my raspberry collecting each day, I'd look up the driveway and barely recognize the entrance to our farm because of the lush growth. Things were starting to look not only settled but well established. My daily walks among the berries were a chance to notice, and to enjoy, and to cross my fingers that it would all last.

52 was on a ranting binge that summer. This meant that the ranting wasn't just sporadic but constant, night after night in a row. He couldn't see me without telling me how selfish I was. One evening, after a particularly lengthy browbeating, I took off my ring when he went down to feed the sheep. We each wore a silver ring on our ring fingers. We didn't have a particular name for the rings. They weren't engagement rings and didn't signify anything other than that we were together. I'd bought the ring for myself and had given a matching one to him for Christmas one year early in our relationship.

I set my ring on his pipe ashtray, where I knew he would see it. It was dark when I drove down the driveway. I didn't know where I was going. I just knew I had to get away. I set off across the river ford, thinking I'd go to Ripley in the next county over, where there were hotels. By the time I got down the road, I decided I was too tired to drive all the way to Ripley. When I got to the highway, I headed back in the direction of the Slanted Little House.

I spent the night in my old bedroom. The house was unlocked, and it was almost as if nothing had changed at all since I'd lived there. My bedding was still on the bed. I woke up in the middle of the night and heard Elvis singing. It freaked me out until I realized the radio had been left on in the cellar porch. My cousin must have been doing something in there that day.

In the morning, I sneaked out without anyone seeing me. I couldn't think of anything to do but go home to 52.

He was up early—and angry. He asked me where I'd been.

"I went to the old farmhouse," I told him.

"You didn't drive out in that direction."

"I didn't know where I was going when I left," I said.

"What are you planning to do?"

I sat down on the porch, shaking. I'd hardly slept, and I was scared for my future. "I don't have a plan."

"You always have a plan. What's your plan?"

I wished I had a real plan. I had hopes and dreams and desperate wishes, fantasies masquerading as plans. I could streamline the animals and take imaginary flights in which I would somehow manage the farm on my own, but a workable plan was nowhere in sight.

"My plan," I told him, "is to stay here as long as I can. It's my home, and it's my children's home."

He sat in his rocking chair, puffing at his pipe. A long beat passed. He was staring straight ahead, at our view across to the hills.

I said, "I'm really disappointed that things have ended this way for us. I think it's time for us to redefine our relationship."

He didn't say anything.

Had I just broken up with him? Another long, long beat passed. I got up and walked inside the house. He had taken my ring from his ashtray and I didn't know where it was. I didn't ask for it back.

The kids were coming home from Texas, and the Chickens in the Road Retreat was looming on the horizon. I got Weston settled into college, started up again with Morgan's sports, and threw myself into the retreat preparations. At first, the mere notion had terrified me. I was going to organize, manage, and host an event bringing in sixty people, providing accommodations, meals, and homesteading-styled workshops over a two-day period? By this time, I'd been throwing a Party on the Farm at Stringtown Rising every fall. I invited any of my readers who wanted to come. And they did, from far and wide and even out of state. I'd ask everyone to bring a dish, and I organized demonstrations of things like cheese making and soap making. The "petting zoo" was open for feeding cookies to the goats, and it was a fun but exhausting time. People never believed me, but I was actually quite shy. Sometimes I spent a good part of the party hiding in the bathroom. I preferred to remain behind my laptop, spinning my stories, but I also knew I needed to connect with my readers face-to-face, and I wanted to be as open as possible with my life and my farm—in spite of the veil I kept over my private secrets.

52 was always helpful with the party, cleaning up the farm, which was usually a mess, so it was our annual "spring" cleaning in the fall. He didn't throw his junk out, but at least he would tidy the piles and stacks. Cindy came ahead of the retreat to help me prepare and stayed for several days following the retreat and the party. She was one of the few people who knew the truth about my relationship with 52. She was smart and practical, and I had come to trust her judgment. The extremely nice and polite veneer 52 presented in front of other people cracked after a few days, and she caught a glimpse of his disdainful treatment of me.

She told me she didn't know how I could stand it. I told her I didn't know how I was standing it either. I couldn't bear the thought of leaving the farm. She encouraged me to find a way out—for me, for my animals, and for my business, but I had no clue what it could be. Winter was coming, and I couldn't survive at Stringtown Rising without 52's help.

After months of working to get Beulah Petunia bred, I was hoping I'd succeeded. I wished Dr. Casto would show up, but the scrapie tests on our sheep had been negative, so we hadn't seen him again. I cast about for an alternative, a country preg checker. As usual, you could find someone willing to undertake any odd farm task if you asked around enough.

Tucker was an older man who worked pipeline when he wasn't poking his entire arm inside a cow for a mere $20. He went in and out of Beulah Petunia's privates about five or six times while I stood by anxiously. He didn't give up easily, but he said he felt nothing in there. Nothing! He punched her side for good measure, and again, came up empty.

Punching a cow's side is an optional method for determining pregnancy. If you know what you're doing, you can feel a calf. I've tried punching cows myself, and any time I do it, I feel the side of a cow (and a sense of guilt for punching a cow). But an experienced cow-puncher knows a calf when he feels it.

I couldn't believe it. How could she not be pregnant by now? I wanted a second opinion and arranged for a vet to pay a visit to the farm. I picked up Morgan after volleyball practice and swung by the vet's office so he could follow me to the farm. It was close to dark, and I knew Beulah Petunia better be ready for him when we arrived. We wouldn't have time to call her up from the hinterlands of her field. She needed to be up at the gate and waiting. I told Morgan to call the house on her cell phone to let 52 know we were on our way. "Tell him to get BP up," I said.

Morgan called the house. 52 answered. Morgan said, "Mom wants you to wake up BP."

Obviously, Morgan hadn't spent much time with the cows.

I imagined 52 out in the field shaking a slumbering cow. "Wake up, BP, wake up!"

I was lucky we didn't roll off the road, I was laughing so hard at her misunderstanding of what I meant when I said I needed 52 to get the cow up. Morgan was a farm girl to a degree and no further. I called her the "donkey whisperer" because she always helped when we moved the donkeys from one field to another. She often helped move the sheep, too, and she was my assistant when I did my annual Christmas photo shoots with Clover, but she was too busy with sports to get involved with the farm on a daily basis, as was Weston. In the summers, when school was out, the kids were with their dad most of the time. They weren't as fascinated with farm life as I was anyway.

I stood by as the vet pulled on the long gloves. This might sound weird, but I wished it was my arm going in there. I wanted to preg check my cow for myself. The vet told me how if the cow sat down, it could break your arm. That put me off a little or I probably would have gone out and bought long gloves. Or gone somewhere to have my head examined. In any case, after months of back and forthing to Skip's, the vet confirmed that she wasn't bred. I didn't know if she was too old to breed again, or if I'd just gotten my timing repeatedly wrong. Glory Bee was nearly old enough to breed by then, but I was tired of taking cows up the road. Fall had arrived. Winter was around the corner, and no way could I take cows back and forth once the snows hit. I didn't know what I was going to do.

My life as a farmer seemed at a standstill.

Sometimes I felt crushed by the hard work of Stringtown Rising. It could be an act of gymnastics just to get a bale of hay to the cows due to the poor layout and management of the farm. But it wasn't my body that was failing me. It was my spirit.

I'd been strong enough to walk away from an unhealthy marriage, but I thought I was being strong by staying in another unhealthy environment at Stringtown Rising?

Your readers think you're so wonderful, but you're not. You're selfish, selfish, selfish.

52 beat those words and similar ones into my head every time he got a chance. If I halfway opened my mouth, he told me to stop

arguing. Often, he put words in my mouth for me. "I know what you're going to say. You think you're perfect. You think you're right about everything." Then he'd take off again for another twenty minutes, responding to my imaginary statements.

Most of the time, I wasn't even sure what brought on his tirades. They seemed to come out of nowhere or stem from some trivial matter. Eventually I stopped trying to figure it out because I felt like an outsider in an argument that didn't involve me.

I got home late one night from one of Morgan's volleyball games. I had e-mailed 52 just before he left work at five to let him know that I'd be going to the game and would be home late. I sat down with him on the porch, and he asked me if I had watched the game.

I said, "No, I read a book." I'm the worst sports mother in the history of sports mothers. I hate sports.

52 said, "Why did you go up there at five if you weren't going to watch the game?"

I said, "I didn't go up there at five. I went up there at seven because I had concession stand duty for the second half, but they weren't done playing because there were three teams there for some reason and they kept playing games and it was like there were three halfs." I know that halfs is not a proper word, but I think it might be in volleyball.

"Then you shouldn't have gone up there at five."

"I didn't go up there at—"

"Stop arguing with me."

Then I just stopped talking and let him finish explaining how I had to be right about everything and thought I was perfect, and not to mention, how I shouldn't have gone up there at five.

When he wound down, I said good night like a good girl and went to bed.

As I opened the door to go inside, he heaved a great sigh and said, "You know that you are a really frustrating person, don't you?"

I said, "Yes, I know. You've told me."

He'd taught me a lot about West Virginia and country life. He knew his way around a farm, and into the woods. I'd take a photo of a wildflower or a tree and show it to him—and he always knew what it was called. He taught me how to hear the whip-poor-wills and see the spring peepers. He helped me learn to light a wood-stove and milk a cow. He was always willing to hop in his truck and drive me anywhere I wanted to explore, especially if it involved a dirt road or an abandoned outhouse. He'd pull down grapevines for a craft or build me a homemade cheese press.

He'd do everything I asked him to do, no matter how nutty, but he couldn't do the one thing I needed him to *stop* doing. He was driven by his own demons that I never completely understood.

I knew there was a good man inside somewhere. I'd known him, and I'd loved him. I believed he loved me, too, but I brought out the worst in him. I know he thought I was annoying, because he told me so constantly. At least once a week, I asked him where the trash cans were. He'd say, "How can you not remember where the trash cans are? They're in the same place they always are and where I told you they were four days ago." Me: "But then I made up a new recipe and now I can't remember." I was flighty and out of his control.

(No matter how many times he told me that my Explorer was an SUV or a truck, I kept referring to it as my car. Calling an SUV a car, how could anyone be expected to live with that?! And toward the end, I did have to start laughing at that kind of anal-retentive obsession over precision because otherwise, how could anyone be expected to live with that?! Laughing did not improve the situation. Except from my perspective.)

I lost my car keys (precisely, my Explorer keys) one time for a month. Luckily it was winter and I couldn't go anywhere anyway. I searched. He even searched. I can't remember where I found them eventually, but it was like on top of my head, the location was so ridiculously obvious, and I came out on the porch laughing so hard at myself that I had tears rolling down my face. When I got out what I thought was so hilarious, "You're not going to believe where I found my car keys!" he bit my head off, explaining that it wasn't funny at all. And probably using the word *car* didn't help.

Despite the rigidity of my family's beliefs, I was raised with a sense of humor and an appreciation for wacky behavior. My dad's idea of a good joke was to tape a homemade bumper sticker to my mother's car that said, "Honk if you're gay." It was difficult for me to relate to someone who couldn't find humor in absurdity. Or who expected me to remember where the trash cans were, to panic if the goats' water bucket was half full (or half empty), or to always remember to say good night before I fell asleep.

Persistence isn't always a virtue.

I'd thought my tolerance of his behavior was my strength, but it was, in truth, my weakness. I tolerated his abuse because I was afraid of losing the farm and my job. I e-mailed Cindy and told her I was afraid I was about to crack.

"You can have a farm anywhere, Suzanne," Cindy wrote back. "Your readers will follow you."

I'd promised 52 that I would never tell him to leave again, but I'd never promised him that I wouldn't be the one to leave.

I couldn't imagine leaving.

I was sitting on the porch one night in mid-October when he came home from work. I thought it was just another ordinary day until he walked up to the porch from his truck and, without preamble, said, "I'm not going to pay my half of the mortgage and the second mortgage anymore."

The words fell out of my mouth. "I'm moving out."

He said, "Where are you going?"

I felt as stunned as he looked.

I said, "I don't know."

CHAPTER 20

I loved Stringtown Rising Farm in the sentimental crazy way that only a sentimental crazy person like me could love a farm that was one of the most inhospitable, inaccessible, and unmanageable pieces of land on the planet. I loved it anyway, and for my love of it, I stayed there longer than I was happy in my personal situation. I couldn't bear to leave the farm, but that night in mid-October I recognized that I had a responsibility to love myself more than I loved the farm or my job.

I didn't know if 52 meant his words. He'd complained and sometimes refused to pay other bills until I'd taken them over, one by one, by myself. His statement that night about the mortgages might have been nothing more than a ploy, a mind game, a way to get me to take over all the rest of the bills, or even simply the latest way to torment me.

I suspected the latter, but it didn't matter whether he meant the words or not. In the three and a half years I'd lived at Stringtown Rising, I had never been able to imagine leaving, but once those words left his lips, I couldn't imagine staying. I'd always felt as if my life at Stringtown Rising was at risk, but the direct threat was the last straw. Even if—or especially if—he didn't really mean it.

I'd spent a solid year or more going over in my mind if there was any way I could possibly remain at Stringtown Rising on my own. I'd made a series of lists of what I would have to buy, build, change, and hire done (regularly) in order to operate the farm alone were I to buy out 52's half (if I could even come up with the money or if he would even agree). The farm was awkwardly laid out due to the terrain, and in the winter, it was at times barely accessible to completely inaccessible, in or out. There was no mail delivery. No trash pickup. The school bus didn't come. In the winter, the river was often either too high or iced over. The road the other way was narrow, icy, steep, with sharp drop-offs and no guardrails. There were also numerous issues with the well and the water supply that were beyond my ability to personally maintain. There was inadequate fencing, inadequate pasture—how much hay did I want to haul and handle by myself because of the inadequate pasture? How would I replenish the hay and feed supply in the winter? How much would it cost to build more storage for winter? How would I get Morgan to the school bus in the winter? There were often stretches of weeks at a time from January to March when I was afraid to even move my vehicle and could only get myself or Morgan out with 52's help. Would I have to send Morgan away to stay with my cousin for three or four months of the year?

The lists were long, and expensive. Stringtown Rising Farm was an adventure fueled by *man*power. To stay alone, I would have to fuel it with a huge infusion of cash for improvements and hired help, and money couldn't buy everything to make a farm like Stringtown Rising more manageable.

Money couldn't buy out winter.

To remain at such a farm alone was a stupid idea, even if I could afford it, and possibly dangerous for a woman on her own—and I could no longer remain there with 52. Stringtown Rising would have to be put up for sale. I stared down the barrel of my greatest fear, and within it, I found the strength I'd been searching for all along.

I looked for a farm of my own that would provide everything I needed to be independent and safe.

I found it about ten miles away, still in Roane County, West Virginia, in an area known as Clio. It was a hundred-acre farm on a hard road. Not only was it a hard road, there weren't even any potholes. No potholes! There was mail delivery. Mail delivery! And the school bus came—right in front of the house! The house was a small but charming 1930s move-in-ready farmhouse that had been restored and maintained, and it came with free gas to keep me warm in the winter.

There was a separate studio in the back that I could use as my second kitchen for classes and other farm-related events. Under the studio was a large stone cellar. There was a mature cherry tree and several mature apple trees in the yard. On the land were wild raspberries, blackberries, sassafras, ginseng, and morels. There were creeks and springs—and a sunny flat space for a garden.

Much of the hundred acres was cleared (and flat!) and fenced, primed for animals to move right in. There were many different fields with connecting gates to allow for rotational grazing, including huge upper meadows. There was a large field near the house perfect for goats, and it came with a goat house. There was a faucet at the goat field for water—no carrying water! There was a good well, and public water was also available.

There was a vintage but sturdy 1890s red barn with a number of stalls, tack room, and paddock. A couple of the stalls were set up as horse stalls in particular, and some of the fields were fenced specifically for horses. Former owners of the farm had had wild mustangs and Percherons. There was a water faucet at the barn, and electric. There were lights in all the stalls and the alleyway. There was a large hayloft with a winch. It was a farm made for animals. It was a *real farm*—and a manageable one. I knew I could handle it by myself.

With the layout of the farm, there was even a very good likelihood that the chickens would go *in the road*.

One of the first few times I went out to the farm, I noticed there was a telephone pole with a light by the road. I was standing by one of the fields across the road (the farm spanned both sides of the road and held the view in every direction), talking to the owner. I said, "Is that a streetlight?"

He said, "Yes."

"Does it come *on*?" I must have sounded as if I'd just landed from Mars, but there was no such thing as a streetlight anywhere near Stringtown Rising Farm.

He said, "Yes. It comes on automatically every night." Noting my excitement, he added, "There's a light at the barn that comes on automatically every night, too."

"Wow."

On the farm at the time lived two men and the sister of one of the men. She lived in the studio. According to her brother, she was a psychic and had owned a metaphysical shop in nearby Clendenin. After I'd been out to the farm a few times, he told me a story. This beautiful farm had been available for two years. During that time, they'd had many takers. Every time they had an offer, the sister said, "They are not the one." And every time, as she predicted, the deal fell through.

After the first time I visited the farm, the brother told his sister about me, and she said, "She is the one."

That farm had waited for me for two years so that it would be there when I needed it. It was the only farm I went to see, and as soon as I laid eyes on it, I knew I would move heaven and earth to make it mine. It looked like it had fallen off the pages of a children's storybook, and it was everything I'd ever dreamed a farm would be.

Moving heaven and earth mostly involved moving money. I had a retirement account that had been awarded to me in my divorce. Early withdrawal came with huge penalties, which was why I'd never broken into it before. I cleaned it out and made the farm mine.

Planning the move was a huge undertaking. I didn't just have to move my furniture and other things, but animals, too. I called the old farmer, Lonnie, who was a friend of Georgia's. He raised cattle and I knew he had livestock trailers. I planned to move the animals the weekend before I moved my furniture and other things, to get them settled in. Lonnie was up in years. He told me, "I'll be there Saturday if I'm still alive."

I asked him how he was feeling. He said he felt okay. He was still alive that Saturday, and longer after that because he helped me move some hay, too. Life with 52 was uneasy in that month between the time I told him I was moving out and the weekend I started moving the animals. I worried about whether or not he would fight me over the animals, though I felt they were all mine. All the animals that had been purchased had been paid for by me from my personal account or had been given to me as birthday gifts other than some of the chickens. He'd bought chicks at the feed store a few times. The animals that had been free had come through readers from my website who had given them to me. He was moving back to the city and would have no place for the animals anyway, even chickens.

He was at turns sad and angry, but he helped load the animals on the trailer, and he even helped me when I started trying to catch the chickens. There were a few stubborn chickens I never could catch. I asked the Ornery Angel if she wanted to come up to the house with her three kids and take home whatever they could capture. She'd become a good neighbor, if not a friend, and I was sad to leave her and all the neighbors in the 'hood, though I don't think she ever cared one way or another about me, which was how it should have been, of course. Approximately 99.9 percent of our relationship had been in my head.

For the first time, we'd raised a couple dozen meat chickens that year, and our last "farm adventure" at Stringtown Rising was to butcher them. Skip came to help with his homemade plucker. It was also 52's birthday, which made it a strange way to spend the day, but he had chosen the slaughter date. The kitchen was already mostly packed up and I didn't make him a cake, but I did buy him a chocolate cheesecake at the grocery store bakery. I think he just wanted the day to be busy. Or maybe killing chickens as the last new thing we did was some kind of fitting punctuation to our life together.

Before I'd started packing up in earnest, I showed the new farm to Morgan, who didn't yet know that we were moving. I picked her up from the bus after school and told her I was taking her somewhere for a surprise. She bugged me with "What is it? What is it?" for a few minutes, then I asked her if she still wanted a horse. Of course she still wanted a horse. She'd wanted a horse all her life, and for many years she'd taken riding lessons. She started complaining about how she couldn't have a horse because we didn't have enough pasture or fencing or a barn.

I said, "What kind of horse would you have if you could?"

She chattered about different breeds of horses and which were her favorites and why for a few minutes. Then I reminded her that we didn't have enough pasture or fencing or a barn. She told me that I was mean to get her talking about a horse when she couldn't have one.

I suggested that she could put our two miniature donkeys, Jack and Poky, together and they'd add up to a horse!

Then I got her talking about what kind of horse she wanted again, and as soon as she got going good I reminded her that she couldn't have a horse because we didn't have enough pasture or fencing or a barn.

We arrived at the farm, and I pulled over to the side of the road and said, "Look at that! This road is such a nice road, isn't it? It doesn't even have potholes! And look at that! Is that horse fencing? And look, there is a mailbox. And do you know what else they have here? A school bus. And isn't that house cute?"

Then I told her to get out of the car and I walked her up the (short and not steep!) driveway. I said, "Look at that! That's a nice barn, isn't it?"

She said, "Yes. Why are we here? Why couldn't you buy a farm like this one?"

She was completely exasperated. I think she wanted to smack me.

I said, "Look at that house again, Morgan. That is your new house."

She stared at me and said, "What?"

I told her again. "That is your new house. This is your new farm. We are moving here."

She flipped around and looked at the barn again, then she screamed. And she kept screaming and then she was screaming and running—to the barn. Her shoes flew off her feet, and she ended up at the barn door in her socks, and she shouted, "This is my barn!"

She looked inside every stall (after she put her shoes back on). She ran upstairs to the hayloft, then back down to the stalls, examining and inspecting every stall all over again, chattering away about what she would need to clean out the stalls and prepare for a horse. Then she ran out to the fields and up to the hay meadow and just everywhere, running and running and screaming.

One night not long before I finished moving out, 52 and I sat at the fire pit at Stringtown Rising. He was helping me burn some things that I didn't want to pack and weren't suitable to give away.

He put his arm around me. "I'm sorry," he said. "I know I didn't treat you right." He told me that he loved me.

I couldn't tell him that he was wrong about how he'd treated me, but at that point, it felt cruel to tell him that he was right. I said, "I love you, too," because it was true. "We did something amazing here, you know? We made this place a farm."

I knew that he meant his apology, and I also knew he would behave badly all over again if we stayed together. If our relationship had been a romance novel, I could have dug into his past, unearthed his motivations, and even transformed him. That was how I always ended my books. But life isn't a romance novel, and real people are much more complex than fictional characters.

We put our arms around each other and for a long, slow beat, just cried together for a dream we'd shared and lost, and for the best of what we'd had. He was headed back to life in the city, and I was headed for a new farm and a new dream. Though we saw each other a number of times after that, that moment was to me our true good-bye. Before I moved out, he left my ring—and his—beside my laptop one day when I wasn't looking. I took them down to the Pocatalico River and threw them in, pieces of my heart left in Stringtown forever.

We were moved in at the new farm by Thanksgiving, along with Beulah Petunia, Clover, and the whole gang down to the chickens. Georgia sat in the middle of the bustle of friends carrying furniture and boxes into my "new" old house. She still loved an outing, even if she couldn't participate in the activity, so of course she had to be there. I told her that as soon as I could I'd break in the new house by canning some jam and I'd bring her a jar. She said, "Well," which in Georgia-speak that day meant she'd get her spoon ready.

Stringtown would always be rising in my heart, but I knew I had finally become a real farmer since I'd found myself capable of such a difficult decision to make myself an independent woman. I had finally passed the only test that mattered—my own—and I would never have to choose again between my happiness and my farm.

I named my new farm Sassafras Farm. First, the word was just fun to say and made me feel happy. Second, there was sassafras on the hill. Third, I was feeling sassy with a farm all my own.

Stringtown Rising had been a great adventure. It had shaped me, changed me, birthed me as a farmer in fire. It was over, but a new adventure was just beginning.

I put on my chore boots and jumped in.

EPILOGUE

I came "home" to the hills of West Virginia in search of my own strength. I fell hard for the farm, my own piece of those hills, but Stringtown Rising was just a conflict to drive the story, not an ending, as 52 was an antagonist to push me, not a hero. He had his own story, and I was only passing through it.

A friend asked me when I realized that I didn't need a man to take care of me.

I said, "When he stopped taking care of me."

The farm taught me in the same way, providing obstacles that forced me to grow.

I had been a novelist, but I was unused to playing the protagonist in my own story. You never think of your own life that way. We see our lives only a page at a time, as we live day by day. When I came to West Virginia, I didn't realize I was living a coming-of-age story of a woman in her forties, and that the woman was me. I was oblivious to most of my story while it was being written in sweat, tears, and even a little blood. It was nearly over before the plot made sense.

In my first year at Sassafras Farm, I got a horse for Morgan, then I got one for me, a little mare named Shortcake, and I learned to ride her. I remodeled the studio behind the house into a health-department-approved kitchen and began holding workshops. I sent Glory Bee and Beulah Petunia to spend a few months at a friend's farm, and Glory Bee came home bred. I let Beulah Petunia retire. I found a hired man to help fix all the fences, install new gates, recoat the old barn's roof, build a chicken house, and transform one of the barn stalls into the nicest milking parlor I'd ever had—weatherproof with lights and access to water. I planted a new garden of ramps.

Ross gave me his old pickup truck when he bought a new one, and I started driving a stick shift and hauling my own hay. At the hardware store, I learned to buy tools, and at home, I learned to drive the tractor. I had all the plumbing in the house replaced when the pipes froze, and I repainted and decorated the entire house. I met new neighbors and found a new community. I incorporated Chickens in the Road, establishing it as a full-fledged business, and I wrote a book about my adventures at Stringtown Rising.

During that year, Faye's husband passed away. She handled it with her usual tough aplomb. I told her one day, for the first time, how much I had always admired her self-reliance, how she had been one of those courageous, capable women I wanted to be more like.

She said, "You're one of those women now."

I know that I'm writing the next story in my life each day, but I only see it by the page—which is the way life should be lived. It makes us better characters if we don't know where our story is headed.

I rise up on the big pasture from the back of a horse, the farm spread out below and around me, animals dotting the fields. Fences stretch out in neat lines. The automatic light on the barn is just barely beaming bright in the deepening dusk. Supper simmers on the stove in my little house. I hear the bleat of a baby goat and the low moo of my cow. In my heart, I feel peace.

And in my hands, I hold the reins.

ACKNOWLEDGMENTS

With my most heartfelt gratitude:

To my agent, Jenny Bent, for believing in this book before it was written, and my editor, Jeanette Perez, for helping me uncover the vision to complete it.

To Mark, Sheryl, and Georgia Sergent, without whom this story could never have happened. Thank you for letting me live in the Slanted Little House and for always being there for me, and especially to Georgia for being my first and most important inspiration of the self-sufficient country woman I wanted to become.

To my moderators on the Chickens in the Road forum—Pete, Deb, Cindy, Dede, and Astrid—for keeping things running smoothly when I was too busy and who are always there with a listening ear. Extra thanks to Cindy Pierce for teaching me to make soap, making me laugh, and for so many other things, and to Dede Kelly for her wisdom about all types of home preserving and her generosity in sharing it. To Debbie Monroe, for not just being a cleaning lady but becoming a friend. And to "my last five friends," Kat, Kacey, Margery, Michelle, and Vicki, for being there for me for so long.

To all my readers, old and new, for reading—this book is for you.

To all my neighbors, old and new, for still speaking to me after I write about them. Unless they don't know. Then let's not mention it.

To Jerry Waters, for driving that huge truck through the rising waters of the river ford in the rain, without which I couldn't have moved from Stringtown Rising, and for his generosity in taking photos of me and some of my recipes for this book.

To my ex-husband, Gerald, for helping me move from Stringtown Rising and for paving the way on short notice for me to buy Sassafras Farm. To my three children, Ross, Weston, and Morgan, for putting up with me as their mother—for all the times they had to walk miles in the snow because I was too scared to drive, all the times they had to carry wood up to the house for the woodstove, all the times dinner was late because I was photographing it, and for moving to West Virginia with me. To my parents, for loving me when they didn't understand me.

Last but not least, to 52, for teaching me to make fire and milk a cow, and for many other things, including loving me the best he could.

RECIPES

RECIPES

RECIPES

GRANDMOTHER BREAD

My grandmother lived on a farm in Stringtown. When she was a little girl, it was her job to make bread every day. She learned to make bread from her mother, and her mother learned it from her mother before her, and so on. She taught her daughters to make bread, and when my mother came to West Virginia as a young bride, my grandmother taught my mother to make that bread, too.

And then she taught me. When I taught it to Morgan, she dubbed it "Grandmother Bread" because I'd told her that her grandmother had taught me the recipe, and it's been known as Grandmother Bread ever since.

This kind of simple yeast-risen bread is what used to be called "light bread" in the old days. It requires nothing more than water, yeast, sugar, flour, and a dash of salt. And, oh yeah, a great, big pat of real butter when it's sliced.

1½ cups warm water
1 teaspoon yeast
2 tablespoons sugar
Dash of salt
3½ cups all-purpose flour

In a large bowl, combine the water, yeast, and sugar. Let sit 5 minutes. Add a dash of salt and stir in the first 2 cups of flour with a heavy spoon. (You can also use a stand mixer.) Continue adding flour a little at a time, stirring until the dough becomes too stiff to stir easily. Begin kneading, continuing to add flour. The exact amount of flour is approximate—your mileage may vary. Continue adding flour and kneading until the dough is smooth and elastic. Let the dough rise in a greased, covered bowl until doubled (usually 30 minutes to an hour).

Uncover the bowl, sprinkle in a little additional flour, and punch down, lightly kneading the dough again. With floured hands, shape the dough and place in a greased loaf pan. The loaf pans I use are 1½ quarts, 4½ inches by 8½ inches. Cover and let rise another 30 to 60 minutes. Bake for 25 to 30 minutes in a preheated 350°F oven.

PEPPERONI ROLLS

The pepperoni roll, a.k.a. the State Food of West Virginia, is one of those simple things that makes life good. I'd never even heard of a pepperoni roll before moving here, but the testament to the pepperoni roll's popularity in the Mountain State is found in every grocery store, bakery, and even gas station convenience store because the pepperoni roll is sold everywhere as if people might not be able to get down the road without one. As the story goes, pepperoni rolls originated with Italian immigrants who came to West Virginia to work in the coal mines. Rolls filled with pepperoni were easy meals to carry with them into the mines. I experimented for months to come up with a recipe of my own, and it fast became a family favorite in my house.

For the dough:

1½ cups warm water
1 teaspoon yeast
½ teaspoon salt
2 tablespoons sugar
1 teaspoon minced garlic
1 large egg
⅓ cup oil
1 cup chopped pepperoni
½ cup shredded mozzarella
4 cups all-purpose flour

For the filling:

Mozzarella or pepper jack cheese (about 2 cups)
Pepperoni, cut into 4-inch-long pencil-width sticks
Banana pepper rings (about 1½ cups)

In a large bowl, combine the water, yeast, salt, sugar, minced garlic, egg, oil, chopped pepperoni, and mozzarella cheese. Let sit 5 minutes. Stir in the first cup and a half of flour with a heavy spoon. Add the next cup of flour a little at a time as needed, stirring until the dough becomes too stiff to continue stirring easily. Add a little more flour and begin kneading. Continue adding flour and kneading until the dough is smooth and elastic. Let the dough rise in a greased, covered bowl until doubled (usually, about an hour).

Uncover the bowl; sprinkle in a little more flour and knead again before dividing in half into two balls.

Working with one half of the dough at a time, roll each ball of dough out onto a floured surface into a rectangle (approximately 8 x 12 inches). Sprinkle flour over the dough to keep from sticking as you roll. Make one slice lengthwise down the dough. Now slicing horizontally, make a slice across the middle, then again, until you have eight pieces. Sprinkle with cheese. Place pepperoni sticks on each piece. Add peppers. Roll up each piece, pinching the seams to seal.

Let rise approximately 30 minutes. Preheat the oven to 350°F. Bake for 20 to 30 minutes. (Watch carefully—the size of your rolls will vary the baking time. They're done when they've browned.)

Makes 16 rolls.

FRIED BOLOGNA SANDWICHES

Fried bologna sandwiches are nothing if not an homage to the country palate, which bears no pride, counts no calories, and uplifts even the lowliest of ingredients to the heights of celestial delight. Which is to say that you can actually find fried bologna sandwiches on sit-down restaurant menus around here and in many other parts of the South.

But the best fried bologna sandwiches are made at home!

Oil for frying
Thick, deli-sliced bologna
Deli-sliced cheese
Great bread
Condiments of choice

The three key points in a fried bologna sandwich are the meat, the cheese, and the bread. Start with good, thick, deli-sliced bologna, not the prepackaged stuff.

Choose your cheese—make it some good, deli-sliced cheese,

too. And then there's the bread. Fried bologna sandwiches are traditionally made on white sandwich bread. Homemade sliced Grandmother Bread is perfect.

Heat a small amount of oil on medium-high in a large skillet. (You can use olive oil, lard, bacon grease—whatever oil you prefer.) Carefully score each slice of bologna. Don't cut the bologna in half—just make a few cuts across the center. (This will help keep the bologna from curling while it's frying.)

Fry 3 minutes per side. If you burn the edges a little bit, you get a nice caramelized flavor.

Here's where it gets really subjective. Anybody who grew up with fried bologna sandwiches will tell you that the only way to eat them is the way their mother made them—with mayonnaise or mustard, ketchup or barbecue sauce. I like mayo and a hot pepper butter. I spread both bread slices with mayo and put hot pepper butter between the bologna and the cheese. I like Colby, but any cheese will do. If you grew up with them, the only right way is how your mama did it, so I understand.

My mother never made fried bologna sandwiches. The first time I was introduced to the fried bologna sandwich was when I was living at the Slanted Little House. One day after church, my cousin made one for me. Now I'm a fan. It's a real comfort food.

Top the bologna with the cheese while still warm and put the sandwich together. If you like, add lettuce, tomato, and onion. Some people even like a fried egg on top. Or if you have a sandwich press, you can grill it.

No matter how you make it, it's hillbilly heaven. Pass the potato chips.

IRON SKILLET UPSIDE-DOWN PIZZA

A meal in a skillet—and it's upside down! I first saw this recipe idea in a West Virginia Department of Agriculture pamphlet, and I've made it many times since with variations. Change up the meat, the cheese, and the other ingredients for a different dish every time. It's a flexible, delicious one-pot dinner. If you don't have an iron skillet, you can also bake this in a greased casserole dish.

½ pound ground sausage
½ pound ground beef
⅓ cup chopped onion
1 tablespoon minced garlic
¼ teaspoon salt
1 teaspoon Italian seasoning
Approximately 2 ounces sliced pepperoni
1½ cups pizza or spaghetti sauce
1 cup shredded mozzarella
2 large eggs
1 cup milk
¼ teaspoon salt
1½ cups all-purpose flour
½ cup grated Parmesan

Preheat the oven to 400°F.

Cook the ground sausage and beef in a 10-inch skillet. Drain grease. Add the onion, garlic, salt, and Italian seasoning and mix in the skillet. Spread the pepperoni over the meat and onion mixture. Pour on the sauce and top with the cheese. In a bowl, combine the eggs, milk, salt, and flour. Mix well and spoon over the sauce and cheese. (That isn't a mistake—no baking powder is required.)

Sprinkle the Parmesan on top (and I like to add some extra herbs for decoration). Bake for about 20 minutes, till the pizza crust top is golden and puffy.

BEANS AND CORN BREAD

To start a pot of beans, rinse and sort (to remove any debris that might be in the bag) dried pinto beans. You can use a colander, or you can just use the pot you're going to cook the beans in. I'm pretty lazy, so I usually don't get out the colander. Either measure out the quantity of beans desired or just pour the beans into the pot straight out of the bag. After rinsing and sorting, pinto beans require soaking before cooking. You can use one of two methods.

Long soak: Place beans in a large pot and cover with water. Cover with a lid. Let sit at room temperature overnight (or at least 6 hours).

Quick soak: Place beans in a large pot and cover with water. Cover with a lid and bring to a boil. Turn off the heat. Leave covered and let sit 1 hour.

Whichever method you follow, after the soak, drain the pot and replace with fresh water. Draining the soaking water helps eliminate the gases that can make beans hard to digest.

Most country bean cooks will put in a ham bone or some bacon, or at the very least some reserved bacon fat. From there, other additions are to your taste, but some good seasonings include garlic powder and chili powder. I like to add ground red pepper and sometimes red pepper flakes. How much seasoning you need depends on how big a pot of beans you're making, but for the size pot I typically make (starting with 5 cups dry beans), I add a couple teaspoons each of garlic powder, chili powder, and ground red pepper.

Don't add salt until the last 30 minutes of cooking. Adding salt directly too early will make your beans tough, and they'll never soften up right no matter how long you cook them. Plus, if you've got a ham bone or bacon in the pot, there's a lot of salt hiding right there. It takes time as the beans simmer for the salt from the meat to permeate the beans. You don't know how salty your pot of beans already is until you give it time. When the beans are soft and close to ready for serving, test the beans and add salt, and other additional seasonings, until you're satisfied. Serve in bowls with chopped onion, hot or mild peppers, shredded cheese, and/ or sour cream as optional toppings.

A big pot of beans takes anywhere from 4 to 6 hours (or more) of simmer time. Test your beans for softness periodically as your time will vary from pot to pot, depending on various minor factors. If you find your water getting low in the pot, just add more. (I add it hot.) You always want the beans covered with water while cooking.

You can also cook beans in a Crock-Pot or a pressure cooker, but there's nothing like beans simmering on the stovetop all day. And it gives you plenty of time to fix the corn bread.

Bacon fat, lard, or shortening
1 cup all-purpose flour
1 cup cornmeal
¼ cup sugar
1 tablespoon baking powder
½ teaspoon salt
¼ cup salted butter (cut up) or oil
2 large eggs
1 cup milk or buttermilk

Preheat the oven to 425°F.

Grease a cast-iron skillet with reserved bacon fat, lard, or shortening. In a mixing bowl, stir together the flour, cornmeal, sugar, baking powder, and salt. Add the butter or oil, eggs, and milk or buttermilk. Stir to combine. Don't overstir. You want a thick, almost-pourable-but-not consistency. Pour the corn bread mixture into the skillet. If you don't have a cast-iron skillet, you can use a greased 8-inch-square pan. Bake for 20 to 25 minutes or until browned.

MAKING FLOUR TORTILLAS

Making tortillas at home is simple, and they're so much more delicious than the ones from the store. These flour tortillas are great for burritos, enchiladas, or just melting butter on them to roll up hot and eat fresh from the skillet.

3 cups all-purpose flour
1 teaspoon salt

¼ cup lard or shortening

1 cup lukewarm water

Mix the flour and salt in a medium-size bowl. Cut in the lard or shortening with a pastry cutter. Stir in the water and mix the dough as much as possible with a spoon. The dough will appear dry. Knead as you would any yeast bread dough until the mixture becomes a pliable ball. Cover the bowl and let rest for about 20 minutes. Sprinkle a bit of flour in the bowl and knead again briefly. Divide the dough into 12 balls. Preheat a cast-iron skillet on medium-high. Because the tortillas are cooked dry, with no oil, cast iron is best.

Taking one ball of tortilla dough at a time, flour waxed paper and stretch the ball a bit to get started. Place the dough on the floured wax paper and sprinkle flour on top of the dough. Roll out each tortilla as thinly as possible without breaking the dough.

If the dough sticks as you pull it up, you aren't using enough flour. It should pull off the waxed paper easily.

Cook each tortilla quickly, about 30 seconds per side. Place cooked tortillas in a tortilla keeper or in foil. Keep wrapped while continuing to cook the remaining tortillas.

This recipe makes twelve 6- to 8-inch tortillas. To make larger tortillas, divide your ball of dough into fewer portions. (Remember to not make larger tortillas than you have a skillet to cook them in.) To store tortillas, place in sealed baggies in the refrigerator. They keep well for a week or more in the fridge. You can vary the recipe in endless ways—substitute whole-grain flour or add crushed hot peppers, chopped olives, anything you like for gourmet tortillas.

FRIED STUFFED SQUASH BLOSSOMS

Even if your garden doesn't burst with produce, most likely, if you've got a garden, there's still too much squash and zucchini. My favorite way of circumventing the sometimes unwelcome bounty each summer is frying up the blossoms. (You can use any kind of squash blossoms, including pumpkin.)

This recipe will stuff 6 to 8 squash blossoms, depending on the size. Note: Squash blossoms are best picked in the morning and they don't keep well. Use as quickly as possible after harvesting. If not using for a day or two, refrigerate.

To make fried stuffed squash blossoms:

Fresh squash flowers
6 ounces cream cheese, softened
1 tablespoon fresh (or 1 teaspoon dried) chives
2 tablespoons onion, minced
1 large egg
½ cup milk
½ cup all-purpose flour
¼ cup cornmeal
½ teaspoon garlic powder
½ teaspoon salt
Dash of pepper
Oil for frying

Pick the squash blossoms. (If you choose male flowers, which grow on longer, thinner stems, you'll avoid reducing your crop . . . if that's what you want to do!) Cut the stems off at the base and clip out the stamens from the inside. Rinse thoroughly, shake off excess water, and let the blossoms air-dry on paper towels.

Combine the softened cream cheese with the chives and onion. Spoon about an ounce into the center of each blossom (less if you're using smaller flowers). Close the blossoms by folding the petals over the mixture. Whisk the egg and milk together in one bowl and mix the flour, cornmeal, garlic powder, salt, and pepper in another. Dip the closed blossoms in the wet then the dry mixture until well coated. Fry in oil over medium heat until browned on both sides. Drain and serve with a creamy dip.

SUMMER VEGETABLE PIE

Even if you don't have a garden of your own overflowing with squash and zucchini, somebody you know does, and he or she will be dropping vegetables off with you by the bagful. Or just setting them on your front porch and running. Not that there's anything wrong with squash and zucchini, but I'm always looking for squash and zucchini ideas.

½ cup halved cherry tomatoes
1 cup yellow squash, chopped
1½ cups zucchini, chopped
1 cup onion, chopped
4 large eggs
1 cup baking mix (such as Quick Mix)
½ cup sour cream
1 tablespoon olive oil
½ cup grated Monterey Jack or cheddar cheese
1 tablespoon minced garlic
½ teaspoon Italian seasoning
½ teaspoon salt
¼ teaspoon pepper

Preheat the oven to 350°F.

Combine the chopped vegetables in a large bowl. Add the eggs, baking mix, sour cream, oil, cheese, garlic, and seasonings. Mix well. Pour into a greased 9-inch pie pan. Bake for approximately 40 minutes.

More ideas: Instead of cherry tomatoes, squash, zucchini, and onion, use 4 cups of whatever you like. Use all zucchini, all squash, or any combination of your favorite vegetables. You can even substitute a cup of cooked, chopped, or ground meat for 1 cup of the vegetables for a main course. Use different cheeses and seasonings. Anything goes in this pie.

COUNTRY-STYLE GREEN BEANS

Everybody's got an opinion about how to cook up a mess of fresh beans, but here's how I do it.

1 quart green beans, fresh
¼ pound sliced peppered bacon, chopped in pieces*
1 medium-sized onion
1 teaspoon sugar
1 teaspoon salt
½ teaspoon seasoned salt
Water

Wash the green beans; drain. Chop the bacon in pieces. Start the bacon frying on medium in a large pot. Slice the onion and add to the pot to cook with the bacon. I love the caramelized taste to the onions that comes from frying them along with the bacon. You can add more or less onion, and slice it any way you like.

When the bacon is about half cooked (just starting to brown a little bit), add the green beans. (Don't drain the bacon grease. Well, you can drain a little bit, if you must, but don't go out of control here.) Add the sugar, salt, seasoned salt, and just enough water to cover. Bring to a boil. Turn the heat down, cover the pot, and simmer for at least 45 minutes.

I like to stop right here, but if you really want to cook them down hard, after the 45 minutes you can take the lid off and turn up the heat. If my cousin is coming over, I keep going until almost every bit of liquid is cooked down because he likes them cooked until dead.

When the beans are cooked to your liking, adjust seasonings to taste. This is a fantastic down-home side dish, or a meal all by itself.

*If you aren't using peppered bacon, you'll want to add some pepper.

POPPING POPCORN

Popcorn is the perfect natural snack, much healthier than chips, and it's cheap, cheap, cheap! But not so cheap if you're buying it in those microwave packages. You can make popcorn for pennies on the top of your stove. You can season it up a thousand different ways to suit yourself and make your own gourmet popcorn.

Making old-fashioned popcorn on the top of the stove is almost a lost art in today's world of microwave popcorn and fancy air poppers. Ask average kids today how to make popcorn, and a good number of them are likely to tell you how many minutes it takes in the microwave. There's a little bit of a trick to making good popcorn, with no burning and few old maids (unpopped kernels), but it's easy once you know how.

The simplest popcorn, flavored with nothing more than butter and salt, is my favorite most of the time, but sometimes I also like to add a little sugar or even some cinnamon-sugar. Occasionally, I get adventurous and try some other spices or herbs. Good ones to try are cayenne, garlic, and pepper. Whenever I make popcorn, I make a big pot and snack on it for days. Store prepared popcorn in an airtight container.

This is the size recipe I make in my 5-quart pot. You can cut the measurements in half for a smaller pot. If you've never made anything but air-popped or microwave popcorn, here's how to make real popcorn, the old-fashioned way.

¼ cup vegetable oil
⅔ cup popcorn kernels
Salt to taste
Butter to taste

Put the vegetable oil in the bottom of a large pot. Place three popcorn kernels in the pot. Turn the heat to medium-high. Watch for the kernels to pop. They'll be popping before you know it—don't go away! Once all three have popped, add all the popcorn and the salt, put on the lid, and remove the pot from the heat for 30 seconds. This allows the rest of the popcorn to warm up before returning to heat, which will mean fewer unpopped kernels in the end.

Note: Adding the salt before popping helps evenly distribute the salt throughout the popcorn. I use two teaspoons of salt.

Put the pot back on medium-high. Using oven mitts to hold the pot, begin shaking the entire pot over the burner. Try to hold the lid on the pot as you shake so that the cover is just slightly cracked—this helps vent steam and make your popcorn crisp. Continue shaking the pot until you don't hear kernels popping anymore. Remove from heat. Drizzle (lavishly!) with butter and/or whatever else suits your fancy. Goodies you can add in to a bowl of popcorn include red hots, M&Ms or other candies, all kinds of nuts but especially cashews and peanuts, raisins and other dried fruit pieces, pretzels, or cereal.

QUICK MIX

You can have an endless array of biscuits, muffins, and pancakes at your fingertips as fast and easy as with a store-bought baking mix, only better because it's homemade.

To make Quick Mix:

5 cups all-purpose flour
¼ cup sugar
¼ cup baking powder
1¼ teaspoons cream of tartar
1 teaspoon salt

Combine all ingredients in a large bowl. I use a large spoon and a whisk to blend the ingredients well. I like to make this mix in 5-cup batches because that quantity fits easily into my mixing bowls for blending. I make multiple batches at once and store it in a large canister on my kitchen counter. Store as you would flour.

BISCUITS:

Per 1 cup of Quick Mix used, add—

¼ cup shortening, salted butter, or lard
⅓ cup milk or buttermilk

Preheat the oven to 450°F.

Using a pastry cutter, cut in the shortening, butter, or lard until the mixture resembles coarse crumbs. Add the milk and knead your biscuit dough. (A secret to great biscuits—knead the dough lightly a few times, adding a pinch of flour if needed to keep the dough from sticking to your hands.) Roll onto a floured surface to an inch thickness and cut out. Bake for 10 to 12 minutes. Depending on the size of your biscuit cutter, this makes approximately 4 to 6 biscuits per recipe using 1 cup of mix. Double or triple as needed.

MUFFINS:

Per 1 cup of Quick Mix used, add—

3 tablespoons sugar
1 large egg
⅓ cup milk
2 tablespoons oil
⅔ cup fruit (optional)

Preheat the oven to 400°F.

Add the sugar, egg, milk, and oil to the Quick Mix all at once. Stir just till moistened. (Batter should be lumpy.) To make fruit muffins, using blueberries, diced apple, and so on, fold in ⅔ cup fruit. Fill muffin cups two-thirds full. Bake approximately 15 to 18 minutes. Per cup of Quick Mix, the batter makes 4 to 6 muffins.

PANCAKES:

Per 1 cup of Quick Mix used, add—

2 tablespoons sugar
1 large egg

¼ to 1 cup milk

2 tablespoons oil

Add the sugar, egg, milk (adjust to make a good pouring batter), and oil. Stir just till moistened. Pour the batter onto a hot, lightly greased skillet or griddle, turning to cook the second side after the first side bubbles on the surface. The 1-cup recipe makes approximately 6 pancakes.

BISCUITS AND GRAVY

Biscuits with sausage gravy is one of my kids' favorite lazy weekend breakfasts, and sometimes we even have it for dinner. One, biscuits. Two, sausage. Three, gravy. How can you go wrong with that combo? It's no surprise it's such a country breakfast staple.

Per dozen biscuits (depending on cutter size):

2 cups all-purpose flour

1 tablespoon baking powder

2 teaspoons sugar

½ teaspoon salt

½ cup shortening or lard

⅔ cup milk

Preheat the oven to 450°F.

Combine the flour, baking powder, sugar, and salt in a mixing bowl (or use 2 cups Quick Mix). Cut in the shortening or lard. Stir in the milk. Roll on a floured surface to about an inch thick and cut. Place the biscuits on a greased pan. Bake 10 to 12 minutes.

For the gravy:

1 pound ground mild or spicy sausage

3 tablespoons all-purpose flour

1 teaspoon garlic powder

3 cups milk

Salt and pepper to taste

Cook the sausage in a large skillet till done; drain, leaving a little bit of the drippings in the pan for flavor. Stir in the flour and garlic powder; add the milk gradually, cooking and stirring over medium heat. When the gravy thickens, turn off the heat and add salt and pepper to taste.

By now, you've got big, fluffy biscuits coming out of the oven.

You might need to eat one of those suckers right away, with some butter, to test them before you let anybody else have them with the gravy. You wouldn't want anyone getting a bad biscuit. And they are awfully good right out of the oven.

Split the biscuits and pour on the gravy. Serve hot!

MAKING LARD

Start with a big bag of fat from when your pig was butchered. If you don't have a big bag of fat, you'll have to go to a butcher shop. Trust me, it's worth it. Making your own lard is easy, and you can do it no matter where you live or how far you are from a farm. Home-made lard is fresh, natural, and not hydrogenated like store-bought lard, and if you raised your own pig, you know exactly what it was fed. It makes the best piecrusts and biscuits in the world. Lard is a real, natural food—don't be afraid of it—and making your own is easy, taking you another step closer to your food and its origins.

To make homemade lard, you'll need:

Pork fat
Water

(Short ingredient list.)

To render lard for baking, the best pork fat is kidney, back, or belly fat. Freeze the fat first to make it easier to handle—cutting up fat is a messy job. Chop it into about 1-inch pieces. (Some people even grind the frozen fat. The smaller the pieces of fat you start with, the quicker it will render.) How much fat you render at once doesn't matter—however much you want to work with at a time and will fit in your pot.

Use a large cast-iron kettle or dutch oven to cook it on the stovetop, or cook it in a Crock-Pot or the oven. Cook the fat any way you choose—the method is similar no matter which way you do it. I prefer a Crock-Pot. Rendering actually produces three products—the mild creamy-white baking lard, what is called savory lard, and the cracklins (which are a guilty pleasure).

First add water to cover the bottom of the pot or pan you're using to cook the lard, then add a layer of fat pieces. (Don't add all the fat yet.) The water will eventually cook out—it's just there at the start while you get the first pieces of fat melting so the fat doesn't stick to the bottom.

Cook the lard slowly. I set my Crock-Pot on low and keep the pot uncovered throughout the process. When you see the first pieces of fat floating and turning white, the rendering has begun.

Go ahead and put in the rest of the fat. You can stir it occasionally, but it doesn't need a whole lot of attention. It knows what it's doing. It doesn't need your help. The pieces will float as the amount of melted fat increases.

Eventually, the pieces of fat will sink to the bottom—those are your cracklins-to-be. Stick a spoon in there and you'll see your nice, clear liquid fat. The cracklings will still have a puffy fatness to them. (Not crispy yet.)

You want to render your good, mild baking lard before you finish the cracklins. When you see the pieces sinking, it's time to get the good stuff. In my Crock-Pot on low, this takes about 12 hours. (It's a good idea to start lard in the evening and let it cook overnight—but be sure you've got it on low.)

Line a colander with cheesecloth. Place the colander over a bowl. Pour the lard into the colander and let it strain through to the bowl. Next, carefully and slowly pour the strained liquid from the bowl to your final container(s). I like to use quart jars to store lard. This first rendering of clarified lard is perfect for piecrusts and other baking uses (and also for soap making). It will be mild and turn a gorgeous white once it sets. Chill it quickly for best texture.

The cracklins, remaining in the cheesecloth, will still look puffy and fat. Return the cracklins to the pot, keeping the heat on low. (No need to add more water.) Continue to cook the cracklins until they're crispy and golden, having released more fat. Again, strain the lard by pouring it through a cheesecloth-lined colander into a bowl. This second rendering is the savory lard. Because it's made from cooking down the cracklins, it has a much stronger flavor. You can use it for various savory cooking purposes—it's just probably not something you'll want in a crust for an apple pie. It will set to a light amber color and should be chilled for best texture, just like the creamy mild lard.

The cracklins, your final product, are delicious sprinkled over salads or on top of casseroles. Or eaten as a snack. Go ahead, you know you want to.

Store your finished lard in a cool, dry place. If you don't have a cool place to store it, you can keep it in the refrigerator. If used within a few months, refrigeration is not necessary.

Note: You can render other types of fat using the same method. Rendered pork fat is called lard. Tallow is rendered beef fat. Chicken fat when rendered is called schmaltz. Suet is the hard, lean rendering of fat from around the kidneys and loins of cows or sheep. All these types of rendered fat find traditional uses in cooking, soaps, candles, and more.

MAKING BUTTER

Making butter is the process of releasing butterfat from the cream. Like cheese making, it's an age-old and delicious way of preserving milk.

Here's how you do it.

Take 1 pint of heavy cream. Not too fresh. It's best to work with cream that's been sitting in the fridge for a couple of days. Set your heavy cream out for several hours to come to room temperature.

When you're ready to start, pour your pint of cream into a quart jar.

Cover tightly with a lid and start shaking. At first, the cream will seem to expand and fill up the jar to where it almost looks as if you can't shake it anymore. Keep shaking—next thing you know, a big yellow blob of butter will appear inside the jar. It's like magic!

Using a spoon to hold the butter in place, pour off the buttermilk, transferring it to another jar, then dump the butter in a bowl. (The most straight-sided bowl you have is best.) Using the back of a big spoon, press the butter, pushing out any remaining liquid. This is still buttermilk, so add it to your buttermilk jar.

Run cold water over the butter, then press again, releasing as much liquid as possible. Dump this liquid—it's watered down now. Repeat this process of washing the butter several times until the water is pressing out clear. After you've washed it for the last time, add salt to taste. (Salt also helps preserve the butter.) Refrigerate and eat with much happiness because you made it yourself.

There are numerous variations on making butter. You can make it with a stand mixer, a blender, or a food processor, too. (Or even the old-fashioned way with a hand-cranked churn.) Main points to remember when making butter:

Be sure to use really good, rich heavy cream.
Don't use cream that's too fresh. Let the cream for butter sit in the fridge a couple days before using.
Don't use ultrapasteurized cream.
Let the cream come to room temperature before starting to make butter.

CANNING IN A BOILING WATER BATH

There is nothing better than a cellar or pantry stocked with home-canned food. It's frugal, it's easy, and it makes for great gifts with the addition of decorative canning lids, labels, and a bit of tied raffia or ribbon.

Note: Boiling water bath canning is for high-acid foods only, which generally include fruits and soft spreads. Figs and tomatoes may be canned in a hot water bath with the addition of a sufficient amount of acid (bottled lemon juice, citric acid, or vinegar). Fermented foods such as sauerkraut and pickles may also be preserved by this method. Standard canning recipes are calculated for altitudes of 1,000 feet above sea level or lower. Always consult expert resources for canning method recommendations for the type of food you are canning as well as for altitude adjustments. For low-acid foods such as vegetables, meats, poultry, and seafood as well as soups, stews, and sauces containing those foods, you must use a pressure canner. The pressure inside this type of canner provides a higher heat to destroy the bacterial spores that emit toxins in low-acid foods. A good beginner resource is the *Ball Blue Book Guide to Preserving,* available at many stores and online.

Supplies you will need: A large canning pot with a rack, a wide-mouth funnel, a jar lifter, and canning jars, lids, and bands. Lids are onetime-use items. Jars and bands can be washed and reused.

Jars must be well washed and hot when you begin filling them. Jars do *not* need to be presterilized as long as the filled jars will be processed at least 10 minutes in a boiling water bath or pressure canner.

1. Before you begin the final preparation stage of the food to be canned, fill the pot half full of water and heat to a simmer (180°F).

   Set the pot on the stove to boil. Use a rack that fits the bottom of the pot and the size jars you are using. (The jars must not be in direct contact with the bottom of the pot. Normally, a rack will come with your canning pot. Canning pots are available at most large stores, such as Walmart, and also at hardware and other specialty stores.) Meanwhile, in a small pan, prepare the jar lids. Lids come in regular and wide-mouth sizes, as do jars. Use real canning jars *only*. Lids should be heated for 10 minutes prior to using. Lids can be heated in a small pan on the stove or in a small slow-cooker that can maintain a temperature of around 180°F. (Do *not* overheat. Do *not* boil. Overheating lids by boiling can result in seal failure.) Remove from the water one at a time as needed.

2. Using a wide-mouth funnel, spoon the food into the jars, filling to the recommended headspace per your recipe.

   Use a plastic or wooden instrument to press the mixture and remove air bubbles. (Always remove air bubbles, even if you think there aren't any. *There are.*)

   Never use metal in a glass jar. The slightest knock of metal against a glass jar could cause an invisible fracture that might cause the jar to break in the canning pot.

   Wipe the jar rims with a damp towel to clean any spillage. This is important because any particles of food remaining on the jar rim can prevent a vacuum seal.

3. Take the lids one at a time from the simmering water with tongs. They do not need to be dried—put them right on the jar.

   You can also buy what is called a magnetic wand to use for removing lids from simmering water to place on jars. But tongs work just fine.

   Place a lid immediately on each jar as it is prepared. Screw on the bands. Use a towel to hold the hot jars as you tighten the bands. Tighten the bands only fingertip tight—meaning stop when there is resistance. Firm and snug—not as tight as you can make it. Overtightening can interfere with the vacuum seal and even cause buckled lids.

4. Slowly lower each jar as you fill it into the simmering pot of water using a jar lifter.

   Make sure the jars remain upright as they are moved. Once all the jars are loaded into the pot, check that the water is at least two inches over the tops of the jars. If necessary, add boiling water to reach the required level. Place the lid on the pot.

5. Time the boil according to the directions for the recipe you are using. After placing the lid on the pot, increase the heat to medium-high and bring the water in the canner to a rolling boil. Begin counting the processing time when the rolling boil begins. Keep the water boiling during the entire processing time.

   When the processing time has expired, turn off the heat, remove the lid, and let the canner cool for 5 minutes.

6. Remove the jars one at a time with a jar lifter and place the jars, not touching and at least 1 inch apart, on a dry surface covered with toweling or layers of newspaper to prevent thermal shock. Keep the cooling jars out of drafts. Do not move the jars or adjust the rings during the resting period.

Allow the jars to rest undisturbed for 12 to 24 hours. You will hear the lids "pop" as they cool and form the vacuum sealing the jars. Store the jars in a cool, dry location after removing the rings from the jars and thoroughly washing the jars in warm soapy water.

Do not store jars with the rings on. The rings may rust onto the jars and become difficult to remove. The rings may also mask a bad seal and result in jar explosion. Always remove the rings on stored jars. (You may want to return rings to jars when transporting or gift giving, but long-term storage with the rings on is not a good idea.)

For storing home-canned goods, most expert sources recommend the standard guideline of one year for optimal quality, though it's not really that simple. Some foods, such as jams, are considered truly best, at least from a flavor standpoint, if used within six months. However, there is no way to give a blanket answer to the storage question because so many different factors affect storage quality, including temperature of the storage location (should be cool, not warm), how clean the fruits/vegetables were when packed in the jars, and whether or not proper processing and handling were followed in every detail. The best advice is to plan what you can. Can what you expect you will use or share within a year, especially if you are a new canner. After all, every year is a new harvest.

WHISKEY-RAISIN APPLE BUTTER

Apple butter in autumn is an Appalachian tradition. Historically, it's a daylong event. Whole families would join together to simmer apple butter in copper kettles as big as washtubs. Apple butter was one of the traditions my father took with him when he left these hills long ago after World War II. I grew up on apple butter and, yes, sometimes I thought it was odd. None of my friends had apple butter at their house. But we did. (We also always—always!—had West Virginia molasses in the house, too.)

Once we moved to the farm, I made a lot of apple butter with free apples, either from farmers' market pig hauls or from the old apple tree behind the Slanted Little House. An adaptation with whiskey and raisins became my favorite version of this West Virginia staple.

Start with however many apples you can get your hands on. A bushel or two is fantastic. (A bushel is 8 gallons.) Most people have a favorite kind of apple, but any type of apple will work. My favorite kind of apple is a free apple. Short of free apples, my next favorite kind is what they sell at the farmers' markets as "canning apples"—boxes of usually mixed varieties of (often bruised) apples that are offered at a cut-rate price.

To make apple butter, core, peel, and slice the apples. Cook apples in a pot of water long enough to soften, then puree into sauce. You can also use a food strainer, like a Squeezo, to prepare the puree, which makes the process even easier. Per 2 quarts prepared puree, add:

4 cups sugar
1 cup raisins
2 teaspoons ground cinnamon

1 teaspoon ground cloves

½ cup whiskey

Combine the applesauce puree, sugar, raisins, and spices in a large pot. Simmer until the mixture thickens and rounds up on a spoon. Stir frequently. Add the whiskey to the pot and stir well. Ladle the hot butter into hot jars, leaving ¼-inch headspace. Add lids and rings. Process in a boiling water bath for 10 minutes. Yield: 3 pints.

CORNCOB JELLY

Corncob jelly is a perfect example of the "waste not, want not" spirit of our ancestors, who knew how to use everything, and I mean everything. Most of us are accustomed to tossing corncobs in the trash or the compost pile, but there are actually many, many ways to utilize them. Corncob jelly is one of the tastiest. Here's a short list of other ideas.

Give them to the animals. Chickens and donkeys love to peck and chew every bit of sweetness out of a cob.

Make a corncob doll.

Make a corncob pipe. (If you're handy and into that.)

Stick a nail or hook in one end of the cob. Slather cob with peanut butter and seeds—tie on a tree branch as a bird feeder.

Boil down for vegetable soup stock. (Similar to the method I outline below for making corncob jelly—use the corn liquid as soup stock instead.)

Potpourri—slice cobs in thin pieces, dry, then sprinkle with scented oil. Makes a very pretty addition to a potpourri bowl.

Dry for fire starters. (You can dry corncobs in the sun, the old-fashioned way, or use a dehydrator.)

In the old days, dried, they were used as pot scrubbers.

Poke a long nail in each end of a dried cob and use as a paint roller to make a neat pattern. (Also can use corncobs held upright as a brush, or cut in half to use the even, cut edge to stamp patterns.)

Corncob wine!

You should never throw a corncob away again.

For this recipe, you can use any kind of corn. Traditionally, (red) field corn was often used, but the corn you plan to serve for supper will also make a delicious jelly.

12 large ears of corn
2 quarts water
2 tablespoons lemon juice
1 1¼-ounce package powdered fruit pectin
Salted butter
Sugar

Cook the corn; cut the kernels from the cobs and store for another use. Measure 2 quarts water into a large pot; add the corncobs.

Bring to a boil. Boil hard for 30 minutes. (If you had the pot covered when you brought it to a boil, take the lid off now. Boil it down uncovered for a more concentrated result.) Turn off the heat and remove the cobs. Strain the corn liquid through cheesecloth or a fine mesh strainer.

Measure the remaining corn liquid. I usually get a little over 3½ cups corn liquid after it boils down. Return the liquid to the large pot. Stir in the lemon juice and pectin. Add a dab of butter to prevent foaming. Bring to a boil. Add the sugar, cup per cup, to match the measure of your corn liquid. Stir to dissolve the sugar. Bring pot to a rolling boil. Boil hard one minute, stirring constantly. Remove from the heat. Ladle the hot corncob jelly into hot jars. Adjust the lids and bands. Process in a boiling water bath for 10 minutes.

Makes approximately 5 half-pints.

This jelly comes out a beautiful pale amber color and tastes surprisingly like a light honey.

FLOWER AND HERB JELLIES

Wildflower jellies are an old-fashioned idea, and the reason for that is we don't think we have time in our rush-rush world to pick flowers for a few hours and separate the petals. It's a slow task, somewhat akin to stringing beans or cracking nuts.

You can make flower and herb jellies using any amount of flowers and herbs, so if you don't want to pick any certain amount, this per cup recipe is helpful. Note: Be sure to check an expert resource when determining what flowers are edible.

This same recipe can be used to make herb jellies. Herb jelly is more than mint! Basil, rosemary, sage, and many other herbs make wonderful herb jellies.

To prepare the infusion, boil water and steep petals/herb leaves overnight, one cup boiling water per one cup petals/leaves. The next day, strain the infusion through cheesecloth to get a clear liquid. When adding up cups of strained infusion, if you're short, add water to round up to the next cup, then make jelly.

For the jelly, per cup strained infusion, add one 1¼-ounce package powdered fruit pectin, ⅛ cup lemon juice, and 2 cups sugar. One 1¼-ounce package powdered fruit pectin will set up to 2 cups strained infusion. For 4 cups infusion, use 2 packages, and so on. (For 3 cups infusion, go ahead and use 2 packages, and for 5 cups, use 3 packages.) There is no natural pectin in flower petals and herbs, so a lot of pectin is required.

To make the jelly, combine the strained infusion, powdered pectin, and lemon juice in a pot according to the per cup measurements. Bring to a boil over high heat. Add the sugar, stirring until dissolved. Return to a rolling boil. Boil hard 1 minute, stirring constantly. Remove from the heat. Ladle hot jelly into hot jars. Add lids and rings. Process in a boiling water bath for 10 minutes.

These jellies come out in beautiful natural colors, but you can add a drop or two of food coloring for a desired effect, if you wish. You can also use this same infusion method as a base for flower or herb syrups, teas, and more.

BANANA SPLIT IN A JAR

I came up with this recipe when I realized I had some bananas on the verge of going bad. I couldn't remember the last time I'd eaten a banana split, but I love the combination of fruit flavors. And the whipped cream. And the fudge. And the ice cream.

And I wondered why I hadn't had one in so long. But, of course, banana splits can be a bit of a hassle to put together. You have to have all the stuff. Then I thought—banana split in a jar!

I created a recipe combining all four of the traditional banana split fruits, ready, able, and willing to go on top of a bowl of ice cream. Just add chocolate syrup and whipped cream.

½ cup lemon juice
2 cups mashed bananas
2 cups crushed strawberries
1½ cups crushed pineapple
1 cup halved maraschino cherries
1 1¼-ounce package powdered fruit pectin
5 cups sugar
½ cup chopped walnuts
½ cup banana rum or dark rum (optional)

Mix the lemon juice into the bananas immediately after mashing to retain the fresh color, then combine all the fruit and the pectin in a big pot. Bring to a boil, stirring frequently. Add the sugar and a dab of butter to reduce foaming. Bring to a rolling boil; boil hard 1 minute. Remove from the heat and add nuts and rum (if using).

Ladle into jars, leaving ¼-inch headspace. Process in a boiling water bath 15 minutes.

Serve over ice cream with whipped cream and chocolate syrup. This also makes a great spread on toast or topping for pancakes or waffles, pound cake or cheesecake, and anything else.

This recipe makes about 9 half-pints.

HOMEMADE VANILLA EXTRACT

You can find whole vanilla beans at farmers' markets, whole food stores, and even many chain grocery stores, but the best deals are available online in bulk. Store vanilla beans triple-bagged in the refrigerator and they will keep fresh up to a year. Scrapings from vanilla beans can also be used in homemade vanilla ice cream and in cookie and other dessert recipes. Add whole split vanilla beans to your sugar container to make vanilla sugar. Don't be afraid to buy vanilla beans in bulk—there are so many ways to use them!

Making your own vanilla extract is very simple, and it also makes great gifts for the bakers in your life. Since I bake a lot, I use a 750 ml bottle of vodka, but the recipe can be downsized if you prefer a smaller batch. For "double-strength" vanilla, increase the number of beans.

12 whole vanilla beans
750 milliliter bottle of vodka
Dark rum (optional)

Using kitchen scissors, split open the vanilla beans lengthwise, leaving about an inch connected (not cut) at one end. The vanilla beans will take up space inside the bottle, so pour out about half a cup of the vodka (or more as needed) and set aside.

Push the beans into the bottle. Add back vodka if necessary to fill up the bottle, or you can also use a little bit of dark rum for additional flavoring if desired.

Screw on the lid tightly, shake well, and store in a cool, dry location. Shake the bottle once or twice a day for the first week or so, then just whenever you think about it. It will take a month or two to steep well enough to use, but you can use it sooner if you're in a rush. Stored properly, it will be good for years and will in fact get better all the time as it grows stronger. If you can wait 4 to 6 months before using, all the better. (Remember to make a new batch well before the old one runs out. If planning for gifts, prepare the extract several months beforehand so your recipient can use it right away.)

CRACKER CANDY

Georgia made big batches of cracker candy every winter. She'd give it away to family and friends and keep a box of it in her refrigerator. "It satisfies all my longings," she'd say.

For a quick treat to put together, it makes pretty good comfort food. All you need for basic cracker candy is crackers (any type will do) and some semisweet chocolate. Melt the chocolate over a double boiler and dip the crackers. Let sit to harden and enjoy.

For toffee cracker candy, a little more involved but worth it, you'll need:

Oil
Crackers (such as Ritz or Club)
1 cup salted butter
1 cup brown sugar
½ cup nuts (optional)
12 ounces semisweet chocolate chips

Preheat the oven to 350°F.

Spray a 9 x 13–inch pan with oil. Spread the crackers evenly over the bottom of the pan. Heat the butter and brown sugar in a small pot. Let boil for 3 minutes. Pour the butter and brown sugar mixture over the crackers. Sprinkle with the chopped nuts. I prefer pecans or walnuts. Bake for 5 minutes. Remove the pan from the oven and turn the oven off. Scatter chocolate chips over the top and place in the still-warm (turned off) oven for a few minutes, long enough for the chocolate to melt. Let sit to cool and harden, then break the candy into pieces.

Don't forget to hide some of it in your fridge for when you have a longing.

RECIPES

MOLASSES COOKIES

Clover's favorite cookies!

1½ cups salted butter, softened

1¼ cups sugar, plus addtional for sprinkling or rolling

2 large eggs

¼ cup molasses

4 teaspoons baking soda

2 teaspoons ground cinnamon

1½ teaspoons ground ginger

1 teaspoon ground nutmeg

½ teaspoon ground cloves

1½ teaspoons salt

1 cup raisins (optional)

4 cups all-purpose flour

Preheat the oven to 375°F.

Three sticks of butter is a lot of butter. That's why these cookies are so delicious. You can substitute margarine or shortening. If you insist.

Cream the butter and sugar. Stir in the eggs and molasses. Add the soda, cinnamon, ginger, nutmeg, cloves, and salt. Stir to combine. (Optional: Add 1 cup of raisins.)

Stir in the flour. Divide the cookie dough into thirds and chill for an hour or two until the dough is easy to handle. Shape the dough into logs for slicing, or use a spoon to scoop off balls of dough. Place the slices on a greased cookie sheet and sprinkle with sugar. If scooping off balls, you can roll the balls in sugar. Bake for 8 to 10 minutes. This recipe makes several dozen cookies, but that depends on their size!

These are actually people cookies, in case you're wondering. But don't be judging if I give them to my goats.

DRUNKEN RUM COOKIE LOGS

When these cookies come out of the oven, they'll make your house smell like you're inside a glass of eggnog, and they are scrumptious. This is a recipe I got from Georgia, only she makes them with rum flavoring. The first time I made them, I took a batch to my cousin and said, "Look, I made your mother's cookies. Only I call them drunken rum cookie logs."

He said, "Why?"

I told him, "I don't use rum flavoring."

He said, "Oh." And took them. Then I delivered some to Georgia and told her the same thing.

She said, "Oh my." (She took them, too.)

For the cookie:

1 cup salted butter, softened
¼ cup sugar
1 large egg
2 teaspoons vanilla extract
2 teaspoons rum flavoring or ¼ cup rum
1 heaping teaspoon ground nutmeg
3 cups all-purpose flour

For the frosting:

3 tablespoons salted butter, melted
½ teaspoon vanilla
1 teaspoon rum flavoring (or a big dollop of rum)
2 cups sifted powdered sugar
A couple tablespoons milk (as much as needed for drizzling consistency)
Ground nutmeg

Preheat the oven to 350°F.

Then start with some rum. Bacardi Gold or Calico Jack spiced rum is good. You should probably test the rum first. You don't want any bad rum going into your cookies.

When you're sure the rum is okay, cream the butter and sugar. You might want to stop now and check the rum again. You can't trust it. It might go bad.

Add the egg, the vanilla extract, and either 2 teaspoons of rum flavoring or ¼ cup rum. Add the nutmeg.

This is when you're about to get up to the real manual labor, so it might be a good time to take a break and test the rum again.

Dump in the all-purpose flour. This makes a pretty heavy cookie dough, so use a sturdy spoon to stir. Divide the dough into four parts and shape each part into a long, loglike roll. Cut into 3-inch pieces with a sharp knife.

Place the cookie logs, lengthwise, on an ungreased baking sheet. Bake for 12 to 15 minutes. Cool before frosting.

This is a good time to test the rum again.

To make the frosting, cream the butter with the vanilla and either 1 teaspoon of rum flavoring or a big dollop of rum. Add the powdered sugar and a few tablespoons of milk until you have icing at a drizzling consistency. Frost the cooled cookies and sprinkle with more nutmeg.

Serve with rum.

SWEET POTATO PIE

My kids think they don't like sweet potatoes, but their easily diverted little minds never make the connection between a pile of sweet potatoes in the pantry and what ends up on their plates. The first time I made sweet potato fries, Morgan said, "Why do these French fries look orange?"

I said, "Oh, it's just some special seasoning I put on there."

She said (suspiciously), "What kind of seasoning?"

I said, "Orange-colored seasoning! Here, you want some ketchup?"

She ate them right up. And so when I make sweet potato pie, I tell everyone it's pumpkin pie. And they eat that right up, too. Ha.

Sweet potato pie does taste very much like pumpkin pie, and this recipe is my favorite.

To start, you need a great piecrust:

4 cups all-purpose flour
1¼ cup lard or shortening
1 tablespoon sugar
2 teaspoons salt
1 tablespoon vinegar
1 large egg
½ cup cold water

Combine the flour, lard or shortening, sugar, and salt in a bowl. Blend with a pastry cutter. Add the vinegar, egg, and cold water. Mix well with a spoon, knead lightly, and divide into four balls. Chill 15 minutes before rolling out into crusts. (Extra pie dough balls can be frozen.)

To make sweet potato pie:

3 large sweet potatoes (about 1 pound)
½ cup salted butter, softened
1 cup sugar
½ cup milk
2 large eggs
½ teaspoon ground nutmeg, plus additional for sprinkling
½ teaspoon ground cinnamon
1 teaspoon vanilla extract
1 unbaked single-crust pie shell

Preheat the oven to 350°F.

Boil the sweet potatoes in their skins until very tender. Drain, then slit the skins with a knife and they'll peel off very easily. Mash the sweet potatoes with the butter, then use an electric mixer to blend well. Add the sugar, milk, eggs, nutmeg, cinnamon, and vanilla. Use the mixer to blend again. Pour the sweet potato filling into the unbaked pie shell. Sprinkle the top with more nutmeg. Bake (mostly on the lowest oven rack) for 1 hour or until a toothpick inserted in the center comes out clean. (Baking pies on the lower oven rack is my secret to properly baked crusts. No gooey crusts! This also prevents the edges from overbrowning.)

Cool and top slices with whipped cream. Then call the kids and ask them if they want some pumpkin pie.

COCONUT-OATMEAL RUM PIE (WITH WALNUTS)

I made up this recipe when I was baking a couple pies and managing with what I had on hand. It's based on a coconut-oatmeal pie recipe, adjusted for the addition of rum and the lack of enough oatmeal, which I replaced with walnuts. The result was intoxicating. This one went right into my holiday pie repertoire.

3 large eggs
¼ cup light corn syrup
¼ cup dark rum
⅔ cup sugar
⅓ cup salted butter, melted
1 teaspoon vanilla extract
½ cup shredded coconut
⅓ cup oatmeal
⅓ cup walnuts, chopped
1 unbaked single-crust pie shell

Preheat the oven to 350°F.

In a medium-size bowl, combine the eggs, corn syrup, rum, sugar, butter, and vanilla. Whisk to mix. Using a spoon, stir in the coconut, oatmeal, and walnuts. Pour into the pie shell. Bake on the lower oven rack for 40 to 45 minutes.

HOMEMADE "POP-TARTS"

My kids love Pop-Tarts, but I don't love to buy them, and one day it hit me that I could just make them, so I did. And wow, they are so good (unlike their rather cardboard-tasting store-bought counterparts), and they're surprisingly easy to make. These are also really fun to make with little (and big!) kids because they can pick out their own flavors and help decorate them.

Use your favorite pie pastry, or try mine. (See my piecrust recipe on page 263.) I use the entire pastry recipe for the Pop-Tarts, splitting the dough in two instead of four balls.

Roll each ball out in two long strips (as far as it will go) that are 6 inches wide.

Cut into 3-inch sections.

Your mileage will vary depending on the pastry recipe you used and how thin you roll the pastry, but you should come out with about 8 to 10 big, full-size, rectangular Pop-Tarts pieces per strip. (You could also cut into smaller pieces for "Pop-Tarts sticks" instead, or cut into triangles, or use a big cookie cutter to make circles, and so on. Think outside the rectangle!)

Place filling in the middle of the strips for the bottom layer.

Filling ideas:

Use a couple teaspoons of the jam of your choice.

For brown sugar 'n' cinnamon Pop-Tarts (my kids' favorite), melt 3 tablespoons butter and combine ⅓ cup granulated sugar, ⅓ cup brown sugar, and 1 tablespoon ground cinnamon in a small bowl. Brush melted butter on each piece, then sprinkle with the brown sugar mixture.

Try a couple teaspoons of melted semisweet chocolate and marshmallow cream.

Preheat the oven to 400°F.

After placing the filling on the bottom strips, using the other strips, place tops on the Pop-Tarts pieces, pinching or pressing

RECIPES

with a fork all the way around the sides to seal. Prick the centers to vent. Transfer to a greased baking sheet using a large spatula.

Bake for approximately 15 minutes, switching oven racks halfway through baking. (Start baking on the top rack, then move the pan to the bottom rack after about 8 minutes.) Cool and top with icing (and candy sprinkles if desired). For brown sugar 'n' cinnamon Pop-Tarts, I add a dash of ground cinnamon to the icing.

Powdered sugar icing: Combine ½ cup sifted powdered sugar, ¼ teaspoon vanilla extract, and enough milk (1 to 2 teaspoons) for drizzling consistency.

APPLE DUMPLINGS

A pan of apple dumplings was Georgia's go-to company dessert. She got the recipe from my great-aunt Ruby, who probably had it handed down to her from my great-grandmother. This old-fashioned delight has been in my family for a long time, and for good reason. It's scrumptious.

For the syrup:

3 cups sugar
½ teaspoon ground cinnamon
½ teaspoon ground (or freshly grated) nutmeg
3 cups water
6 tablespoons salted butter

For the dough:

5 cups all-purpose flour
5 teaspoons baking powder
2½ teaspoons salt
1⅔ cups lard
1¼ cups sweet milk

For the filling:

12 medium-sized apples
2 cups sugar
Cinnamon for sprinkling

You know it's an old recipe when it calls for sweet milk. Sweet milk is the old-time way of saying regular milk, not soured or buttermilk. You can substitute margarine for the butter and shortening for the lard, but you'll be sorry. Lard is the secret to a tender, flaky pastry, and butter is the secret to happiness. For the nutmeg, if you can use fresh grated, that's the best!

For the syrup, combine the sugar, cinnamon, nutmeg, and water in a medium-sized pot and bring to a boil. Turn the heat to low and simmer about 3 minutes. Turn off the heat, dump in the butter to melt, and let the syrup cool while you continue with the recipe.

Preheat the oven to 350°F.

To make the dough, place the flour, baking powder, and salt in a medium-sized bowl, cut in the lard, then stir in the milk and knead lightly.

Divide the dough into four parts, then divide each part into four balls for 16 dumplings. Peel, core, and slice the apples. If you want to prepare the apple slices in advance, you can sprinkle fruit protector on them to prevent browning and refrigerate until you're ready.

On floured parchment paper, roll each ball of dough into a 6-inch circle. Place a cup of apple slices on each center. Sprinkle ⅛ cup sugar and a dash of cinnamon on top of the apples. Fold the dough up around the apples to make a sort of pouch.

Divide the dumplings between two greased 9 x 13-inch pans. Pour the syrup over the dumplings. Bake for about 45 minutes or until lightly browned.

This recipe has comfort food written all over it, but it is also so stunningly delicious that no wonder it was Georgia's most frequent offering to guests, often tripled to serve at her parties, and is even worthy of showing up on a holiday table.

Note: You could easily add some raisins and/or chopped nuts to the apple filling if you like for an even more festive dumpling, although the simplicity of the recipe is pretty darn perfect as is.

STRAWBERRIES AND CREAM COFFEE CAKE

2 cups all-purpose flour

2 teaspoons baking powder

⅓ cup sugar

¼ teaspoon cream of tartar

¼ teaspoon salt

½ cup salted butter, margarine, lard, or shortening

1 cup strawberries, chopped

⅔ cup milk

4 ounces cream cheese, softened

4 ounces strawberry jam

Preheat the oven to 375°F.

Place the first five ingredients (or 2 cups Quick Mix or other baking mix, with the addition of a tablespoon of sugar) in a large bowl and cut in the butter, margarine, lard, or shortening with a pastry cutter. Mix in the fresh chopped strawberries. Add the milk and stir to combine.

Place the dough on a floured surface. Sprinkle more flour on top and roll into an approximately 12 x 8-inch rectangle. Spread the cream cheese down the center, then top with the strawberry jam.

Make cuts, about an inch and a half apart, all along both long sides. Lift the cut strips of dough and crisscross them over the top of the cream cheese and jam. Pinch the ends to seal. Transfer to a greased baking sheet or 13 x 9-inch casserole pan. I use two big spatulas to move the unbaked coffee cake. Bake for 25 minutes or till nicely browned. Cool, then top with powdered sugar icing.

RECIPES

Powdered sugar icing: Combine ½ cup sifted powdered sugar, ¼ teaspoon vanilla extract, and enough milk (1 to 2 teaspoons) for drizzling consistency.

Slice to serve. Perfect for breakfast, lunch, dinner, and midnight snacks. Don't tell anyone you made it and you can have the whole thing! Add some ice cream and it's even dessert.

PUMPKIN BREAD

Whether you're fixing holiday gift baskets to share, or just a sweet, warm treat to enjoy at home, pumpkin bread is irresistible. You can make this recipe with canned pumpkin, but it's so much better with fresh.

The most common pie and baking pumpkins include Sugar or Sweet Pie, Small Sugar or New England Pie, and Sugar Baby. Choose a pumpkin that is heavy for its size, which means more moisture and lower chances of the flesh being dry or stringy. Don't refrigerate unless cut. Stored in a cool, dry place, pumpkins can be kept for a couple months before being used. Depending on the size of the pie and baking pumpkin you choose, you can count on getting 2 to 4 cups of puree per pumpkin.

If you're planning to prepare puree for baking, cut out the stem then slice the pumpkin in half. Scoop out the seeds with your hands or a spoon and scrape out the strings. Rinse in cold water.

Pumpkin can be cooked in the microwave, on the stovetop, or in the oven.

Microwave—place each pumpkin half, cut side down, on a microwave-safe plate and cook on high for approximately 15 minutes.

Stovetop—boil in a cup of water in a large covered pot approximately 30 minutes. (It's not necessary for the water to cover the pumpkin.) Or steam pumpkin for about 15 minutes.

Oven—place pumpkin halves, cut side down, on a cookie sheet and bake at 350°F for an hour to an hour and a half.

However you cook the pumpkin, test for doneness with a fork. Pumpkin is ready when it's tender and a fork slides easily through outer skin.

To prepare puree, scoop cooked pumpkin out of skin. Puree with a masher or food processor. Pumpkin puree should be the consistency of mashed potatoes. Fresh pumpkin puree can be substituted in equal amounts in recipes calling for solid-pack canned pumpkin. Use immediately or store in the refrigerator for up to a week. For longer storage, place in freezer bags or containers for as long as twelve months.

For pumpkin bread, you'll need:

$\frac{2}{3}$ cup shortening
2 $\frac{2}{3}$ cups sugar
4 large eggs
2 cups canned pumpkin or fresh pumpkin puree
$\frac{2}{3}$ cup water
3 $\frac{1}{3}$ cups all-purpose flour
2 teaspoons baking soda
$\frac{1}{2}$ teaspoon ground cloves*
1 teaspoon ground cinnamon
$\frac{1}{2}$ teaspoon salt
$\frac{2}{3}$ cup nuts
2 cups raisins

Preheat the oven to 350°F.

In a mixing bowl, cream the shortening and sugar. Add the eggs, pumpkin, and water. Mix thoroughly. Stir in the flour and the rest of the dry ingredients, then add the nuts and raisins. Spoon into greased loaf pans. Bake 1 hour for standard-size loaves or 25 minutes for miniloaves. Makes 2 standard-size loaves or 15 miniloaves.

For holiday pumpkin bread, add 2 cups raisins and candied fruit, mixed, to the batter, instead of just raisins. Press a candied cherry into the top of each loaf before baking.

*Add up to 2 teaspoons of ground cloves, if you like it spicy.

NUT CAKE

The origins of nut cake go all the way back to medieval times. American settlers brought the tradition with them and claimed it in their own way. The basis for all the competing nut cake variations is the plain nut cake that is but a simple and delectable cake with nuts.

We forget how rare treats were in the days when sugar was limited. Nuts were also a treat in and of themselves. They were harvested in the fall and time-consumingly cracked, the nut meats carefully extracted and lovingly stored to show up on holiday tables at Thanksgiving and Christmas and on other special occasions through the year. Pioneers weren't buying nuts—they were using what was available to them where they lived.

In West Virginia, that meant black walnuts. In other areas, the nut cake might have had English walnuts or pecans because that was what was available. And traditional old-time nut cake is just that—a simple nut cake made with what is available to you.

Nut cake is an amazing cake that deserves a comeback. It's a truly versatile recipe, and its longevity speaks for itself.

½ cup salted butter, softened
1 cup sugar
3 large eggs
1 teaspoon vanilla extract
¼ cup milk
2 cups all-purpose flour
2 teaspoons baking powder
1 teaspoon ground cinnamon
1 teaspoon ground nutmeg
½ teaspoon ground ginger
½ teaspoon ground cloves
1 cup chopped nuts (any)

Preheat the oven to 350°F.

Cream the butter and sugar; stir in the eggs and vanilla. Using a sturdy spoon (or an electric mixer), alternately mix in the milk with the flour, baking powder, and spices. Stir in the nuts. Transfer to a greased pan (or pans) and bake for about 30 minutes (depending on pan size).

You can use any type of pan(s) you want. When I did this in loaf pans, I divided the batter into two large loaf pans. You could also do two 8- or 9-inch cake rounds, an 11 x 9-inch cake pan, a tube or Bundt pan, or a cupcake pan.

For the cream cheese frosting:

8 ounces cream cheese
½ cup salted butter (or margarine), softened
1 teaspoon vanilla extract
16 ounces powdered sugar, sifted

In a bowl, beat together the cream cheese, butter or margarine, and vanilla till light. Gradually add 2 cups of the powdered sugar, beating well. Beat in the rest of the powdered sugar a little bit at a time until you reach spreading consistency. (You may or may not need the whole 16 ounces.)

BURNT SUGAR CAKE

If you don't recognize the name of the cake, you'd likely recognize the flavor. It's a cake you had sometime in your childhood, while visiting older family members or at a church supper somewhere. Burnt sugar cake has a unique taste that just spells home and country roads and a day when people spent more time in the kitchen. But there's a reason burnt sugar cake isn't so popular anymore—it does take time. There is no cake mix that will give you the flavor of burnt sugar. You have to "burn" the sugar yourself and make the cake from scratch.

But let me tell you—it's worth it.

I started out with a little old lady's recipe in an old spiral-bound church cookbook. The recipe included the list of ingredients, with some measurements (but not all), and directions that were incredibly lacking. (In which she instructs about ingredients that aren't even mentioned in the list of ingredients and measurements.) You know, it's one of those recipes—the type where they all knew what they were doing and only halfway wrote it down because you were supposed to know too. It gave absolutely no instructions for burning the sugar.

Lost, I turned to the Internet and studied burnt sugar cake recipes I found online. I chose one and made it. . . . It was quite different from the "authentic" recipe I had from the elderly lady, but hey, at least it had directions. Unfortunately, the cake was terrible. It baked up dry and dense and just utterly unacceptable.

Not to be deterred, I took what I'd learned from the online recipe and went back to the "authentic" one. Armed with at least a sense of how burnt sugar is created and the process of this cake, I tackled the old-time recipe again, filling in the gaps with my own experience. You know, the experience the incomplete recipe assumed I had to begin with. The two recipes were different in several ways, and by and large my second attempt was based on the old-time recipe. However, where measurements were incomplete in the old-time recipe, I filled in with my own guesses from my baking background, and what I ended up with was a delicious, moist, light cake that fulfilled all my burnt sugar cake dreams.

Start by making the burnt sugar syrup:

1⅓ cups sugar
1⅓ cups hot water

Dump the sugar in a skillet on the stove. Turn the heat to medium-low. You don't actually "burn" the sugar—you melt it. Stir only occasionally. The less you stir, the better. Once the sugar is melted, add the hot water, continuing with your heat on medium-low. When you add the hot water, the melted sugar hardens again, but as it continues to cook, it transforms into a syrupy mixture.

Turn off the heat and set the sugar syrup aside to cool to room temperature while you start preparing the cake. The syrup is thin while it's hot, but as it cools, it thickens. By the way, if you're ever snowed in and need pancakes, this makes a pancake syrup in a pinch. Add a bit of maple flavoring if you have some on hand and it's make-do maple syrup. Just remember, however much you want to make, use equal parts sugar and water. Using 1⅓ cups sugar and 1⅓ cups water, you're going to end up with approximately 1¼ cups burnt sugar syrup after it cooks down in the process. Your exact mileage may vary.

To make burnt sugar cake:

3 cups all-purpose flour
2 teaspoons baking powder
½ teaspoon salt
¼ cup salted butter, room temperature
1½ cups sugar
2 large eggs, separated
½ cup burnt sugar syrup
1 teaspoon vanilla extract
½ cup water (minus 1 teaspoon)
¼ cup milk

Preheat the oven to 350°F.

Combine the flour, baking powder, and salt; set aside. In another bowl, cream the butter and sugar. Add the egg yolks and beat again. In a small bowl, beat the egg whites till fluffy. Pour or spoon the burnt sugar syrup in a 1-cup measuring cup. Add the vanilla extract, then add enough water (cool to lukewarm) to add up to a cup. To the bowl with the creamed butter/sugar/egg yolks, add the flour mixture, the syrup mixture, and the milk. Beat well. Gently fold in the egg whites. (Do not beat again.) Divide into two round, greased cake pans.

Bake for 25 to 30 minutes or until a toothpick inserted near the center comes out clean. (Don't overbake!) Cool and frost with burnt sugar icing.

For **burnt sugar** icing:

16 ounces powdered sugar
⅔ cup to ¼ cup burnt sugar syrup (however much you have left)
¼ cup salted butter, room temperature
1 teaspoon vanilla extract
Pecan halves

Combine the powdered sugar, burnt sugar syrup, butter, and vanilla and beat till smooth and spreadable. If your icing is too stiff because you found yourself on the low side with your remaining burnt sugar syrup, add a bit of milk or water. Frost the cake and decorate with pecan halves. Serve with vanilla ice cream.

MRS. RANDOLPH'S STRAWBERRY CAKE

1 cup salted butter, softened
2 cups sugar
6 eggs, separated
3 cups all-purpose flour
1 teaspoon baking powder
½ teaspoon ground allspice
½ teaspoon ground cinnamon
½ teaspoon ground nutmeg
¼ cup buttermilk
½ teaspoon baking soda
8 ounces strawberry jam

Preheat the oven to 350°F.

Cream the butter and sugar in a large bowl. Beat the egg yolks, add to the mixture, and mix well. Combine the flour, baking powder, allspice, cinnamon, and nutmeg in a medium-size bowl.

Mrs. Randolph called for 2 small teaspoons each of baking powder, allspice, cinnamon, nutmeg, and baking soda. *What was a small teaspoon?*

Teaspoons don't come in small, medium, and large. They come in quarter, half, and full.

I looked up some other cake recipes, checking out the baking powder and baking soda measurements. This wasn't all that helpful since every cake recipe I looked at called for something different. I wanted the cake to rise, of course, but I didn't want to go overboard. I also thought the spices were a bit much if she really meant a "scant" teaspoon. Maybe to Mrs. Randolph, a small teaspoon was a quarter teaspoon? I went with the measurements in my ingredients list above. If you want it spicier, go for it. I could be wrong! If I'm wrong, it's Mrs. Randolph's fault.

Combine the buttermilk and baking soda. Add flour/spice mixture and buttermilk/soda mixture alternatively, mixing well. Mrs. Randolph didn't say to beat this, but I did.

Fold in the strawberry jam, mixing well, then fold in the egg whites. This makes a huge bowl of cake batter. Mrs. Randolph didn't suggest a baking pan size, but I ended up going with a large tube pan (greased). She didn't tell me at what temperature to bake it, either, so I used 350°F.

Bake until a toothpick comes out clean, which took an hour and a half for me. (Put aluminum foil over the top after about 40 to 45 minutes so it doesn't overbrown.) Of course, if you're baking this in round cake layers or in a 13 x 9-inch pan, your baking time will vary. If you bake it in round cake layers, I think it will take three pans!

Mrs. Randolph suggested a caramel icing, but, of course, didn't provide a recipe.

RECIPES

CRAFTS

CRAFTS

HOT PROCESS SOAP

To make hot process soap just like Great-Grandma but without the iron kettle:

1. Weigh each fat/oil in your recipe. Place fats/oils in a Crock-Pot on low. Heat until completely melted. Turn the Crock-Pot off.

2. Put on your goggles and gloves. Weigh the lye and the water. Always add lye to water, not the other way around. Mixing the lye and water is best done outside in the fresh air. Slowly pour the lye into the water. Stir with a slotted spoon and hang back so you don't inhale the fumes. The mixture will appear cloudy at first, then quickly clear.

3. Still wearing goggles and gloves, take the mixture back inside and slowly pour it into the melted fats/oils in the Crock-Pot. Stir briefly with a spoon, then begin mixing with a stick blender. Use the stick blender on and off so you don't burn out your tool. (Run the stick blender for a few minutes, then turn it off and hand-stir with the stick blender, and so on.) Most recipes take 5 to 10 minutes to trace.

4. When your mixture traces, it will be sort of like a soft pudding where you can draw a line in the mixture and see the "trace" you left behind.

5. Set your Crock-Pot to low, and put on the lid to start the cooking process. The soap will gradually take on a waxy appearance. The edges will appear dryer than the middle as they push up the sides of the Crock-Pot. Stir occasionally—this keeps the soap mixture cooking evenly. As it nears finishing, it will look like waxy mashed potatoes. You should continue to wear goggles and gloves when stirring the soap until it tests noncaustic (see below). The cook time of soap recipes will vary with the fats/oils involved. Most recipes will cook in about an hour.

6. Test soap with a pH strip. Finished soap should test between

7 and 10. You can also test soap using 1 percent phenol-phthalein solution. (This is my preferred method.) To use the solution, remove a very small bit of soap (a half teaspoon is plenty) from the pot to a nonreactive surface. Add one drop of the solution to the soap. If the soap turns pink, it's not done. (Throw away the test sample—don't return it to your pot. Be careful not to touch the solution or get it on your skin or eyes. You can use a paper towel to wipe away the sample and dispose of it.) If the soap remains clear when the solution is dropped on it, it's finished. (You can purchase 1 percent phenolphthalein solution online—put the words in a search engine to find places where it is available.)

7. Once the soap tests finished, you can get rid of the goggles and gloves and touch the soap all you want. It's soap!

8. Quickly mix in any additives or colorant, adding fragrance last, then scoop the soap into a mold. Bang the mold down a few times to settle the soap. Wait about 12 hours for the soap to harden enough to cut.

I often use the same base recipe with different additives, colorants, and fragrance. Once you've found a recipe that you like, there's no need to recalculate it when changing the additional elements as long as you do not change the fats and oils. Be sure to run any recipe through a soap calculator if changing the fats or oils.

As a rule of thumb, when including dry additives, a maximum of ½ cup dry additives in a 2-pound batch is recommended. (More may make your soap crumbly.) If using a nondry additive like honey, add 2 tablespoons per 2-pound batch.

Coloring: I prefer liquid soap colorant. I find dry pigments are more difficult to blend evenly. Be sure you're using soap colorant (not food dye or candle dye, for example). Soap colorant can be purchased from soap-making suppliers. Use as many drops as it takes to reach your desired effect. You can also color soap naturally in a variety of organic ways, and keep in mind that some additives (such as ground cinnamon) will color your soap.

CRAFTS

Fragrance: Use no more than 1 ounce fragrance oil or essential oil per 2 pounds of soap. (More may make your soap oily.)

Molds: Molds can be anything! When making hot process soap, by the time you put the soap in the mold(s), it's soap. You may line the mold (I use freezer paper) to protect the mold (for example, a wood mold) from the oils in the soap and to make the soap come out easily.

To make round soaps, I use Pringles cans. Just tear the can away when hardened and cut the soap. In this case, you don't have to line the mold. Be sure to wipe out crumbs thoroughly before using as a mold. Quart cardboard cartons can also be used without lining.

Molds must be chosen much more carefully for cold process method soap where the mixture is not yet saponified and the still-caustic soap may react with various materials (including the interior of Pringles cans). These suggestions are for hot process method soap only.

SOAP RECIPES

All my recipes make gentle soaps with light lather and soft conditioning. They're "grocery store" soaps, meaning most of the ingredients can be found in any large grocery store. Each recipe makes a 2-pound batch.

To make the soap, follow the instructions for making hot process soap in a Crock-Pot, mixing in the additives and fragrance oil at the end before scooping into your mold(s).

APPLE-OATMEAL SOAP

Soap:

Crisco, 9.6 ounces or 272.155 grams
Olive oil, 9.6 ounces or 272.155 grams
Lard, 6.4 ounces or 181.437 grams

Coconut oil (76-degree melt point), 6.4 ounces or 181.437 grams

Distilled water, 12.16 ounces or 344.73 grams

Lye, 4.463 ounces or 126.524 grams

Additives and fragrance:

¼ cup rolled oats, ground

¼ cup sugar

1 tablespoon ground dried apple peels

1 ounce apple fragrance oil

LAVENDER-BASIL SOAP

Soap:

Crisco, 6.4 ounces or 181.437 grams

Coconut oil (76-degree melt point), 6.4 ounces or 181.437 grams

Olive oil, 6.4 ounces or 181.437 grams

Lard, 12.8 ounces or 362.874 grams

Water, 12.16 ounces or 344.73 grams

Lye, 4.483 ounces or 127.077 grams

Additives and fragrance:

1 tablespoon finely crushed dried basil

1 ounce lavender essential oil

WILD MINT AND HONEY SOAP

Soap:

Lard, 22.4 ounces or 635.029 grams

Olive oil, 9.6 ounces or 272.155 grams

Distilled water, 12.16 ounces or 344.73 grams

lye, 4.24 ounces or 120.195 grams

Additives and fragrance:

½ cup brown sugar
2 tablespoons honey
1 tablespoon finely crushed wild mint*
1 ounce spearmint fragrance oil or peppermint essential oil

*If you don't have wild mint, you can use any kind of cultivated mint.

CHOCOLATE CREAM FACIAL MASK

This facial mask is deliciously moisturizing and well worth it. It's a fun and easy beauty trick to create—right out of your cupboard.

Cocoa powder is for the antioxidants along with honey for nourishment, cream cheese for moisturizing, and oatmeal for conditioning.

⅓ cup cocoa powder
3 tablespoons cream cheese
¼ cup honey
3 teaspoons oatmeal

Combine all the ingredients in a blender or food processor and blend till smooth. It makes a dark, rich concoction that looks like you could frost it on a cake. Transfer to a container.

Use a small spoon or mini Popsicle stick to dip into the container and spread it all over your face with your fingers. Let sit for about 15 to 20 minutes, then rinse. Store in the refrigerator. It will keep several weeks.

BEESWAX MOISTURIZING CREAM

Beeswax is produced by honeybee "worker" bees. They secrete it from glands on the underside of their abdomens, then chew it up

CRAFTS

and mold it into the cells of the combs. That's why they call them worker bees. It's a big job for the beekeepers, too, who collect it from the hives and melt it down into cakes. (At least they don't have to chew it.) For every 100 pounds of honey harvested, a beekeeper will get only 1 to 2 pounds of beeswax. It's not easily come by, but maybe that's also why beeswax is so very, very wonderful.

For these recipes, you can use a small spoon or mini Popsicle stick as an applicator to avoid contamination of the contents of your container.

The following measurements are by volume, except for the beeswax, which is by weight (weighed before melting).

4 ounces sweet almond oil
1 ounce beeswax
2 ounces water
8–10 drops essential oil (optional)
8–10 drops vitamin E

Melt the almond oil and beeswax. Remove from the heat and stir in the water. Stir in the remaining ingredients. Stir as it cools—before it becomes too cool to pour, transfer to a container (or divide between smaller containers).

You can also make a super-easy petroleum jelly–type moisturizer by combining ½ cup baby oil per ounce beeswax. After you melt the beeswax, remove from the heat and stir in the baby oil. (You can add a few drops of essential oil, too, if you want more scent. I really like beeswax just how it smells naturally.)

BEESWAX LIP BALM

The measurements in this recipe are also listed by volume, except for the beeswax, which is by weight (weighed before melting).

1 teaspoon grated beeswax
2 teaspoons coconut oil

½ teaspoon lanolin

Liquid from one vitamin E capsule

2 drops lemon or orange essential oil (optional)

1 teaspoon honey

Melt the beeswax, coconut oil, lanolin, and vitamin E in a microwave-safe bowl. If you don't want to use the microwave, you can also place the ingredients in a little custard cup inside a pot of water on the stove; heat gently to melt. Remove from the heat and stir in the essential oil and honey. Transfer to a small container. (This even tastes good.)

CONTAINER CANDLES

Homemade candles are so much less expensive than store-bought candles. What you need to get started:

Candle wax

A double boiler

Thermometer

Wicks

Fragrance oil (optional)

Candle dye (optional)

Containers

You can make container candles out of various types of wax, such as soy, gel, paraffin, or specially prepared container wax. I prefer "one-pour" container wax. (One-pour means the wax is for-mulated to form a smooth top with one pour, eliminating the need to top off to fill holes formed when regular wax settles as it cools. Candle wax is available from large craft stores or candle-making suppliers, which are easy to find online.)

Start by preparing your containers—you can use anything that will withstand heat. I have plenty of glass canning jars with lids to seal and retain scent for the candles I won't use right away. You can buy prewaxed wire wicks, which makes wicking easy. Put a dab of glue or cool wax on the bottom and it will make the wick stick to the bottom of your jar nicely so you don't have to worry about it moving around when you're pouring the wax.

Pour water inside the base of a double boiler, add the wax pot, and heat the wax to the degree directed for your specific wax (for container wax, 180 degrees).

When the wax reaches its pouring temperature, add candle dye, which comes in liquid or solid form. (The dye package will direct how much to use for its specific formulation.) If you're using solid dye, cut it up finely before adding it so that it will melt faster.

After the dye is mixed in, turn off the heat, let cool slightly, then add the fragrance oil, if using. You can use one scent or a combination to create custom scents. Most fragrance oils recommend 1 ounce of fragrance per pound of wax.

Pour the wax into the containers, being careful to keep your wicks centered. (If not using a one-pour wax, leave room in the jar and reserve wax to top off later after the candle cools.)

Let cool for several hours. Reheat reserved wax to pouring temperature, then top off the candles, if necessary.

Trim the wicks and you're ready to light up.

For cheap, cheap container candles, recycle old candles. Ask all your friends and family to save their old candles for you that have burned too low to light again. Scrape or melt out the old wax, removing the wicks. Combine leftover wax from multiple candles and melt it down to pour into a new jar with a new wick for a brand-new (free) candle. Best of all, the dye and scent are already included! (You may get some interesting combinations of color and scent. You can add more fragrance oil also, if you wish.)

HAND-DIPPED TAPERS

Hand-dipped tapers are easy to create—though time-intensive. There's a reason hand-dipped tapers are expensive! Even so, it's

CRAFTS

a simple and very satisfying project that can be done cheaply at home, and the sheer charm of hanging paired candles makes them a great gift, too. (Give them in pairs, uncut, and your recipients will hate to burn them!)

To make tapers, you'll need taper wax and small flat braid wick sized for tapers. Taper wax is a hard wax with a high melting point, which provides a cleaner-burning result. You can find taper wax, sold in blocks, at large craft stores or online candle-making suppliers. Flat braid wick is sold in rolls, also at large craft stores or online. If you like, add scent and dye.

You'll need some kind of setup to hang your candles between dips. The height you'll need depends on the height you're planning to make your tapers. For example, an average spaghetti box propped on quart jars works well for six-inch tapers. Set two quart jars about 10 inches apart on a protected surface. (Use newspaper, aluminum foil, or wax paper.) Place the box of spaghetti (empty or full, doesn't matter) on top of the jars and hang the tapers over it with the non-dipped center across the box. You could also use a paint stir stick, a piece of wood, or anything else you can find that will work.

The candles are dipped in pairs, so after determining the height of your tapers, measure off double that width (for two tapers) then figure the length in between. (Your tapers will hang in pairs from the portion of unwaxed wick left in the middle.) For six-inch tapers, cut lengths of about 18 inches. Six inches of wick for each candle plus 6 inches for the nondipped center between the candles from which the tapers will be hung while drying. Cut the number of lengths you're intending to use.

To get started, melt the wax in a double boiler at the temperature specified in the packaging instructions for the type of wax you're using. You need enough wax in the pot to reach the depth required for dipping your tapers, so you'll need a pretty full pot. Holding the strand of wick doubled over evenly, dip the two wick ends to the height you've planned for your tapers. (You can mark the wick using a pen, if you like.) On the first dip for each wick length, hold the dip for a full minute to really soak the wick.

Hang the length of wick to cool, keeping the two tapers separated, and continue on until you've done the initial dip for each length you've cut. Go back to the first pair and dip again—this time, only for about 3 seconds. Hang to cool and go on to the next. Gradually with each round, the wax starts building up.

Each dip builds the coating surrounding the wick, turning it into a taper. As you dip the candles, blobs of wax will build up on the bottoms of the tapers. You can stop periodically, cut the blob off with a knife, and drop the extra wax back into the pot.

Dip your candles however many times you need to in order to get the result you want. This is the time-intensive part. It takes dozens of dips to build up to the width of a standard-size taper that will fit your average candlestick holder. (Set aside a couple of hours to work on this project.) A standard taper has a ⅞-inch base, but candlestick holders may vary. As you get close to that size, test-fit your taper in your candlestick holders and dip to the perfect size for your use.

As a finishing touch, you can do the last few dips in different colors of wax to add stripes. You can also roll the candles flat (except for the last inch or two) and twist them while they're still warm for a special effect. Or leave them plain for an authentic, rustic look.

Hang the candles to harden for a day before burning. To use, cut the tapers apart and trim the wicks.

Leftover wax in the pot will be too shallow to dip long tapers, but you can use it to dip homemade birthday candles.

CANDLE JARS WITH PRESSED WILDFLOWERS

You can decorate a jar for all sorts of purposes, from holding your pencils to storing your herbs, but flowers and candles go together like . . . flowers and candles!

The simplest way to press flowers is the same way you did it when you were a kid. Separate flowers from the stems and carefully lay them down on a sheet of paper, cover with another sheet of paper, then press between the folds of a book. Stack up more heavy books on top. Most light, delicate flowers will press flat in a matter of hours or overnight, but you'll need to keep them pressing longer to thoroughly dry out. How long it takes flowers to dry varies by the flower type, but you can speed it up by drying them in the microwave. (Press the flowers at least a few hours or overnight before drying in the microwave.)

To dry flowers in the microwave, place the pressed flowers between sheets of paper on a microwave-safe plate. Place something else, microwave-safe, on top. Heat them in short bursts, 15 seconds on high, until dry. Let the flowers cool completely between bursts of heat. Light, delicate flowers will dry quickly by this method.

To adhere pressed, dried flowers to a glass canning jar, use a clear craft glue. Thin the glue with water. This isn't rocket science or brain surgery—don't worry too much about how much water and how much glue. Add several squirts of glue to about a quarter cup of water and stir it up with a small painting brush.

With the jar resting on its side, brush a small amount of the thinned glue on the outside of the jar where you intend to place the flowers. Transfer the dried flowers carefully—tweezers are a good way to move them. Place each flower and press down lightly with the back of a spoon. (It's better not to use your fingers.) As you place each flower, brush lightly over each one with the thinned glue mixture to seal.

The nice thing about this method, as opposed to using a varnish, is that if you ever want to do something else with the jar, you can simply wash it with hot water and soap to remove the flowers.

You can apply the flowers in any design you like, all on one side of the jar or wrapping around the jar. Get as creative as you like. You could add all sorts of other dried materials, including leaves. Fill the jar with candle wax and a wick to make a unique gift or something pretty to keep for yourself.

CRAFTS

HOMEMADE LAUNDRY DETERGENT

Make laundry detergent at home. You can! It's easy, frugal, and doesn't even take very long. The ingredients are simple and inexpensive—borax, washing soda and/or baking soda, and any supersudsing, hard-grating soap (such as Fels-Naptha, Ivory, or Zote). Even better, start with your own homemade plain soap.

To make a homemade batch of soap for laundry detergent use:

Lard, 16 ounces or 453.592 grams
Coconut oil (76-degree melt point), 16 ounces or 453.592 grams
Distilled water, 12.16 ounces or 344.73 grams
Lye, 5.191 ounces or 147.155 grams

Vegetarian version:

Crisco, 16 ounces or 453.592 grams
Coconut oil (76-degree melt point), 16 ounces or 453.592 grams
Distilled water, 12.16 ounces or 344.73 grams
Lye, 5.134 ounces or 145.538 grams

Follow the directions for making hot process soap. These recipes make 2 pounds of soap. If you want to add scent, add 1 ounce fragrance oil before placing the soap in the mold.

Borax, washing soda, and baking soda are all natural laundry boosters that help remove soils, fight stains, and freshen laundry—they're soap enhancers. You can find borax, washing soda, and the laundry-size baking soda in the laundry aisle at most grocery stores.

To make a dry laundry soap mixture:

2 bars (approximately 4–5 ounces each) plain soap
2 cups borax
1 cup baking soda
1 cup washing soda

CRAFTS

Grate the soap as finely as possible. Combine the grated soap with the other ingredients and mix well. Store mixture in a container. Use 1 to 2 tablespoons per load. Double or triple the recipe to make large batches.

Laundry detergent is highly personal. Everyone has different issues. You may want to use more or less of any given ingredient depending on your needs. If you wash a lot of whites, you may want to add OxiClean (or a generic oxygen cleaning equivalent) to brighten whites. I work on a farm and I avoid whites like the plague, so that's not a big problem for me. If it is for you, you could add it to your mixture, or add it separately for specific loads according to the product's directions. You can add $1/4$ to $1/2$ cup (or, you know, just a big splash, which is what I do) of white vinegar to the rinse cycle for softening. Vinegar also helps to remove any remaining soap. Take any homemade laundry detergent recipe as a starting point—once you start experimenting, you'll come to know what works best for you.

SIMPLE HOMEMADE CLEANERS

For most basic homemade cleaners that will tackle almost every job in your house, you'll need these standard supplies (along with water):

White vinegar
Ammonia
Rubbing alcohol
Lemon juice
Olive oil
Baking soda

Buy plain spray bottles to use for your homemade cleaners, or save old store-bought spray bottles to wash out and reuse. Be sure to label everything and store cleaners out of the reach of children and pets.

Undiluted white vinegar works wonders by itself. It's very good

CRAFTS

for cleaning hard water deposits or soap scum. You can use ½ to a full cup of vinegar in the rinse cycle to soften laundry instead of store-bought fabric softener. (It won't leave any vinegar smell on your laundry.) You can also use straight vinegar to remove mold and mildew. (Lemon juice works well for this, too.)

Vinegar is also a great stain remover on many surfaces. (Tip: Run ¼ cup vinegar in with a pot of water through your coffeemaker to remove stains on the carafe.) The wonders of white vinegar go on and on. Buy it in the bulk size.

This first recipe is very basic and is what I call "Kitchen Cleaner" because it's great for cleaning countertops, appliances, backsplashes, and so on. It's also great in the bathroom and effective on many carpet and other stains.

KITCHEN CLEANER

Use equal parts—

Water
White vinegar

My all-time favorite and most-used cleaner is glass cleaner.

GLASS CLEANER

1 cup water
1 cup rubbing alcohol
1 tablespoon white vinegar*

An easy furniture polish is ½ cup lemon juice per 1 cup olive oil. It will make your house smell so good, you'll want to polish your furniture more often.

For vinyl floors, use 1 cup white vinegar in a gallon of water. For wood flooring, use ½ cup white vinegar in a gallon of water.

If you want any of your homemade cleaners to have fragrance, you can add a drop or two of any essential oil. For example, love the orange scent of some store-bought cleaners? Add a drop of orange essential oil. Or whatever scent you love.

CRAFTS

Once you get the idea of how homemade cleaners are put together, you can experiment to make your own recipes for specific cleaning tasks. Ammonia is a strong cleaner for tough jobs. Olive oil adds softening and protection. Lemon juice dissolves dirt and eliminates odors. Alcohol is added to glass cleaner for the "evaporating" aspect, leaving your windows and mirrors clear and streak free. (Also good for many shiny fixtures.) Baking soda is a mild abrasive and deodorizer. Vinegar is also a deodorizer and a gentle cleaner (and adds shine to floors). A liquid soap (like Dawn dish liquid) can add extra cleaning and sudsing power when you need it.

Note: In case you get a hankering to include bleach in any of your homemade cleaners when you are experimenting, please note this: DO NOT combine bleach with ammonia or vinegar as this can create toxic fumes.

*You can use ammonia instead of vinegar if you need a stronger glass cleaner.

RUFFLED CROCHET DISHCLOTH

This is a very simple project that can be completed in a couple hours with one skein of yarn.

You can make this dishcloth smaller or larger by adding or removing from the starter chains. Just be sure to chain an odd number and single crochet across your first row in an even number and go from there. You could even add additional edging rows in single or half double crochet before doing the final double crochet ruffle. It's an easy pattern to adapt.

Finished size: Approximately 9-inch square

Materials:

100% cotton worsted weight yarn (2 ounces)
Crochet hook, size F

CRAFTS

Directions:

Row 1. Make a slip knot and chain 27. Single crochet (sc) in back ridge of second chain from hook and in each chain across. You should have 26 sc.

Row 2. Chain 1, turn; skip first sc, 2 sc in next sc, *skip next sc, 2 sc in next sc; repeat from * across. 26 sc in each row.

Repeat until work measures to an approximate 6¼- to 6½-inch square.

Round 1. (Do not turn work from this point forward.) Chain 1 and crochet evenly around all four sides in sc. (Stop periodically to make sure you are crocheting evenly so that work stays flat.) Make 3 sc in each corner and join last corner with a slip stitch.

Round 2. Chain 1, sc in each sc all the way around, making 3 sc in the middle sc of each corner. Join with a slip stitch.

Round 3. Chain 2 and half double crochet (hdc) in each sc all the way around, making 3 hdc in middle sc of each corner. Join with a slip stitch.

Round 4. The ruffly round! Chain 3. Make four double crochet (dc) in every other hdc stitch as you go around—except in the corners. In each corner, in the first hdc of the corner, make three dc. Chain 3. Skip the second corner hdc and make three dc in the third hdc of the corner. (After making each corner, skip one hdc stitch, then carry on with making four dc in every other hdc stitch.) Join with a slip stitch at the last corner and finish off.

HOMEMADE FLOWER FOOD

Per quart of cool water, combine 2 tablespoons sugar and 2 tablespoons lemon juice or vinegar. Stir to mix well and dissolve sugar, then pour into the container where you'll be placing flowers. You can measure to be exact, or just eyeball it. If your vase is smaller or larger, adjust your quantities to match.

The sugar is the food for the flowers. The lemon juice or vinegar is used to keep the flower water fresh and free of bacteria. An old-fashioned method for keeping flowers fresh was to drop a copper penny in the water. (Copper is a fungicide.) People also used to (and sometimes still do) drop an aspirin in the water for the same reason. I like to use a little lemon juice or vinegar. The point is to add something antibacterial, antifungal, and/or acidic to the water to keep it fresh. Use whatever you have on hand. I've even heard of people using lime soda. You could also use citric acid crystals. Whatever you have!

A few more tips for keeping flowers fresh longer: put flowers in cold water, not warm. Also, be sure to remove all the excess foliage below the water line to reduce the risk of rotting foliage in the water. If the vase water gets cloudy, replace it with fresh flower food water. If you got your flowers from the store, be sure to give them a fresh cut, at an angle, when you get them home, and cut them under water.

APPLE SPICE SIMMERING POTPOURRI

When making apple butter or other recipes using apples, I save the peels and cores, and even a few slices, for the dehydrator—to eventually become simmering potpourri.

Cinnamon sticks
Ginger slivers
Whole cloves
Dried apple peels, cores, slices

Use one cinnamon stick, broken, three slivers of fresh ginger, and about a teaspoon of whole cloves per batch, then add enough dried apple to make a heaping cup.

Place mixture in a pot and pour water into the pot until it's about two-thirds full. Bring to a simmer. Your house will smell like apple pie.

WINTER CITRUS POTPOURRI MIX

I conjured up this potpourri mix for homemade Christmas gifts our first winter at Stringtown Rising, utilizing what was available to me, and have made some version of it every winter since. Think creatively and adjust the recipe to suit what you can get your hands on where you are. Using what you have around you makes the potpourri personal.

I always have a surplus of cinnamon sticks in my pantry, so this puts them to good use. The pinecones come from Georgia's yard. She has tall pine trees all around her house. The hickory nuts can be picked up off the farm, and the white pine comes from the cuttings off our Christmas tree after trimming—making each gift of potpourri a piece of our tree. This usually leaves me with only the cost of the fruit.

And by the time I make up a huge turkey-roaster size pan of potpourri, the cost of that fruit goes pretty far in filling about a dozen bags of potpourri to go into gift baskets for family and friends.

What you need to make winter citrus potpourri:

Oranges
Lemons
Limes
Whole cloves
Cinnamon sticks
Hickory nuts
Pine cuttings
Pinecones
Fragrance oil
Quart-size Ziploc bags

CRAFTS

The quantity of each item is up to you. Make as little or as much as you want, and weight each item in the mix according to what you have available or your personal preference.

Slice fruit thinly. Place in single layers on baking sheets. Poke cloves in orange slices if desired. Dry in a low oven (about 200°F) for several hours. (Watch fruit to make sure it doesn't turn too brown.) If you have a dehydrator, follow your dehydrator's directions for drying citrus fruit. After the fruit slices are dried and cooled, place them in a large bowl or pan (such as a roasting pan if you're making a large quantity) and add cinnamon sticks, hickory nuts, and pine cuttings. Add a few drops of fragrance oil per cup of mix and toss. (For this mix, I like orange or lemon oil or cinnamon oil.) Measure 2 cups mix per quart bag, placing one pinecone in each bag. Seal bags to allow fragrance to steep for at least several days before using.

Poke cloves into whole oranges to make pomanders for potpourri centerpieces. To give as gifts, pack the orange pomanders separately from the dry mix. To display, 2 cups mix with one large pinecone makes a nice-sized bowl or small platter of potpourri when you add the orange pomander.

INDEX

INDEX